Mildred Trotter and the Invisible Histories of Physical and Forensic Anthropology

Mildred Trotter and the Invisible Histories of Physical and Forensic Anthropology

Emily K. Wilson

CRC Press
Taylor & Francis Group
Boca Raton London New York

CRC Press is an imprint of the
Taylor & Francis Group, an **informa** business

Cover: Trotter wearing several leis, ready to leave Hawaii on the S.S. Mars, August 20, 1949. VC170-i170183, Becker Medical Library, Washington University School of Medicine.

First edition published 2022
by CRC Press
6000 Broken Sound Parkway NW, Suite 300, Boca Raton, FL 33487-2742

and by CRC Press
4 Park Square, Milton Park, Abingdon, Oxon, OX14 4RN

CRC Press is an imprint of Taylor *& Francis Group, LLC*

Library of Congress Cataloging-in-Publication Data
Names: Wilson, Emily K., author.
Title: Mildred Trotter and the invisible histories of physical and forensic anthropology / Emily K. Wilson.
Identifiers: LCCN 2021048789 (print) | LCCN 2021048790 (ebook) | ISBN 9781032180908 (hardback) | ISBN 9781032180892 (paperback) | ISBN 9781003252818 (ebook)
Subjects: LCSH: Trotter, Mildred, 1899-1991. | Women physical anthropologists—United States—Biography. | Women forensic anthropologists—United States—Biography. | Physical anthropology—United States—History. | Physical anthropology—Social aspects—United States—History. | Forensic anthropology—United States—History. | Forensic anthropology—Social aspects—United States—History.
Classification: LCC GN50.6.T76 W55 2022 (print) | LCC GN50.6.T76 (ebook) | DDC 301.092 [B]—dc23/eng/20220211
LC record available at https://lccn.loc.gov/2021048789
LC ebook record available at https://lccn.loc.gov/2021048790

ISBN: 9781032180908 (hbk)
ISBN: 9781032180892 (pbk)
ISBN: 9781003252818 (ebk)

DOI: 10.4324/9781003252818

Typeset in Sabon
by codeMantra

Contents

Acknowledgments

Thank you to the Bernard Becker Medical Library and Archives at the Washington University School of Medicine for preserving and making Trotter's collection available, particularly to Ashley Chase for her repeated assistance and to Philip Skroska, as well as to Andrew Heuer for digitizing a portion of the collection. Thank you to Jim and Dave Trotter, for taking the time to chat with a random person about their Aunt Mamie; I hope to one day meet you in person and see the farm.

I am so grateful to Christine Dougherty and Kaustubh Kulkarni for being such warm and exhausting hosts in St. Louis, to Susan Steele D'Alonzo Jaques for her continued encouragement, and to Nancy Lundblad for her support and for locating more delightful Wallis mystery novels. I appreciate the editors and reviewers from the *Yearbook of Physical Anthropology*, the *American Journal of Physical Anthropology*, and *American Anthropologist*; certain chapters benefitted greatly from your insights. Many thanks are due to my editor, Mark Listewnik, and the editorial team for turning this manuscript into a real book, as well as the anonymous reviewers. Thank you to everyone at the Defense POW/MIA Accounting Agency; I am professionally and personally indebted to so many of you, and it broke my heart to leave Hawaii. I am so thankful for all the friends and colleagues who spoke with me on this and many related subjects, including, but certainly not limited to: Megan Ingvoldstad, Willa Trask, Audrey Scott, Mary Megyesi, Nicolette Parr, Greg Berg, Joe Hefner, Laura Cutter, Jeff Johnson, Craig Schneider, and Quinn Curnow.

I am, of course, forever grateful for the love, support, and advice of my mom and dad, Jody and Ned, and my sister and brother-in-law, Joanna and Henry De Los Santos. Thank you also to my Michigan family. My deepest gratitude is due to my relentlessly kind and buoyantly supportive spouse, the incomparable John Linabury. And though I did not know it when I started out, I am particularly thankful for our mochi, Eve, who gave me extra purpose and a deadline during a global pandemic.

Notes on Terminology

Partly because I am writing at once about the past and the present, this book includes a mix of older and newer language. I sometimes use "female" and "male" as adjectives for people, but use them as nouns only when referring to skeletal research collections and data, and similarly use "sex" to denote biology. The terms "sexism" and "sexist" indicate prejudice or discrimination on the basis of sex and/or gender. I use "Black" and "White" to denote socially constructed racial descriptions. I put other historical terms in quotes, as taken directly from written descriptions. I do not use the term "race" to imply the validity of biological race, but rather to represent the concept as it is understood socially and as it was used, unscientifically, in science.

Author Biography

Emily K. Wilson has worked as a forensic anthropologist with the Defense POW/MIA Accounting Agency in various capacities since 2013. Prior to this, she worked at the National Museum of Health and Medicine outside DC and as a forensic technician for the NYC Office of Chief Medical Examiner's World Trade Center recovery operation. She has published on a variety of subjects related to skeletal identification, museum curation of human remains, and the history of science.

CHAPTER 1

Introduction

Mildred Trotter's disarmingly serene expression stands out among the portraits of the current and past laboratory directors lining a wall at the Defense POW/MIA Accounting Agency (DPAA), on Joint Base Pearl Harbor–Hickam in Hawaii. With few exceptions, portraits of Trotter all capture this placid affect, even as a baby. Not only is she the only woman pictured, but also her calm expression seems to belie the general impressions modern anthropologists often have of her. Though Trotter's name is well known in forensic anthropology, not much is actually known about her. What is remembered of this anatomist who excelled in a male-dominated field indicates a tenacious personality, that of a person who gave unabashed critiques to Army Colonels and insisted on her own promotion to full professor at Washington University in St. Louis. Beyond just being one of the very few women in the discipline at the time, she has also had a considerable and lasting influence on the field. For these reasons, even when people know nothing more than a few basic facts, she often attracts interest.

This is a book that I sincerely wish I could have just read, but it did not exist. This sentiment is shared by others, particularly those in her growing and now majority-female field. Physical/biological anthropology and, in one of its more specific forms, forensic anthropology have experienced a boom in popularity and recognition with programs such as *Bones*, *CSI*, and *NCIS*, as well as true crime series and podcasts. Not only are more people intrigued by the details of forensic anthropology, but this has also resulted in an influx of young students, mostly women, who consider pursuing careers in this field. To historians of science though, Trotter is not likely to be widely known. A more comprehensive accounting of this one person's life is long overdue. So, I wrote this book for anthropologists curious about Trotter and for the increasing number of people investigating the overlooked histories of women and marginalized people in science.

I have worked as a forensic anthropologist at the DPAA laboratory since 2013, first as an Oak Ridge Institute for Science and Education fellow, then as a civilian employee of the Department of Defense, and currently as a remote contractor. As with most others at DPAA, I was always

DOI: 10.4324/9781003252818-1

Studio portrait of Trotter taken in 1950. VC170-i170024, Becker Medical Library, Washington University School of Medicine.

well aware of Trotter's existence and understood the gist of her time and influence within the Army's identification efforts after World War II. I was also vaguely familiar with Trotter's connection to the Robert J. Terry Anatomical Collection from doing a master's degree at George Washington University. Osteology courses relied on the Collection at the National Museum of Natural History, assiduously taught by David Hunt and Marilyn London. When I was first there, the Terry Collection was still housed on the National Mall, in some of the original olive drab cabinets that Trotter had shipped all the way from Missouri.

Like any historical figure, Trotter remains somewhat of an enigma due to the limitations of surviving documentation. Once I started searching, I found there were very few readily available secondary sources to turn to for more information. Most of it was piecemeal, and none of it was truly in-depth. Her story will always be incomplete, but she did leave behind ample primary materials to explore. Trotter maintained extensive correspondence with countless colleagues, which are archived in St. Louis at the Bernard Becker Medical Library of the Washington University School of Medicine. Also preserved there is her oral history, a loose transcript of which is available on the Library's website, and her unpublished history of the anatomy department at the University. Her obituary was published in the *American Journal of Physical Anthropology*, and several anthropologists have written briefly about her. My sources also include Washington University publications, Trotter's own scientific publications, newspaper and magazine articles, and other archival sources. Her papers at the Beaver County History Center unfortunately only consist of genealogical material (Alice Kern, Personal Communication, October 4, 2019), and I did not access the small amount of materials related to Trotter that are present within the archival collection of her attorney, Lucile W. Ring, at the St. Louis Mercantile Library of the University of Missouri – St. Louis. I did have the opportunity to speak with her nephew, James Trotter, and great-nephew, David Trotter, who were kind enough to share their memories and stories of their dear Aunt Mamie. Some time periods are particularly well covered because she saved an excess of documentation when, presumably, she felt they were important parts of her life and career. Other specific time periods are featured just by dint of available documentation. More personal content is only preserved by chance and memories. This variability of detail on different aspects of her life is unavoidable.

Trotter's story is, in short, that of a woman raised on a farm in Pennsylvania, who graduated from Mount Holyoke College, earned a PhD in anatomy, became the first woman to be full professor at the Washington University School of Medicine, was one of only two women who were founding members and the first woman to serve as president of the American Association of Physical Anthropologists (now the American Association of Biological Anthropologists), authored more than 100 academic works, shaped and improved the military's ongoing process of human identification, developed widely used stature estimation references, expanded and secured the preservation and accessibility of the Terry Collection at the Smithsonian, and taught more than 4,000 medical students over nearly five decades. J. Lawrence Angel named her as the one founding mother, among all the founding fathers, of physical anthropology.[1] But this is not a hagiography; I do not intend to portray Trotter as a mythical origin figure, devoid of faults and flatteringly blurry from a distance. She was human and had all the attendant strengths and weaknesses. This fact will already be obvious to anyone who may be familiar with Trotter's work, knowing that she made and continued to miss a major and now well-known error in her tibia measurement in her renowned stature estimation research, which I will specifically address.

This book is at times more of a history of anthropology through Mildred Trotter than it is strictly a standard biography. While I provide the details of her life, her experiences, and her scholarship, these topics bring up broader themes in physical anthropology and science that are sometimes ignored, such as scientific error, the historical experiences of women and marginalized people within the discipline, sexism, and scientific and social racism. Though women are now better represented, the discipline continues to suffer from disparities and a distinct lack of diversity. Where pertinent, I branch out into further details on these subjects, even when they stray momentarily from Trotter. When I deviate in this way, I am attempting to give her story more substance through the relevant and parallel experiences of others connected to her in various ways. I explore the vast and commonly overlooked domains of professional women and underrepresented people. From these perspectives, I hope to fill in the world she inhabited from multiple angles, some of which she may, and some of which she may not, have been aware of at the time.

When writing a story about the past, we are always necessarily also writing a story about the present. The timing of a biography can affect its contents nearly as much as the original events and experiences themselves. I hope to be sensitive to that, and also to open myself and readers up to other perspectives on the topics in this book. Trotter was just as much a product of her time as we are, and as much as this book must be. Certainly, I will fail to pursue questions that would have been more apparent if I were writing at another time or if I were another person.

Trotter was an organized person, and so I want to present her life in an orderly way, but it will not be strictly chronological. Please be patient then if I initially mention important concepts only in passing; I will return to these later. Because one aspect of Trotter's life is likely of greatest interest and familiarity to many readers – the year she spent working for the military in Hawaii – this is where her story will begin. And for anyone who is not already familiar with Trotter, this time consulting as an expert for the Army serves as an excellent introduction to her professionalism and character. It was also during this appointment in Hawaii that Trotter collected much of the data for her seminal publication on stature estimation. Trotter was certainly humble, but also uncompromising and resolute in her approach to obstacles on matters for which she held authority. As Trotter described her career, "I really don't think I have done anything more than establish an endurance record."[2] That distillation may be partly accurate, but there is so much more to her story.

NOTES

1 J. Lawrence Angel, "Symposium in Honor of T. Dale Stewart, 75th Birthday Celebration," *American Journal of Physical Anthropology* 45, no. 3 (1976): 519–530, p. 521.

2 Quoted in Twink Cherrick, "Named Lectureship, Portrait to Honor Anatomy Professor Mildred Trotter," *Washington University Record* (May 22, 1975), p. 4.

CHAPTER 2

Hawaii and the Army

For many biological anthropologists today, the defining moment for Mildred Trotter stems from her work identifying US war dead, though it counted as only a brief amount of time in her life and career. In many other narratives, this period is only presented as a side note to the life of an accomplished anatomist, professor, and founding American physical anthropologist. But this particular episode is what brought her prominence and a legacy within the history of physical and forensic anthropology. Here, we follow the story of a middle-aged professor in St. Louis who suddenly found herself on an US island territory in the Pacific, identifying the remains of World War II casualties, writing harsh critiques of military processes to Army officials, and undertaking the most comprehensive stature estimation project of the time.

In 1948, at the age of 49, Trotter accepted an approximately 1-year appointment as the anthropological consultant to the US Army at a laboratory dedicated to the identification of World War II dead. Identification efforts have been a national priority since the Civil War, usually under the operation of the American Graves Registration Service (AGRS). For a brief history of these efforts, see Emanovsky and Belcher.[1] The first central identification point was established in Strasbourg, France for World War II European theater remains in 1946, headed by Harry L. Shapiro from the American Museum of Natural History in New York. A laboratory for the Pacific Theater was started in Hawaii, first overseen by Charles E. Snow from 1947 to 1948. From June 1948 to June 1949 Trotter then served as the lead anthropology expert. This work has continued on, in various forms throughout the world, and today is undertaken by the Defense POW/MIA Accounting Agency (DPAA) laboratories at Joint Base Pearl Harbor-Hickam in Hawaii and at Offutt Air Force Base in Nebraska.

Trotter was offered the position in April of 1948, just a couple of months prior to the start date. Before accepting, she was careful and firm in negotiating her salary and other conditions of employment. She wrote to a fellow anthropologist, Stella Leche Deignan, that she had requested a higher rating than they first offered her, and she got it.[2] Her annual

DOI: 10.4324/9781003252818-2

salary would be $8,578.50 and designated a "P-6," which was categorized as comparable to a field-grade officer.[3] She was required to list her current salary on an application document. Although only 2 years previously she had, with her hard-won promotion to full professor, received a 25% salary increase, the dean of the medical school told her to claim yet a higher sum. When she returned to St. Louis after the year in Hawaii, she did not get a raise to reflect that amount, and she suspected that the dean had perhaps simply been "ashamed to have the Army know how little my salary was."[4] Her Washington University salary at that time was $6,500.[5] Trotter's biggest point of negotiation for Army employment in May of 1948 was access to her car, and despite extensive issues securing its shipment, she refused travel to Hawaii without it.[6] After she gave her final acceptance, her specialized training consisted of 2 days spent with Charles E. Snow at the University of Kentucky.[7] Snow had completed his PhD at Harvard under Earnest A. Hooton in 1938, and prior to his identification work for the AGRS had contributed to an anthropometry (human measurement) project for the US Department of Agriculture.[8]

That May, the Mount Holyoke Club of St. Louis honored Trotter with a luncheon prior to her departure.[9] In June, she drove to California to drop her car off for shipment. A former student drove her to the Army base where she then flew by military cargo plane to the Territory of Hawaii with a steamer trunk, a footlocker, and one suitcase. At some point, she underwent a physical exam and received required immunizations for her overseas posting.[10] She reported her height at 5 feet 4 inches and her weight at the very precise sum of 118 pounds.[11] Military travel instructions provided to her cautioned travelers "not to expect luxury accommodations." The flight instructions began with a lengthy assurance, filled with strangely concocted statistics, that "while this may be your first airplane trip," there is no need for concern because air travel has an extremely low fatality rate.[12] Considering that Trotter personally knew at least one woman who had previously died as a stowaway on a mail plane and two men who would die in peacetime US aircraft crashes within the next 8 years, this reassurance may have been welcome.[13] The flight instructions also stated that women must wear slacks in order to be fitted for the parachute harness "without undue embarrassment," and ended by wishing civilians traveling for the Army overseas "Happy Landings!".[14] After she arrived in Hawaii, she learned that, though she had been found to have excellent credentials, there had been a 2 day delay while the Army created waivers for her age and gender.[15] She would live in the nurses' quarters on the base where she worked, Schofield Barracks.

Efforts to identify the remains of US war dead began immediately. Two temporary mausoleums were erected at Schofield, where caskets of remains still unidentified from throughout the World War II Pacific Theater came to a hub. Remains that reached this laboratory had already

Technicians at work in the main processing laboratory, CIL, Schofield Barracks, Oahu, Hawaii, ca. 1948. VC170-i170400, Becker Medical Library, Washington University School of Medicine.

proven difficult or impossible to identify at the time of recovery or at intermediate processing stations, and constituted an estimated 6% of all recovered remains. One mausoleum housed the Central Identification Laboratory (CIL), a 9,000 sq ft space designed like a medical school dissection room. Here, Trotter and staff processed the skeletal remains to determine a biological profile (of characteristics such as age at death, sex, stature, and race) and make other observations that could be compared to antemortem medical records. The staff included Trotter as the sole anthropologist, two Army supervisors, 23 licensed embalmers, two dental technicians, a chemist, a photographer, an X-ray technician, several typists, clerks, and many laborers.[16] Remains were cleaned, inventoried, measured, and x-rayed. Commingled groups were segregated into individuals. Skeletons were examined for individually identifying features, such as antemortem fractures, evidence of surgeries, dental work, and pathological conditions. Measurements of long bones were taken and compared to formulas derived from an 1888 French study by Rollet to produce stature estimates, as well as the 1899 Karl Pearson statistical tables derived from Rollet's work, tables produced by Wilton M. Krogman, and an unspecified chart brought from the previous identification point in Strasbourg, France.[17] Other measurements were used for weight estimates. Race determinations were based on observed cranial traits.[18] Age estimates were based on markers of bone development on long bones and the pelvis. Sex determination was not generally done; Trotter noted that, expectably, no female remains came through the laboratory during her time there.

Trotter and staff made these postmortem analyses "in the blind," which would then be compared to antemortem records of casualties by a military review board. The board made the ultimate identification, without further input from or even notification to the laboratory, and was headed by an "ambitious young captain, who had attended a 2-year college in Texas."[19] After being unsuccessfully pressured by this officer to sign reports, she did not scientifically agree with, two officials arrived from DC to observe the laboratory. Trotter was asked her opinion on the entire process and apparently had a forceful and convincing response because she claimed that "the change that followed my 'explosion' caused the disappearance of the Captain."[20]

She was working long hours and later remembered that "my ankles were like balloons every night from standing so long in the lab, I couldn't sleep etc--. But, I'd do it again if asked."[21] The year she spent in Hawaii, "opened [her] eyes to the military world in peacetime and to the idyllic ways of an island in Paradise of the Pacific."[22] Trotter appreciated and found meaning in the mission, telling colleague T. Dale Stewart that, "you have my most heartfelt thanks for advising me to undertake this job. Don't misunderstand me, it is not a cinch for it is physically exhausting, but at the same time mentally stimulating."[23]

She learned the nuances of working with the military staff assigned to her, many of whom she regarded as being quite spirited compared to her academic colleagues and students. Some even played pranks on her, which was uncommon, though not unheard of, from her Washington University students, such as switching the batteries around on her flashlight tool.[24] Perhaps this was a departure for the woman who taught her medical students first and foremost to respect cadavers and "would not tolerate any levity or foolishness" in the laboratory in St. Louis.[25] She compared the relationships she had with embalmers to that of student and teacher.[26] But, of course, her new military cohort had very different and complex recent wartime experiences than she and her students in Missouri had, and would certainly have related differently to both the human remains and the work itself.

While on Oahu she also enjoyed swimming, hosting friends who visited from the mainland, and took a trip to the Big Island of Hawaii.[27] When she spent Thanksgiving on a beach, she felt that she "wouldn't mind seeing a snow flurry."[28] She experienced her first earthquake during her first week on the island.[29] She was present for the dedication of the new Tripler Army Medical Center.[30] She even took to closing some of her correspondence during this time with a warm "Aloha."

In the summer of 1948, it seems that Trotter quickly discovered the unique challenges facing an academic working within the confines of the American military establishment. Thomas McKern, a future collaborator with

T. Dale Stewart during similar identification efforts for the Korean War who had also recently begun a short consultancy for the Army in Saipan, shared some of these experiences. They commiserated via letters over the difficulties they encountered, and as McKern wrote to Trotter, "for the first time I realize the disadvantages which [arise] as the result of the Army vs. civilian standard. It is our biggest problem and to me a great disappointment. It is impossible to maintain qualified [personnel] if they are not granted a certain amount of respect. I cannot understand the Army's attitude."[31] They were learning the definition of red tape. One obstacle, in particular, was a thorn in Trotter's side from the beginning. Both she, and later T. Dale Stewart, would later express regret that Trotter had not negotiated one further condition prior to accepting employment: that she be given the necessary permissions to conduct a stature research project.[32]

Almost immediately upon arriving in Hawaii, and in addition to her identification duties, Trotter had begun to solicit permission to undertake her stature estimation research. Indeed, she had accepted this position in Hawaii in no small part specifically because the opportunity for this research was so enticing. T. Dale Stewart and Charles E. Snow had helped to encourage Trotter to take this post by promoting the wealth of physical data she would be able to collect for the purpose of improving stature estimation methods.[33] Stewart and Trotter, longtime colleagues and friends, had already corresponded about a large potential stature estimation project in 1946, when Stewart was unsuccessfully seeking funding from the FBI expressly for this purpose.[34] He was Trotter's most trusted and frequent professional correspondent. Thomas "Dale" Stewart (1901–1997) was the Curator of Physical Anthropology at the Smithsonian's National Museum of Natural History and a regular consultant for the FBI on forensic anthropology cases. He was a prolific publisher and committed much of his later career to encouraging the development of and education in forensic anthropology. From 1954 to 1955, he would work in Kokura, Japan to identify Korean War dead. He combined this with research on determining age at death, similar to what Trotter had accomplished with World War II remains and stature, resulting in the 1957 manuscript, *Skeletal Age Changes in Young American Males*, coauthored with Thomas McKern. It was Trotter's indefatigable work and accomplishments that laid the groundwork for Stewart's research through the Army. Stewart credited his ability to undertake age-at-death determination research in Kokura to "the administrative break-through achieved by Dr. Trotter in Hawaii."[35]

In early April of 1948, the American Association of Physical Anthropologists (AAPA) had held a symposium on applied physical anthropology. This included Stewart's paper, "Medico-legal Aspects of the Skeleton I. Age, Sex, Race, and Stature" and Snow's description of the Army's process of identifying remains, "The Identification of the

Unknown War Dead."[36] Stewart touted the value of such a project, stating that "unlike sex, age, and race, wherein the subjective factor and experience play such prominent roles, stature can be determined by anyone who can measure bones and handle correlation tables or formulae," and encouraged anthropologists to do this research on the documented collections at Western Reserve and Washington University.[37] Snow's appointment with the AGRS was ending, and the Army was looking for a replacement.

Back in 1947, after 27 years in the anatomy department at the Washington University School of Medicine in St. Louis, Trotter claimed that she had been at a critical juncture. She had already starting looking into a possible leave of absence, either staying in St. Louis or possibly taking a short position at the Bishop Museum in Honolulu.[38] While at the same 1948 AAPA meeting where Stewart and Snow held their symposium, she had a casual conversation with a quiet young Army soldier who was present at a "smoker" social event. She discovered that he had apparently been sent by the Quartermaster to help identify Snow's replacement. Once others realized this soldier's scouting purpose, more anthropologists began to speak with him. But Trotter was the intended and leading candidate.[39] When Trotter discussed the prospect with Stewart, he appealed to Trotter to take the job. He claimed he would go himself but already had other commitments. Snow also encouraged Trotter and would maintain communications with her for decades, particularly to seek her advice on hair research topics. Trotter would later explain to a colleague, in specific reference to her work with the Army, that she had once seen a friend grieve the loss of a child, and she felt it important to give families closure.[40] With this perspective in mind, with Snow's and Stewart's support and recommendations, and with her previous experience consulting for the US Public Health Service from 1943 to 1945, Trotter accepted the post.

Stewart specifically encouraged her to use this as an opportunity to perform the research he had outlined in the 1948 applied physical anthropology symposium. The main argument was that stature estimation tables were still based on measurements from an 1888 study by Étienne Rollet on a sample of only 100 French cadavers, consisting almost entirely of elderly individuals.[41] Trotter had access to the Terry Collection of skeletons at Washington University, one of the few large and well-known, documented research samples, for her stature study. But the Terry Collection was derived from civilian deaths, consisted mostly of older individuals in variable states of health, and at that time overrepresented Black males compared to the living population. The representation of individuals between the ages of 18 and 25 in the Terry Collection was then only 2 White males and 44 Black males.[42] The military identification project offered the possibility to collect stature data from a much larger sample of young, otherwise relatively healthy American males from many backgrounds. This is a population that does not ordinarily die with such frequency, and resulting data would be more reliable and relevant to contemporary anthropological forensic cases than that from collections like the Terry.

The project would require taking systematic measurements of specific bones of individuals with known identities and comparing the resultant bone measurement data to records of living measured statures. She would measure the long bones (such as the femur of the thigh and the humerus of the upper arm) from this military population, as well as from the Terry Collection at Washington University. The Terry skeletons were derived from individuals with known statures, as measured from the cadavers. For the military sample, Trotter used only men whose "identities had never been questioned," and therefore had reliable antemortem statures available in their military medical records.[43] She would, with a statistician, produce mathematical stature estimation formulas which correlate the long bone measurements to the known stature measurements. These formulas could then be applied to skeletal cases where the living stature of a deceased individual is not known. The results would provide anthropologists with a more relevant and accurate height estimation method, which would aid in the overall process of identifying the remains of unknown deceased individuals in military, legal, academic, and other cases.

Though the military had a history of employing anthropologists to undertake anthropometry in order to meet the needs for an immediate requirement, such as uniform sizes, it had not previously allowed research exclusively for future reference or for the sole purpose of research.[44] During her time in Hawaii, Trotter would therefore have to work hard to explain her objectives and to get the approval to undertake her project. Her efforts sometimes bypassed normal military channels. As she characterized the attitude toward her strategy, "the Army can't understand how anybody can be so ignorant of the pattern as this civilian."[45] When Trotter relayed to her ally within the Quartermaster Corps, Captain O.W. Greenwood, Stewart's advice that she should not give up too easily, the officer found this humorous. Greenwood on the contrary thought that Trotter already had "too much tenacity for a woman" and didn't need any added encouragement.[46]

Always an avid and effective communicator, she canvased inside and outside the Army for advocates who could help her in this task. She sought advice and professional support from other anthropologists on her intended methodology. She wrote to and spoke with representatives for the Quartermaster Corps and its sub-department, the AGRS. She appealed to Colonel Stone at the Office of the Surgeon General and Lewis Weed at the National Research Council that she was "increasingly impressed with the thought that a great opportunity, here for the taking, is being neglected," and that "not being a member of the Army, I am not certain of the channels through which a recommendation, or better a plea of this kind, should be made, or even if it should be made at all. I realize that the only objective officially recognized is the return of remains."[47]

She seems to have encountered a revolving door of military officials whom she had to convince. When she was able to successfully make her case to one officer, anthropologist, or other influential person, she would then enlist him to solicit higher authorities on her behalf. She tried to appeal to emotion and obligation, stating (or, more accurately, *over*stating) that "if our knowledge of man can be increased through study of the remains of our war heroes, then it can truthfully be said that our boys have not died in vain."[48] If problems with her methods or plans were raised, Trotter devised remedies. In one response to a letter sent in support of Trotter from the Secretary of the Smithsonian Institution, the Quartermaster General responded that "we have been forced to withhold approval at this time. We could not conscientiously permit the diversion of personnel and funds from the immediate pressing mission for which they were authorized."[49] Her subsequent entreaties, with this response in mind, then included assurances that her work would in no way impede current identifications.

On the advice of anthropologist Kenneth Emory at the Bishop Museum in Honolulu, Trotter took advantage of a cocktail party invitation in late November 1948 at the house of the Commanding General of the Army's Pacific Command, Lieutenant General John Hull. Trotter later wrote to the head of the anatomy department at Washington University, that "fortified with a highball (you know a little goes a long way with me)," she approached Hull and made her case. He seemed to appreciate her argument and asked her to send him a letter to the same effect, marked "Personal."[50] She did. In the letter, after summarizing her research intentions and stressing that they would not detract from current identifications, she detailed the names and positions of the many civilians and military officers who explicitly support her research concept, methods, and the project's value to military and civilian skeletal identification.[51] Within 2 weeks, Trotter was approved to take the measurements, provided that "no additional funds or personnel will be required and that operating efficiency will not be impaired."[52]

Trotter had first requested official permission for the project in July of 1948. She received approvals and was able to measure the first bone for the study on Christmas Eve, December 24, 1948.[53] She had determined that the remains actively arriving in the laboratory were not as suitable for research as earlier skeletons had been, so she decided instead to use remains that were already identified and were being stored on Pearl Harbor while they awaited burial.[54] This specific plan was quickly approved, and she got started taking measurements of the long bones of individuals with known identities. She completed the military measurements in 1949 before ending her post. Ahead of her still remained the measurements of the Terry Collection skeletons, comparison of antemortem biological information to her measurements, and developing formulas to estimate stature.

Trotter had wanted Stewart to be included in any publications for this project, presumably for his notable role in generating the concept and perhaps also for consulting on methods.[55] By February of 1949, the military had decided that it should be an "Army endeavor," and that Trotter alone would be provided with funding to complete the work.[56] The field of physical anthropology at large had also received Stewart's and Snow's calls for better stature estimation studies, and C. Wesley Dupertuis had started a similar project using the collection at Western Reserve University.[57] Stewart and Trotter expected his project, later published in 1951, to bolster, not detract from, Trotter's planned work on a military population and the Terry Collection.[58] Yet Trotter still did not have official permissions and access from the Army to the other data that was vital to her work—the antemortem height measurements. Her campaign for approvals had to continue.

Writing to Colonel Waldron of the Quartermaster Corps, Trotter noted that "there is a crying need for a better approach to height estimation on Americans," and "it is regrettable that data on the living… have not been made available to us."[59] She was routed and re-rerouted through different channels, with no certainty of who even had the authority to give her the necessary approvals. When later given advice on how to "sell" her future research plans to the military, Trotter untangled an underlying problem: "it will be difficult to 'sell Memorial Division on' any investigation which might contribute to more accurate identification of unknown war dead. The Memorial Division assumes that an excellent job has been done with the knowledge already available."[60]

Eventually she was sent to Francis E. Randall, the lead anthropologist with the Quartermaster Corps, who had completed a joint PhD in Physical Anthropology and Biology at Harvard under Earnest Hooton in 1942 and worked on anthropometry projects for the Army.[61] Trotter, and possibly also Stewart, were suspicious of his intentions to potentially co-opt the research for himself. She had heard that, with Randall as advisor, two Army officials had a plan to have Trotter's collected data sent to an undetermined board, which Trotter seemed to suspect might include Stewart and Randall, in DC to undertake the actual analysis. Trotter made her stance known, that she "certainly [does] not propose to take a lot of measurements out here and turn them over to Randall.

And I shall be annoyed if I take measurements and then cannot acquire stature measurements from the files."[62]

In early correspondence, Randall seemed somewhat territorial about Trotter's work. He prepared his own prospectus on the project and planned to set an outline of investigations. He did not seem to understand that the work was already started and that she was not seeking any assistance in methods or plans from him; Trotter then made it clear to him that she simply needed official approvals for access to the antemortem records.[63] Randall had even held a "confidential meeting" in January of 1949 with Stewart and Krogman to ensure they were not seeking any credit and approved of Trotter's project.[64] But months later, in October, Randall wrote to Trotter stating that he would not approve her work until he first checks with Stewart and Krogman that they also approved of it.[65] Randall certainly underestimated the anthropologists' communication and openness among each other since Trotter was already aware of the earlier February meeting. His efforts may have been innocent or they may have been motivated by some unrelated and unknown military pressures, but no one would find out. Stewart wrote in November 1949 that "whether or not he was taking advantage of the situation for his purposes, we may never know," Randall had been killed in an airplane crash near DC the previous week.[66] She had to start over in her efforts to attain approvals for access to antemortem records, which would then be assisted by the new Quartermaster Corps anthropologist, Russell Newman.

Sometime before February of 1950 Trotter received her permissions for Army personnel records, and was still requesting Navy and Marine records.[67] By that point she was even back in the same city as most of the antemortem records she was not allowed access to, which were housed at the Military Personnel Records Center in St. Louis. It took until the summer of 1950 for her to receive the final approvals to actually access them. She also located original directions for height measurement at military induction for Army and Navy service members. Her work was not finished, but she finally had access to collect all of the data she needed.

All of these efforts to secure permissions are put in another perspective by the work of Franz Vandervael, from the University of Liege. During the 3 years that he worked and volunteered for the AGRS in Europe after World War I, he undertook research on aging using the remains of American soldiers, some of which he included in a 1952 book on skeletal age estimation.[68] When Trotter asked him in 1953 whether he too had a difficult time obtaining Army approvals for his project, Vandervael replied that "I had no difficulty at all for the reason I did not ask permission to anybody."[69] Certainly this tack would not have worked for Trotter, both as an American citizen and with the long-term aim to maintain a positive, ongoing relationship between the military and physical anthropologists in order to improve upon the processes of military identifications. Furthermore, with this information from Vandervael, Trotter surmised that he had never actually received the records of known ages from the Army, which made his conclusions and stature estimations entirely suspect.[70] Trotter's endeavors, though difficult and circuitous, were unquestionably worthwhile.

In early 1949, while still in Hawaii, Trotter was called on to make identifications for remains recovered from the USS Oklahoma, which sank during the Pearl Harbor bombings on December 7, 1941. Historian Heather Harris compiled a detailed description of this project, explaining Trotter's contributions to maintaining scientific integrity and the validity of identifications.[71] Trotter determined that the remains, which had been previously buried, disinterred, processed, reprocessed, and were heavily commingled, could not be individually identified. Further practical issues had arisen, such as what conditions justified a group burial versus individual unknown burials, and whether identifications should be made on solely a cranium and/or mandible when additional parts are likely present. Trotter found that in these USS Oklahoma cases, any association of a set of skeletal elements with an individual name lacked clear scientific evidence and only served to mislead people.

In response to her recommendation that these individual identifications were not scientifically possible at that time, the command simply decided to eliminate the requirement for an anthropologist to sign off on identifications. However, Major Stewart W. Abel heard Trotter's argument and found this unacceptable. With an insider proponent to maneuver within the acceptable military channels, and many discussions, it was eventually determined that the Army would follow Trotter's professional expertise and bury the remains as unknowns at the National Memorial Cemetery of the Pacific (Punchbowl) in Honolulu. Approval for the exhumation of the previously unidentified remains was granted in 2015 to the current iteration of the laboratory. Most have now been identified with the benefit of DNA comparisons, physical space, time, personnel, and other resources that Trotter did not have.

In 1951, while settled back in St. Louis, she was again called on to serve as an anthropological expert, this time with World War II remains from the Japanese POW camps at Cabanatuan in the Philippines. She was pleased to be asked because "it was implied that the Army had been satisfied with my work in Hawaii and it also promised adventure."[72] She went against the discouragement of her superiors in the Washington University anatomy department to accept the temporary job, which arose inopportunely at the beginning of the fall semester. As she wrote to a friend just before leaving St. Louis, "keep your fingers crossed for

Major Abel, Mildred Trotter, and Captain Kelly, Schofield Barracks, Oahu, June 22, 1949. VC170-i170254, Becker Medical Library, Washington University School of Medicine.

me. I'm not a bit enthusiastic about this undertaking."[73] She was in some ways excited but also knew that there are complications in these exploits, both physically and professionally. She slept under mosquito netting in a Quonset hut with two secretaries.[74] She did at least enjoy a picnic on an island in the polluted Pasig River eating local foods and was surprised, despite warnings from a local physician, that she did not get sick.

In a letter expressing the Army's pleasure at her temporary reappointment to Manila, the Chief of the Memorial Division of the QMC wrote that "no other echelon of the Armed Services has been called upon to perform a service with such delicate and far-reaching public relations aspects as the return of World War II Dead."[75] He continued, lauding that Trotter's "efforts in achieving accurate and positive identifications of World War II deceased have, in many instances, resulted in the elimination of any existing doubts and have played an essential part in easing the hearts and minds of the next of kin of those deceased."[76] This was important, as families of the deceased had early on expressed concern about the quality of identifications, handling of remains, as well as confusion about what expectations were reasonable from the identification efforts. In 1948 a reminder went out, compelling caution to avoid misinformation because "irresponsible comment regarding exhumations, concentrations, storage and shipping of remains has caused wholly unnecessary anguish for the next of kin of war dead" and that "inaccurate information… have caused next of kin to expect rights to which they are not entitled under the law and to neglect to ask for rights which are lawfully theirs."[77]

And yet despite the Army's confidence in Trotter, she was again thrust into a scenario that she could not fix. But when hired specifically to make individual identifications for a highly commingled group of remains in extremely poor condition from Cabanatuan, she had the expertise and resolve to say it could not properly be done. Heather Harris again thoroughly described the chaotic earlier identification attempts with the Cabanatuan remains, a history of which Trotter had also compiled by hand in order to better understand the predicament.[78] The project was plagued by poor planning, lack of anthropological expertise, and naiveté regarding the complexities of such an undertaking. This included the recent unsuccessful attempts of a young and relatively untrained anthropologist, Charles P. Warren, whose role consisted solely of following specific directions from AGRS staff in DC. Expectably, the project was floundering by the time Trotter was brought in.

When the caskets were exhumed from the cemetery in Manila for her to examine, water seeped from them due to the intervening years of seasonal monsoon rainfall. "We saw one casket held high in the air by the jaws of a crane with a stream of water running from it."[79] This issue will be unpleasantly familiar to anthropologists who have more recently worked on disinterments at the Manila American Cemetery. She and her assistants worked in a temporary building made of sheet metal. Colonel Abel, whom she had worked with and befriended in Hawaii when he was a Major, told her that "this place makes Hell feel like a deep freeze, doesn't it, Doc?"[80] She soon discovered that the work environment did not much matter, since the remains were in such a poor state. She furthermore described that they were "jumbled beyond belief."[81]

Yet again, the skeletons were not in good enough condition for Trotter to accomplish identifications at that time. She determined that the remains could not be individually identified through scientific bases and should therefore be buried as unknowns; she would not claim identifications which she could not find scientifically valid. The Army accepted her decision and reinterred the remains in Manila. Though she did not give the Army the individual identifications they had hoped for, Colonel Clearwater wrote to Trotter that "I have such complete confidence in your professional knowledge and honesty of purpose that I accept the outcome of the investigation without reservation. I feel that we now have a confident and indisputable judgment that the work of identification cannot reasonably be pursued further."[82] Trotter then used the opportunity to appeal for improvements to the overall AGRS methods, which would mostly include increased input from trained anthropologists earlier in the process.

Trotter had already named some of these failings and had recommended changes in 1949. At the end of her year-long post from 1948 to 1949, Colonel Waldron of the Quartermaster Corps requested a written critique of the AGRS identification process. Trotter provided a very candid one, which apparently left Colonel Waldron "shocked."[83] She explained the problems of using top level Army personnel who have no specific training for this work and are replaced at regular intervals due to their tours of duty, yet they are the ones who determine the process and make final identification decisions. Furthermore, work by the anthropologist was done not just in the blind, but "in the dark." Trotter's analyses of the remains were compared to antemortem information of unaccounted for individuals by a board of military officers, without further input from Trotter or other anthropologists. This was done deliberately in order to "test" her abilities, though it only served to further confound the process. As she expressed it, any tests should have been done prior to hiring her, since there was too much expense and too much at stake during the identifications, and it created unnecessary possibilities for errors. Trotter had already successfully argued that this protocol was counterproductive and it had been discontinued by July of 1949. She went on to note in her critique that at times the direction of efforts went toward making identifications not based on proof, but because they could not be disproven. Her final recommendation was the most compelling. She noted that much work was undertaken by improperly or completely untrained personnel, even if well-intended and working to the best of their ability. "If properly trained personnel are not to be found within the ranks of the Army then for the sake of accuracy the entire responsibility for the C.I.L. (administration and execution of the project) should be taken out of Army jurisdiction."[84]

Unfortunately, on the advice that with materials like this one could either "forward it or file it,"[85] Colonel Waldron filed it. Expectably then, these same issues have been recurrent throughout the long history of US identifications, and certain parts of the letter read as though they could have been written decades later. It became clear that the task of identifying war dead would continue as the Korean War soon began. Trotter and Stewart had found that military personnel were completely unprepared for anthropological work, but also that even most anthropologists within the relatively new field were not properly trained for the specific type of work needed for this and other forensic cases. They wanted to train young anthropologists because, as Trotter put it, "the ways of the army are tricky and it was my experience that they feel about physical anthropologists as they do about privates, i.e. the Army has complete control over them even in scientific matters."[86]

To proactively confront some of these issues, Trotter and Stewart decided to hold the summer seminar, starting in 1955, on human identification. This would encourage forensic-specific research, catalyze specialized forensic education for anthropologists, as well as paid fellowships to provide military identification-specific training to young PhDs. Trotter and Stewart maneuvered to get these fellowships funded by the Army, since the

Trotter seated at Schofield Barracks, Oahu, June 17, 1948. VC170-i170021, Becker Medical Library, Washington University School of Medicine.

issue had become a "long range" problem for the military.[87] This would be the precursor to the lab's longtime, ongoing relationship with the Oak Ridge Institute for Science and Education (ORISE) fellowship program, which brought many young anthropologists to the laboratory. Trotter also established and maintained military interest in forensic anthropology, inviting quartermaster corps officials to the AAPA meetings and the summer seminars. Trotter's and Stewart's work has shaped training, capability, and research, and has improved the quality of identification work possible at the Defense POW/MIA Accounting Agency.

At the end of her initial 1-year appointment to Hawaii in 1949, Trotter had enough time to take a vacation before returning to Missouri for the start of the fall semester. In late summer 1949, Trotter visited Japan and was the first woman arriving as a tourist after the war while the US still occupied the country.[88] She was able to visit a former student who was at the time in charge of a medical unit in Tokyo. She returned to the US by ship, via Honolulu. Once back in St. Louis, Trotter treated herself with a new Ford Custom Coupe, in sea mist green "with a heater and a radio."[89] Trotter always took pride in her cars, and in her entire lifetime had exclusively owned Fords, beginning with her first purchase in 1931.[90] She would also own a 1969 Fairlane and a 1975 Granada.

Her courses at Washington University started back up in early September. She also continued her work to complete the stature estimation research. She began her measurements of the Terry Collection long bones, which had documented biological information about the deceased, including stature and race, immediately available to her. She had acquired measurements of military deceased, and would eventually gain access to the antemortem files, in order to compare living statures to the skeletal measurements to create stature estimation formulas. To accomplish this last part, she also needed a statistician who could correlate the two sets of data – antemortem stature with postmortem long bone measurements.

Trotter found Goldine Cohnberg Gleser, who had just finished a PhD in psychology and also had an AM in mathematics at Washington University. Gleser described Trotter as "an unmarried woman about 50 years old with white hair and meticulous attire."[91] Indeed, Trotter was known for her polished appearance, and she even subscribed to *Vogue* magazine for years.[92] Gleser felt that she and Trotter "quickly developed a mutual liking for each other. I admired her scientific precision in everything she did, and she was constantly astonished that I could catch on so quickly to the problems involved with physical measurement and the identification of human remains. She particularly respected my ability to handle and organize her data and the fact that I discovered generational trends as well as age-related changes in stature from the data in addition to developing the equations."[93] Gleser impressed so many that after attending one AAPA annual meeting in conjunction with this project, she was invited to join the Association.[94]

Prior to completing their stature estimation research, in 1951, Trotter and Gleser published a study of the Terry Collection, looking at stature trends across ages. Among other details, they were the first to establish

Trotter standing outside the St. Louis Art Museum, January 1948. VC170-i170066, Becker Medical Library, Washington University School of Medicine.

that after attaining maximum height, individuals become shorter as they grow older.[95] This research made its way into popular press, with several headlines like "The Older You Get – The Shorter You Grow," and stating that Trotter confirmed, "if you're past 30 and you think you are getting shorter, you are probably right."[96] That same year Trotter and Gleser also published an article documenting generational variation in stature within the Terry Collection.[97]

Trotter and Gleser's larger project resulted in the 1952 publication of "Estimation of Stature from Long Bones of American Whites and Negroes" in the *American Journal of Physical Anthropology (AJPA)*. Here, Trotter and Gleser provided formulas to be used by inputting measurement data from unknown skeletal remains, which provide reliable stature estimates within ranges. They created these formulas by comparing this large sample of individuals with known heights to their postmortem bone measurements. Their sample included males from both the military and the Terry Collection, and females from the Terry Collection, totaling 1,619 individuals. In 1958, Trotter and Gleser published an expansion of this study with male data collected during subsequent Korean War identifications, "A Re-Evaluation of Estimation of Stature Based on Measurements of Stature Taken during Life and of Long Bones after Death." This relied on the measurements and data collected in the early 1950s by a team of anthropologists and technicians employed at the AGRS laboratory in Kokura, Japan.

These stature estimation papers have been an invaluable resource for decades and continue to be used today, particularly through a statistical computer program, *FORDISC*, created by Richard Jantz and Stephen Ousley.[98] Due to its obvious populational relevance, the data is still in heavy use at the Defense POW/MIA Accounting Agency laboratory. To provide just one extremely rough proxy for significance, according to Google Scholar, the 1952 publication had 1,907 citations, and the 1958 publication had 1,506 as of December 2021. These numbers continue to grow when periodically checked. In the 1970s, French anthropologist Emmanuel Eliakis published a kind of disc-shaped abacus of the formulas to make estimations easier, though Trotter and Stewart did not find its results to be entirely accurate.[99]

Though it is not well-known outside of physical anthropology and related circles, this research has had a least a couple of extracurricular appearances. It was somehow publicized enough to be noted in a *Cosmopolitan* magazine cartoon in June of 1953, referring to the relationship between long legs and height.[100] And the work was mentioned in a 1972 murder mystery novel, *The Body of a Girl*, by British attorney and author Michael Gilbert, which surprised and delighted Trotter.[101] She recommended the book to many friends and colleagues. More recent popular writing involving forensic science has included at least passing reference to Trotter and Gleser's work, including, to give a broad swath of examples: Susan Sheehan's 1986 *A Missing Plane* about the identification of remains from a World War II bomber, Jon Zonderman's 1990 *Beyond the Crime Lab*, and even Anne Marie Duquette's 1996 mystery romance novel *She Caught the Sheriff*.[102]

NOTES

1 Paul D. Emanovsky and William R. Belcher, "The Many Hats of a Recovery Leader: Perspectives on Planning and Executing Worldwide Forensic Investigations and Recoveries at the JPAC Central Identification Laboratory," in *A Companion to Forensic Anthropology*, ed. Dennis Dirkmaat (West Sussex: Wiley-Blackwell, 2012), 567–592.

2 Letter, Trotter to Mrs. Herbert Deignan, April 12, 1948, Series 3, Box 4, Folder 6, Mildred Trotter Papers, Becker Medical Library, Washington University School of Medicine.

3 Letter, R. E. Smyser, Jr. to the Commanding General, San Francisco Port of Embarkation and The Chief of Transportation, May 26, 1948, Series 3, Box 4, Folder 23, Mildred Trotter Papers, Becker Medical Library, Washington University School of Medicine.

4 Draft, Trotter, "The Department of Anatomy in My Time," p. 61, No Date, Series 1, Box 1, Mildred Trotter Papers, Becker Medical Library, Washington University School of Medicine.

5 Draft, Trotter, "The Department of Anatomy in My Time," p. 2, Appendix 1, No Date, Series 1, Box 1, Mildred Trotter Papers, Becker Medical Library, Washington University School of Medicine.

6 Letter, Trotter to Major Bryant, May 28, 1948, Series 3, Box 4, Folder 18, Mildred Trotter Papers, Becker Medical Library, Washington University School of Medicine.

7 Letter, Charles E Snow to No Recipient, May 17, 1948, Series 3, Box 4, Folder 16, Mildred Trotter Papers, Becker Medical Library, Washington University School of Medicine.

8 William M. Bass, "Charles Ernest Snow, 1910–1967," *American Journal of Physical Anthropology* 28, no. 3 (1968): 369–372, p. 369.

9 Mount Holyoke Club, *St. Louis Post-Dispatch*, May 9, 1948, 3G.

10 Letter, H. H. Iaggi to Medical Officer in Charge "Re: Medical Examination, Trotter," May 5, 1948, Series 3, Box 8, Folder 5, Mildred Trotter Papers, Becker Medical Library, Washington University School of Medicine.

11 Application for federal employment, Trotter, September 13, 1950, Series 3, Box 8, Folder 5, Mildred Trotter Papers, Becker Medical Library, Washington University School of Medicine.

12 Document, "Travel Information for Department of the Army Civilian Personnel Proceeding Overseas," November 3, 1947, Series 3, Box 4, Folder 23, Mildred Trotter Papers, Becker Medical Library, Washington University School of Medicine.
13 These Included Carol Skinner Cole (Draft, Trotter, "The Department of Anatomy in My Time," p. 6, No Date, Series 1, Box 1, Mildred Trotter Papers, Becker Medical Library, Washington University School of Medicine); Francis Randall (Letter, T.D. Stewart to Trotter, November 7, 1949, Series 3, Box 4, Folder 16); and Colonel Wall (T.D. Stewart to Trotter, July 17, 1956, Series 3, Box7, Folder 19).
14 Document, "Travel Information for Department of the Army Civilian Personnel Proceeding Overseas," November 3, 1947, Series 3, Box 4, Folder 23, Mildred Trotter Papers, Becker Medical Library, Washington University School of Medicine.
15 Marion Hunt, "Mildred Trotter: 'With Honor in Her Own Country'," *Outlook Magazine, Washington University School of Medicine* 17, no. 1 (Spring 1980): 8–13, p. 11.
16 Document, Mildred Trotter, "Operations at Central Identification Laboratory, A.G.R.S," Series 5, Box 15, Folder 5, Mildred Trotter Papers, Becker Medical Library, Washington University School of Medicine.
17 Letter, Trotter to T.D. Stewart, July 20, 1948, Series 3, Box 7, Folder 17, Mildred Trotter Papers, Becker Medical Library, Washington University School of Medicine.
18 Document, Mildred Trotter, "Operations at Central Identification Laboratory, A.G.R.S," Series 5, Box 15, Folder 5, Mildred Trotter Papers, Becker Medical Library, Washington University School of Medicine.
19 Draft, Trotter, "The Department of Anatomy in My Time," p. 62, No Date, Series 1, Box 1, Mildred Trotter Papers, Becker Medical Library, Washington University School of Medicine.
20 Draft, Trotter, "The Department of Anatomy in My Time," p. 62, No Date, Series 1, Box 1, Mildred Trotter Papers, Becker Medical Library, Washington University School of Medicine.
21 Letter, Trotter to T.D. Stewart, November 10, 1954, Series 3, Box 7, Folder 18, Mildred Trotter Papers, Becker Medical Library, Washington University School of Medicine.
22 Draft, Trotter, "The Department of Anatomy in My Time," p. 62, No Date, Series 1, Box 1, Mildred Trotter Papers, Becker Medical Library, Washington University School of Medicine.
23 Letter, Trotter to T.D. Stewart, July 20, 1948, Series 3, Box 7, Folder 17, Mildred Trotter Papers, Becker Medical Library, Washington University School of Medicine.

24 Letter, Trotter to Thomas McKern, August 20, 1948, Series 3, Box 4, Folder 23, Mildred Trotter Papers, Becker Medical Library, Washington University School of Medicine.
25 Richard Hudgens, quoted in "Lasting Lessons," no author, *Washington University Magazine and Alumni News* 69, no. 2 (Summer 1999): 8.
26 Document, Mildred Trotter, "Operations at Central Identification Laboratory, A.G.R.S," Series 5, Box 15, Folder 5, Mildred Trotter Papers, Becker Medical Library, Washington University School of Medicine.
27 Letter Trotter to Thomas McKern, August 20, 1948, Series 3, Box 4, Folder 23, Mildred Trotter Papers, Becker Medical Library, Washington University School of Medicine.
28 Letter, Trotter to Edmund Cowdry, November 26, 1948, Series 3, Box 4, Folder 23, Mildred Trotter Papers, Becker Medical Library, Washington University School of Medicine.
29 Draft, Trotter, "The Department of Anatomy in My Time," p. 63, No Date, Series 1, Box 1, Mildred Trotter Papers, Becker Medical Library, Washington University School of Medicine.
30 Letter, Trotter to Lewis H. Weed, September 16, 1948, Series 3, Box 2, Folder 23, Mildred Trotter Papers, Becker Medical Library, Washington University School of Medicine.
31 Letter, Thomas McKern to Trotter, July 30, 1948, Series 3, Box 4, Folder 23, Mildred Trotter Papers, Becker Medical Library, Washington University School of Medicine.
32 T. Dale Stewart, *Essentials of Forensic Anthropology: Especially as Developed in the United States* (Springfield, IL: Charles C. Thomas, 1979), pp. 12–13.
33 T. Dale Stewart, *Essentials of Forensic Anthropology: Especially as Developed in the United States* (Springfield, IL: Charles C. Thomas, 1979), pp. 12–13.
34 Letter, T.D. Stewart to Trotter, November 5, 1946, Series 3, Box 7, Folder 17, Mildred Trotter Papers, Becker Medical Library, Washington University School of Medicine.
35 T. Dale Stewart, *Essentials of Forensic Anthropology: Especially as Developed in the United States* (Springfield, IL: Charles C. Thomas, 1979), pp. 12–13.
36 T. Dale Stewart, "Medico-legal Aspects of the Skeleton, I. Age, Sex, Race, and Stature," *American Journal of Physical Anthropology* 6, no. 3 (1948): 315–321; Charles E. Snow, "The Identification of the Unknown War Dead," *American Journal of Physical Anthropology* 6, no. 3 (1948): 323–328.
37 T. Dale Stewart, "Medico-legal Aspects of the Skeleton, I. Age, Sex, Race, and Stature," *American Journal of Physical Anthropology* 6, no. 3 (1948): 315–321, p. 319.

38 Draft, Trotter, "The Department of Anatomy in My Time," p. 61, No Date, Series 1, Box 1, Mildred Trotter Papers, Becker Medical Library, Washington University School of Medicine.
39 T. Dale Stewart, *Essentials of Forensic Anthropology: Especially as Developed in the United States* (Springfield, IL: Charles C. Thomas, 1979), p. 12.
40 Ann Randolph Flipse Gerber, "*Remarks Prepared for the Memorial Service for Mildred Trotter*, Ph.D. 1899–1991," October 9, 1991, http://beckerexhibits.wustl.edu/mowihsp/bios/FlipseMemTrotter.htm.
41 Étienne Rollet, *De la Mensuration des Os Longs des Membres* (Lyon: Storck, 1888).
42 Letter, Trotter to Russell Newman, April 12, 1951, Series 3, Box 4, Folder 16, Mildred Trotter Papers, Becker Medical Library, Washington University School of Medicine.
43 Trotter to Francis E. Randall, October 8, 1949, Series 3, Box 4, Folder 16, Mildred Trotter Papers, Becker Medical Library, Washington University School of Medicine.
44 For a history of anthropometry in the military at the time Trotter began her work, see F. E. Randall, "Anthropometry in the Quartermaster Corps," *American Journal of Physical Anthropology* 6, no. 3 (1948): 373–380.
45 Letter (unsent), Trotter to Francis E. Randall, no date (likely early 1949), Series 3, Box 4, Folder 23, Mildred Trotter Papers, Becker Medical Library, Washington University School of Medicine.
46 Letter, Trotter to T.D. Stewart, November 30, 1948, Series 3, Box 4, Folder 17, Mildred Trotter Papers, Becker Medical Library, Washington University School of Medicine.
47 Letter, Trotter to Col. William S. Stone, October 15, 1948, Series 3, Box 4, Folder 23, Mildred Trotter Papers, Becker Medical Library, Washington University School of Medicine.
48 Letter, Trotter and O. W. Greenwood to Commanding General USARPAC, August 6, 1948, Series 3, Box 4, Folder 23, Mildred Trotter Papers, Becker Medical Library, Washington University School of Medicine.
49 Letter, T.B. Larkin to A. Wetmore, October 29, 1948, Series 3, Box 4, Folder 18, Mildred Trotter Papers, Becker Medical Library, Washington University School of Medicine.
50 Letter, Trotter to Edmund Cowdry, November 26, 1948, Series 3, Box 4, Folder 23, Mildred Trotter Papers, Becker Medical Library, Washington University School of Medicine.
51 Letter, Trotter to Lt. Gen. John E Hull (Commanding General, USARPAC), November 24, 1948, Series 3, Box 4, Folder 23, Mildred Trotter Papers, Becker Medical Library, Washington University School of Medicine.

52 Letter, Norman E. Waldron to Trotter, December 15,1948, Series 3, Box 2, Folder 23, Mildred Trotter Papers, Becker Medical Library, Washington University School of Medicine.
53 Letter, Trotter to Francis E. Randall, October 8, 1949, Series 3, Box 4, Folder 16, Mildred Trotter Papers, Becker Medical Library, Washington University School of Medicine.
54 Letter, Trotter to T.D. Stewart, November 30, 1948, Series 3, Box 7, Folder 17, Mildred Trotter Papers, Becker Medical Library, Washington University School of Medicine.
55 Letter, Trotter to T.D. Stewart, July 20, 1948, Series 3, Box 7, Folder 17, Mildred Trotter Papers, Becker Medical Library, Washington University School of Medicine.
56 Letter, Marshall T. Newman to Trotter, February 7, 1949, Series 3, Box 4, Folder 17, Mildred Trotter Papers, Becker Medical Library, Washington University School of Medicine.
57 C. Wesley Dupertuis and John A. Hadden, "On the Reconstruction of Stature from Long Bones," *American Journal of Physical Anthropology* 9, no. 1 (1951): 15–54.
58 Letter, T.D. Stewart to Trotter, April 26, 1949, Series 3, Box 4, Folder 16, Mildred Trotter Papers, Becker Medical Library, Washington University School of Medicine.
59 Letter, Trotter to Norman E. Waldron, March 4, 1949, Series 3, Box 4, Folder 23, Mildred Trotter Papers, Becker Medical Library, Washington University School of Medicine.
60 Letter, Trotter to Russell Newman, April 12, 1951, Series 3, Box 4, Folder 16, Mildred Trotter Papers, Becker Medical Library, Washington University School of Medicine.
61 Robert M. White, "Francis Eugene Randall, 1914–1949," *American Journal of Physical Anthropology* 8, no. 1 (1950): 113–117.
62 Letter, Trotter to T.D. Stewart, February 3, 1949, Series 3, Box 4, Folder 17, Mildred Trotter Papers, Becker Medical Library, Washington University School of Medicine.
63 Letter, Francis E. Randall to Trotter, October 11, 1949, Series 3, Box 4, Folder 16; and Letter, Trotter to Randall, October 15, 1949, Series 3, Box 4, Folder 16, Mildred Trotter Papers, Becker Medical Library, Washington University School of Medicine.
64 Letter, Marshall T. Newman to Trotter, February 7, 1949, Series 3, Box 4, Folder 17, Mildred Trotter Papers, Becker Medical Library, Washington University School of Medicine.
65 Letter, Francis E. Randall to Trotter, October 11, 1949, Series 3, Box 4, Folder 16, Mildred Trotter Papers, Becker Medical Library, Washington University School of Medicine.
66 Letter, T.D. Stewart to Trotter, November 7, 1949, Series 3, Box 4, Folder 16, Mildred Trotter Papers, Becker Medical Library, Washington University School of Medicine.

67 Letter, Trotter to Hoyt Lemons, February 8, 1950, Series 3, Box 4, Folder 16, Mildred Trotter Papers, Becker Medical Library, Washington University School of Medicine.
68 Franz Vandervael, *Critères d'estimation de l'âge des squelettes entre* 18 et 38 ans (Bologna: La Grafica Emiliana, 1952).
69 Letter, Franz Vandervael to Trotter, February 21, 1953, Series 3, Box 8, Folder 16, Mildred Trotter Papers, Becker Medical Library, Washington University School of Medicine.
70 Trotter's handwritten notes over Letter, Franz Vandervael to Trotter, February 21, 1953, Series 3, Box 8, Folder 16, Mildred Trotter Papers, Becker Medical Library, Washington University School of Medicine.
71 The Defense Prisoner of War/Missing Personnel Office, World War II Division Memo, To: Geographic File, From: Heather Harris, dtd 1 March 2010, last update 10 April 2012. Re: History of the Sinking of USS Oklahoma and subsequent attempts to recover and identify her crew.
72 Draft, Trotter, "The Department of Anatomy in My Time," p. 81, No Date, Series 1, Box 1, Mildred Trotter Papers, Becker Medical Library, Washington University School of Medicine.
73 Letter, Trotter to "Donna," September 19, 1951, Series 7, Box 25, Folder 11, Mildred Trotter Papers, Becker Medical Library, Washington University School of Medicine.
74 Draft, Trotter, "The Department of Anatomy in My Time," p. 82, No Date, Series 1, Box 1, Mildred Trotter Papers, Becker Medical Library, Washington University School of Medicine.
75 Letter, James B. Clearwater to Trotter, June 19, 1951, Series 3, Box 4, Folder 16, Mildred Trotter Papers, Becker Medical Library, Washington University School of Medicine.
76 Letter, James B. Clearwater to Trotter, June 19, 1951, Series 3, Box 4, Folder 16, Mildred Trotter Papers, Becker Medical Library, Washington University School of Medicine.
77 Memorandum, Norman E. Waldron, "To: All Military and Civilian Members of this Command, Subj: Irresponsible Talk Regarding AGRS activities and Policies," September 20, 1948, Series 3, Box 4, Folder 23, Mildred Trotter Papers, Becker Medical Library, Washington University School of Medicine.
78 The Defense Prisoner of War/Missing Personnel Office, World War II Division Memo, To: Philippines Geographic File, From: Heather Harris and Lisa Breckinbaugh, dtd 13 Oct 2005, Revised 20 Feb 2014. Re: Casualties of Cabanatuan Prisoner of War Camp #1 and the history of their burials. See also The Handwritten Notes by Trotter, Series 3, Box 4, Folder 19, Mildred Trotter Papers, Becker Medical Library, Washington University School of Medicine.

79 Draft, Trotter, "The Department of Anatomy in My Time," p. 82, no date, series 1, box 1, Mildred Trotter Papers, Becker Medical Library, Washington University School of Medicine.
80 Draft, Trotter, "The Department of Anatomy in My Time," p. 83, No Date, Series 1, Box 1, Mildred Trotter Papers, Becker Medical Library, Washington University School of Medicine.
81 Letter, Trotter to James B. Clearwater, November 1, 1951, Series 3, Box 4, Folder 19, Mildred Trotter Papers, Becker Medical Library, Washington University School of Medicine.
82 Letter, James B. Clearwater to Trotter, January 3, 1952, Series 3, Box 4, Folder 16, Mildred Trotter Papers, Becker Medical Library, Washington University School of Medicine.
83 Letter, Stewart W. Abel to Trotter, September 2, 1949, Series 5, Box 12, Folder 10, Mildred Trotter Papers, Becker Medical Library, Washington University School of Medicine.
84 Letter, Trotter to Norman E. Waldron, August 18, 1949, Series 3, Box 4, Folder 22, Mildred Trotter Papers, Becker Medical Library, Washington University School of Medicine.
85 Letter, Stewart W. Abel to Trotter, September 2, 1949, series 5, box 12, folder 10, Mildred Trotter Papers, Becker Medical Library, Washington University School of Medicine.
86 Letter, Trotter to Sherwood Washburn, August 28 1951, series 13, box 8, folder 14, Mildred Trotter Papers, Becker Medical Library, Washington University School of Medicine.
87 Letter, Trotter to Hastings, April 17, 1956, series 3, box 7, folder 19, Mildred Trotter Papers, Becker Medical Library, Washington University School of Medicine.
88 Mildred Trotter, interviewed by Estelle Brodman, May 19, 1972 and May 23, 1972, transcript, Becker Medical Library, Washington University School of Medicine; Draft, Trotter, "The Department of Anatomy in My Time," p. 38, no date, series 1, box 1, Mildred Trotter Papers, Becker Medical Library, Washington University School of Medicine
89 Letter, Trotter to Don C. Herr, September 20, 1949, series 3, box 4, folder 16, Mildred Trotter Papers, Becker Medical Library, Washington University School of Medicine.
90 Letter, Trotter to D.C. Lesseg, September 29, 1983, series 13, box 7, folder 3; and Letter, Trotter to "Anne," July 19, 1969, series 13, box 43, folder 3, Mildred Trotter Papers, Becker Medical Library, Washington University School of Medicine. Mildred Trotter Papers, Becker Medical Library, Washington University School of Medicine.
91 Goldine C. Gleser, *Getting It All* (Seattle, WA: Keepsake Editions, 2000), p. 90.

92 Letter, Trotter to *Vogue*, March 2, 1970, series 13, box 7, folder 5, Mildred Trotter Papers, Becker Medical Library, Washington University School of Medicine.
93 Goldine C. Gleser, *Getting It All* (Seattle, WA: Keepsake Editions, 2000), pp. 96–97.
94 Goldine C. Gleser, *Getting It All* (Seattle, WA: Keepsake Editions, 2000), p. 97.
95 Mildred Trotter and Goldine C. Gleser, "Trends in Stature of American Whites and Negroes Born between 1840 and 1924," *American Journal of Physical Anthropology* 9, no. 4 (1951): 427–440.
96 "The Older You Get – The Shorter You Grow," *The Sunday Herald*, Sep 23, 1951; "Old, Fat Men Weather Life Better," *Wilmington News*, September 18, 1951.
97 Trotter, Mildred, and Goldine C. Gleser, "Trends in Stature of American Whites and Negroes Born between 1840 and 1924," *American Journal of Physical Anthropology* 9, no. 4 (1951): 427–440.
98 Richard L. Jantz and Stephen D. Ousley, *FORDISC 3* (Knoxville, TN: The University of Tennessee, 2005).
99 Emmanuel Eliakis, "Présentation d'un Abaque Servant à la Détermination de la Stature d'après la Longueur des Os Longs," *Bulletins et Mémoires de la Société d'Anthropologie de Paris* 9, no. 3 (1972): 177–182; Letter, T. Dale Stewart to Trotter, May 18, 1973, series 13, box 6, folder 12, Mildred Trotter Papers, Becker Medical Library, Washington University School of Medicine.
100 Letter, Amram Scheinfeld to Trotter, June 1, 1953, series 3, box 7, folder 9, Mildred Trotter Papers, Becker Medical Library, Washington University School of Medicine.
101 Letter, Trotter to Joan Kahm (Harper and Row), October 18, 1972, series 3, box 6, folder 14; and Letter, Trotter to T.D. Stewart, May 30, 1973, series 13, box 6, folder 12, Mildred Trotter Papers, Becker Medical Library, Washington University School of Medicine.
102 Susan Sheehan, *A Missing Plane* (New York: Putnam, 1986); Jon Zonderman, *Beyond the Crime Lab: The New Science of Investigation* (New York: Wiley, 1990); Anne Marie Duquette, *She Caught the Sheriff* (Toronto: Harlequin Books, 1996).

CHAPTER 3

The Tibia

Of this defining moment in Trotter's career within physical anthropology, her measurement of one particular bone for her stature estimation publication has drawn sustained notoriety. Something strange had happened with the tibia (also known as the shinbone) and the stature formulas related to it. Despite the publication being in frequent use throughout the intervening decades, it took a very long time to come clearly to light. In the 1990s, a few years after Trotter's death, this error was finally discovered, and the formulas have since been modified in the attempt to mitigate the problem. It became a widely known and fixating error within anthropology. Contrary to the later emphasis given to this one particular failure, Trotter had been known throughout her career to be quite meticulous. As one editor of the *American Journal of Physical Anthropology (AJPA)* wrote to her, "I only wish that everyone took as much pains as you do in the preparation of text, tables, and figures."[1] Another stated that "this is so much better than most of what we get."[2] But with this expansive project, Trotter did indeed make and continue to miss a major error. The synopsis is that the way Trotter described her tibia measurement and the way she actually measured the tibia were not the same.

For her 1952 stature estimation publication, Trotter personally took measurements of long bones of World War II and Terry Collection skeletons. She seems to have used an assistant to record her measurements. She provided written descriptions for each measurement technique so that anthropologists using the resultant stature estimation formulas could replicate them. Trotter's published 1952 description of the maximum length of the tibia explains that it is to be taken with the

> end of malleolus against vertical wall of the osteometric board, bone resting on its dorsal surface with its long axis parallel with the long axis of the board, block applied to the most prominent part of lateral half of lateral condyle.[3]

DOI: 10.4324/9781003252818-3

This description appears to include the medial malleolus (the bony prominence on the inside of the ankle). She omits any reference citation for this particular method, unlike every other description she provides. For the second tibia measurement, "ordinary length," which is not used in the later 1958 publication, she cites only personal communication with Krogman. This was "measured with spreading calipers from the center of the articular surface of the lateral condyle to the center of the inferior articular surface," and does not include the malleolus.

For the follow-up 1958 study, data was provided by measurements of Korean War deceased, which Trotter did not personally collect. Anthropology technicians working with Korean War remains measured all bones according to her 1952 written descriptions. For the tibia, only maximum length was included for this second paper. Trotter noted various inconsistencies in the data and results for most long bones between the two studies in the 1958 publication, explaining that "errors in such an involved undertaking are bound to be multiple since they can arise from so many possible sources [...] It is likely that errors are random and thus have not biased the averages of stature and bone lengths."[4] But of all the long bones, the tibia showed the greatest difference and the only significant variation between the 1952 and the 1958 studies. The Korean War tibias were 5.6–7.68 mm longer, while other bones only varied from 0.0–1.57 mm. The average living statures of the individuals did not change significantly between the two groups. And for the 1958 studies, tibia measurements of individuals were longer than fibulas, which was opposite of the findings from 1952.

Trotter recognized that there was a problem with the tibia, but her only explanation in 1958 was that

> possibly this difference between the two studies may be accounted for by different technicians measuring the maximum length of the tibia (from the end of malleolus to the most prominent part of the lateral half of the lateral condyle) which, of all the long limb bone lengths, is the most difficult to reproduce.[5]

Trotter and Gleser had decided that

> such a difference could result from either a change in the stature-tibia relationship (i.e., the tibia is actually longer relative to stature and, also, to lengths of other long limb bones in White males of the present series than of the World War II series) or from variation in the technique of measuring the tibia. The latter explanation

> seems more likely since a corresponding difference is not found in the length of the companion bone, the fibula.[6]

They were correct that the problem was the measurement, but they did not at that time recognize that it was actually Trotter's 1952 measurement that varied from the description, and not the Korean War technicians'. Trotter did not probe further into the discrepancy at the time, and throughout her life she makes no further mention of it in the literature.

In 1994 and 1995, Richard Jantz, David Hunt, and Lee Meadows Jantz determined that Trotter's 1952 maximum length measurement description was not written in accordance with the actual method she used to measure the tibia.[7] In this landmark research, Jantz et al. (1995) compared records of Trotter's measurements of the Terry Collection to updated measurements of a selection of the same individuals taken by one of the authors (Hunt) following Trotter's written description. They found that Trotter's tibia measurement was an average (across groups) of 10.18–12.83 mm smaller than the measurement taken in the 1990s by Hunt. Trotter's actual method was, unlike her description, more consistent with a measurement which excludes the medial malleolus. Measurements of other long bones (such as the femur) were closely reproducible by Hunt.

Anthropology technicians who measured the tibias for the 1958 publication did so following her 1952 written description, which, based on this 1995 research, must have varied from her actual method. In the absence of the same Korean War remains from the 1958 study for re-measurement, the authors compared the relationship of two bones from Korean War data (measured by technicians), and found that the tibia measurements were longer than those of the fibula. This would be consistent with including the malleolus, and with Trotter's written description. Results of my 2017 study comparing historical and modern measurements from exhumed Korean War remains confirm that the tibias for the 1958 study were consistently measured including the medial malleolus.[8] Trotter and Gleser had noticed this reversal of the tibia-fibula relationship as well in 1958. The tibias were longer than the fibulas in the 1958 study because they were measured with the malleolus, following the 1952 description; the "smaller" tibias in the 1952 study were likely measured without the malleolus, contrary to Trotter's description. Though they noticed the discrepancy, Trotter and Gleser did not pinpoint the underlying cause.

This inconsistency, of course, has had ramifications for stature estimates derived from this data. Using Trotter and Gleser's original formulas to estimate stature requires that an anthropologist replicate the measurement method used to create those formulas. If an anthropologist follows Trotter's written measurement description and uses the 1952 formulas, the resulting stature estimate would be inaccurate, over-estimating the height of the individual. Trotter at the time, and decades later, recommended using the original World War II formulas for American White and Black samples, wrongly believing this to be, in light of these inconsistencies, the more accurate data of the two studies.

Once Jantz et al. discovered the tibia error, the data and formulas have been modified to mitigate the problem. Trotter's stature data, including this correction, is most widely used to this day in a computer program, *FORDISC*. The *FORDISC 3* help file states that "Trotter's measurements of the tibia have been adjusted in *FORDISC* for the correct measurement of the tibia" based on the 1994 and 1995 research of Jantz et al.[9] These are 'corrected' measurements, produced by adding 10 mm to each tibia length, as opposed to actual re-measurement to provide the "correct" length, which is not possible. The *FORDISC* data was more recently, in 2019, found to have inadvertently been overcorrected for years by 20 mm instead of 10 mm.[10] Even now that the data has been re-adjusted to the intended 10 mm, the tibia continues to provide stature estimates that are not in line with those calculated from other long bones. So, unfortunately, even attempts to remedy the original tibia measurement error have been unsuccessful, and indicate that adding one set millimeter amount to each tibia length is still inaccurate. Once an error like this is made, it is difficult to retroactively solve it to any adequate satisfaction. Trotter's error has had longstanding repercussions, and the tibia measurement should be avoided for stature estimation from her data when possible.

Along with their specific findings, Jantz et al. concede that they cannot know how the error occurred and went uncorrected. They do, however, offer some rebukes of Trotter. The authors note that she "apparently had not received any formal instruction in measuring techniques," since she was trained at a medical school as an anatomist.[11] Indeed, she had never taken a course specifically in physical anthropology until she audited one after her retirement at Washington University.[12] But the same could be said of most other prominent physical anthropologists at the time. Of the 83 founding members of the American Association of Physical Anthropologists (AAPA), the plurality (28) held MDs, 23 were PhD anatomists, 18 held PhDs in other disciplines, 8 were unidentified, and only 6 actually held PhDs in anthropology.[13] Stewart himself held an MD, as well as Hrdlička and Robert J. Terry. It was standard within the discipline at the time to view anatomical training as perhaps the best qualification for physical anthropologists.[14]

Jantz et al. (1994) went on to state that

> it is hard to imagine why someone as experienced as Trotter would have chosen to depart from established

> practice and her own prescriptions. She never remarked on the change in her procedures, and we suspect that, strange as it seems, she was simply unaware of it. She seems to have been genuinely perplexed by the tibia-fibula inconsistencies between the WWII and Korean War studies. Her unsystematic references to measurement technique also suggest an inattentiveness to detail.[15]

While indeed Trotter departed from her own measurement description in the 1952 paper, and 'maximum' lengths included the malleolus, there was not necessarily one definitive, established practice for her to deviate from.

Jantz et al. cite Hrdlička (1952) and Martin (1957) as established references for tibia measurement (although both editions cited post-date Trotter's original work, the measurement descriptions did not change much from earlier formats). The most commonly prescribed measurements for the greatest length of the tibia, in their various formats, included the medial malleolus. Though she provided no citation for maximum length, and personal communication with Krogman for ordinary length of the tibia, for all other bones in the 1952 study, Trotter cited Hrdlička (1947) and Martin (1928).[16] These sources provided multiple variations of tibia measurements with the malleolus, with one name indicating different measurement techniques, sometimes difficult wording, and very few diagrams. Hrdlička described two tibia measurements, both of which included the malleolus. Martin provided four measurements, only one of which excludes the malleolus and which is measured with calipers (which would correspond more closely to Trotter's "ordinary length"). The other anthropologist undertaking a similar study at Western Reserve University around this time, Dupertuis, used Martin's measurement description for maximum length of the tibia (including the malleolus). Rollet in 1888 had used a measurement that included the malleolus, and Pearson developed regression formulas from Rollet's data with the malleolus in 1899. And this was the reference data Trotter had available to her for estimation of stature prior to her 1952 publication. Though measurement descriptions and names for the tibia were variable, the standard was to include the malleolus.

But Trotter's avoidance of citing Hrdlička (1947) or Martin (1928) for the tibia was clearly intentional, and not likely due to "inattentiveness to detail." Because the existing standards for tibia measurement were more inconsistent and provided more options than the standards for other bones did, along with any of her own unfamiliarity with the measurement, Trotter actively sought to identify the best method of measuring the tibia for stature estimation, even if that might stray from conventions. Her sources did not seem to agree that a tibia measurement that included the malleolus was the most useful for its relationship to stature, or on the particular details of how to take those measurements.

Consistent with the inconsistency in the literature though, it appears that she was measuring tibias throughout this time using multiple methods to suit her immediate purposes.[17] At least one type of measurement was used for comparison to older data (with the malleolus) for identification work, as well as other measurements that she surmised would correspond to newer research and better correlate to stature (usually without the malleolus). While she ultimately selected one style for the maximum length of the tibia for the 1952 research, she unfortunately recorded it as another. Why this did not by 1958 occur to her as even a potential explanation for the problem of the reversal of tibia-fibula relationship is unknown. She did think to question the later Korean War technician's measurements, but does not appear to have questioned her own.

While Jantz et al. (1995) considered that it could be plausible that Trotter may simply have "misconstrued the measurement definition" due to her ignorance of methods, they did not find it possible for her to have been as truly baffled as she seemed in print. They suspected that she may have realized her mistake, but had intentionally chosen to conceal it. To support this, they cited personal correspondence between Trotter and Henry McHenry from 1974 that demonstrated her implied understanding of the maximum length of the tibia as including the malleolus decades after this publication. All indications I have found in her correspondence and publications also show that she indeed did believe her maximum length of the tibia included the malleolus. But this in itself is not evidence to support the assertion that she concealed any possible knowledge of her error.

Trotter openly made other corrections when they were brought to her attention. When evidence of an unrelated error in her data came to light in 1976, Trotter and Gleser corrected a mistake from one individual's radius and ulna measurement data and its effects on the resultant stature formulas.[18] The error was discovered by T. Dale Stewart and Lucile E. St. Hoyme at the Smithsonian. Trotter was not eager to hear the criticism at first, and her initial reaction to a vague question about a possible anomaly with the radius was to ask Gleser to explain the variation to "satisfy" Stewart and St. Hoyme.[19] Stewart stressed that the one individual's measurements would only be plausible in cases of gigantism.[20] Trotter then readily shared her notes and data so that Stewart and St. Hoyme could check the problem by re-measuring that specific skeleton from the Terry Collection themselves, as Jantz et al. would also do decades later for their research on the tibia. After this, Trotter was quick to correct the error in print, publishing a corrigenda to the 1952 paper in 1977 in the *AJPA*. As this demonstrates, Trotter was open to admitting and correcting mistakes, particularly when it could improve the accuracy of her stature formulas. Her omission of a correction to the tibia problem, then, is not consistent with deliberate concealment. Gleser even commended Trotter and others for correcting the radius and ulna mistake: "congratulations on a great detective job! Tracking down an error after 25 years is no small accomplishment."[21]

Stewart had been looking into stature formulas in advance of his 1979 book *Essentials of Forensic Anthropology* and wrote to Trotter, "believe it or not, errors in two formulas (by different authors) for estimating bone age have been brought to my attention."[22] Even in this careful review which highlighted an issue with the radius and ulna, Stewart too did not specifically identify any one problem with the tibia—even with access to the Terry Collection to retake measurements for comparison. He had, of course, corresponded repeatedly in 1948 with Trotter specifically on the difficulties with the tibia, and was also aware of the general tibia problem in the 1958 paper. Stewart and Trotter were not shy to thoroughly question and critique one another. But the underlying basis of the tibia problem escaped them both.

Unlike the more easily uncovered typos for the radius and ulna (e.g., 335 vs. 235 mm), the tibia problem did not result from a random blip. The differences Trotter and Gleser themselves found between World War II and Korean War tibias ranged from 5.6–7.68 mm. This was much smaller, and possibly less alarming, than the 10.18–12.83 mm Jantz et al. later found for the Terry Collection when remeasuring the same individuals. There likely was some noise to this data caused by, among other uncontrollable variables as stated by Trotter, the numerous technicians measuring the Korean War tibias and that these were the tibias of different individuals.

Identifying the issue alone did not point to a clear cause or actionable solution though. She and Gleser had noted the inconsistencies between tibia measurements in 1952 and 1958 studies, they just did not pinpoint the underlying problem, and therefore any resolution. Perhaps the issue with the tibia was too systematic of an error, making it more difficult to identify one specific mistake or solution, as was possible in the case of the radius and ulna. The data looked organized and systematic because this was an inherent error in her work that affected every single tibia. To Trotter and Gleser, it simulated secular change, populational variation, or age-related proportional changes, and they never sorted out the source of the error. This is further affirmed by Jantz et al.'s (1995) surprise that future anthropologists using the formulas didn't pick up on the issue, even when they specifically identified odd discrepancies with estimations derived from the tibia compared to other bones. Once the error was made, it was insidious, and Trotter was not the only one deceived by the data for decades.

Her correspondence and publications during this time do not suggest that Trotter attempted to conceal a known problem. She unabashedly lists problems encountered in compiling the data to everyone involved. In official quarterly progress reports, Trotter submitted to the Army throughout the preparation of the 1958 publication, she openly relays data problems, and notes the tibia discrepancy, in particular, and describes her efforts to investigate each.[23] She was also dealing with many other variables that complicated the data. She noted or discussed this particular tibia inconsistency, along with others, in all her preparatory work with the Army, in correspondence with Quartermaster Corps anthropologist Russell Newman, with Gleser, and explicitly in the final 1958 publication. She reached out to other anthropologists, such as Stewart, who had worked with the Korean War remains and the technicians who measured them. The tibia problem appears to have been a genuine mistake that confounded Trotter and others involved in the project.

'A VERY TROUBLESOME BONE'

'How do you measure the tibia?' – Trotter asked this direct question in the summer and fall of 1948 in letters to fellow physical anthropologists. She had begun the 1-year contract with the US Army in the Territory of Hawaii that June and had been measuring bones only for identification work and not yet for research. She had accepted the job with the hope of using the opportunity to undertake this project. But her lead time was minimal – less than 3 months after she first discussed the job with an Army representative, she departed for Hawaii. She did not have a set research plan until after she arrived. To start her stature estimation project, she wanted to be certain of her methods. While temporarily out in the Pacific, she did not have immediate access to all available articles, books, and colleagues that would have provided her with proper references. So she sought, in addition to reference materials and a reference skeleton, the guidance of colleagues. She maintained her already very active correspondence, surveying for general advice, input on what would assist her in her work, and, from a few, specific advice on measurements. Almost immediately upon starting work in Hawaii, she sought particulars from respected colleagues on the technical details of certain bone measurements for the study. Most of this correspondence concerned the tibia. The tibia is an oddly shaped bone which has historically been measured in a variety of manners, and at that time did not have, unlike many other bones, a singular, established protocol for maximum length.

Measurement descriptions included or excluded the tibial spine, used the medial or lateral condyles, and oriented the bone in a variety of ways. She wrote to Stewart and Krogman for information on how the measurement is most commonly described, how the bone is measured in practice, and how they think it *should* be measured. She sought not only their opinions on the measurement and the best reference for measurements, but also which measurement they believed would be best correlated to stature.

In July she wrote to T. Dale Stewart asking for advice. He responded:

> The only criticism I have… is in the third paragraph where the method of measuring the tibia is described. There, in the second line, the words, 'or medial malleolus', should be deleted. Everyone has recognized that the tibia should be measured between the articular extremities; that is, without the spine or medial malleolus. However, in practice everyone, like Rollet, has eliminated the spine but not the malleolus.[24]

He re-emphasized that the "tibia should be measured without either spine or malleolus, i.e. between articular extremities." Stewart knew that the malleolus was usually included, but he recommended here, and in a handwritten correction to her previous letter, that the malleolus should *not* be included for Trotter's project.

In August, she reached out to Wilton M. Krogman at the University of Pennsylvania and then-current President of the AAPA, "should not the spine and medial malleolus be excluded in taking the length? How do you measure the tibia?"[25] In the letter she also requests reprints to be sent along, a reminder that she was on an island in the Pacific and did not have full or immediate access to reference materials at that moment. He wrote back, writing directly on her original letter, "Yes." He also drew a schematic, writing "lat cond depth" at the proximal end and "depth on dist. end."[26] This image unambiguously denotes the distance between articular surfaces, excluding the medial malleolus. His sketch indicated that calipers, and not an osteometric board, be used for this particular measurement. Krogman did not name this measurement and it did not conform to any of his measurement descriptions, including a similar "physiological length," which involved the *medial* condyle. This letter appears to be what Trotter cited in the 1952 measurement description for the "ordinary length" of the tibia.

In November of 1948 she wrote yet again to Stewart:

> But what about the Tibia? Krogman, I gather, measures it with spreading calipers. He didn't say so in so many words but he

> implied that he took the shortest length between the inferior articular surface and the lateral condyle (of the head).
>
> Please tell me what measurements to take on the Tibia. I find it a very troublesome bone. Here we are measuring from the rim of the lateral condyle to the tip of the medial malleolus. Even though our osteometric board has no slit in the stationary end through which the medial malleolus can slide. I can eliminate both spine and medial malleolus, but then I'm measuring from the rim of the lateral condyle to the rim of the distal articular surface.[27]

This makes it clear that Trotter had been measuring the tibia with the malleolus included for identification casework, since she had not yet begun her measurements for the research project. This was the measurement she could compare to Rollet and Pearson data. She also had ideas for how to measure without the malleolus on an osteometric board. Both Krogman and Stewart had by that point advised her to take measurements excluding the malleolus, with calipers or an osteometric board, though they of course do not describe it as 'maximum length'.

She prodded Stewart again for a clarification that December when she found out that the approval to start her project was imminent: "I'm anxious to know your ideas on taking the length of the tibia."[28] Stewart then replied:

> Greatest length of the tibia is indeed an annoying measurement. Apparently the older measurements were taken on an osteometric board which had a hole in the vertical head piece to accommodate [read: omit] the spine. . . . In the field… I have measured from the medial side of the proximal articular surface to the tip of the malleolus. If time permits, I would suggest that you take this measurement and also one connecting the centers of the superior and inferior articular surfaces. The first of these measurements would be useful for comparison with the older records. The second might yield a closer correlation with stature. The main thing to remember, however, is that you should have a clear idea of what you are measuring and stick to it. As long as others know exactly what measurements you took they can use your data.[29]

But it seems that consistency is one thing she did not accomplish. Douglas Ubelaker later described that "research by Jantz et al. suggests that while Stewart's advice was frequently sought, it was not always followed."[30] But Stewart had twice indicated to her that taking the tibia measurement without the malleolus was the more modern and likely useful measurement; and measuring with the malleolus was beneficial mostly only for comparing to older data. But here he indicated that she should also take one measurement with the malleolus. Of course, she also received varied and sometimes contradictory advice from other sources. In the end, she decided to include two measurements, likely intended to capture the variation in opinions: "ordinary" (with calipers from proximal and distal articular surfaces, excluding the malleolus) and "maximum" (with an osteometric board, allegedly including the malleolus). But whether she intended to include the malleolus for her maximum length or not, at some point in time she lost sight of the fact that she had in actuality excluded the malleolus while describing it for future anthropologists as being included. She confused her actual technique and her description.

Throughout her time in Hawaii, Trotter had been measuring tibias for her research project differently than for identification casework, and she seems to have varied how she took measurements for different purposes. She used at least four different variations of measurement techniques across that year to measure the tibia. She also struggled with the quality of her assistants, and later cautioned Stewart to find a better one than she had: "I was thwarted at every turn and was always given the least intelligent person to record figures."[31] It is less surprising then, though no less problematic, that she mixed up which specific tibia measurement she used for these particular bones. More confusing is how she made the same mistake for the Terry Collection too, which she measured back in St. Louis. It appears that Trotter measured the World War II tibias in the same manner that she measured those from the Terry Collection, as evidenced by the tibia-fibula relationship, so at least that means all of her 1952 data was consistent. For much of her identification casework though, it appears she used the maximum length of the tibia, including the malleolus. She did this in order to emulate the methods of Rollet (1888) and Pearson (1899) that she used for stature calculation.[32] She clearly measured the USS *Oklahoma* remains from around February to March 1949 *with* the malleolus, as evidenced by the nearly identical lengths when comparing her measurements to those taken at DPAA starting in 2016 following their exhumations.[33] For 417 left and right tibias, Trotter's measurements are a mean difference of 0.50 mm larger (ranging from 11 mm smaller to 10 mm larger) than DPAA's measurements. This is less than the variation for 226 left and right fibulas, with Trotter's measurements being a mean of 0.86 mm larger (ranging from 6 mm smaller to 12 mm larger). When she was definitively taking the maximum (or condylar-malleolar) length of the tibia, she was doing it properly, so the error was not a misconstrued technique or mis-application, it was Trotter taking the wrong measurement. It seems she wanted to use a measurement that excluded the malleolus because she believed it might be more closely correlated with stature. Unfortunately, in the end she took two measurements without the malleolus, not just one, but recorded her technique incorrectly.

Nothing was noticed to be amiss for the 1952 paper. The average difference between her ordinary length (excluding the malleolus, between articular surfaces) and maximum length (incorrectly described as including the malleolus) was only approximately 10 mm. This similarity of measurement, too small to account for the length of a malleolus, went unnoticed. When preparing the Korean War data for the 1958 publication though, Trotter and Gleser began to encounter more questions stemming from the data comparisons. When asking Stewart for details of stature estimation with Korean War remains, he responded that "I am ashamed to say that I am confused now as to whether I recorded stature as estimated from the combined femur and tibia or that based on all the bones."[34] So Trotter was not the only one who experienced an overload of information while working on multiple projects under tight timelines for military identification efforts in a foreign land, along with research. He further attested that "I doubt you need to worry about the technique of bone measurements. At least when I was over there the procedure was fully standardized and the results seem to be comparable." Nothing seemed immediately wrong between the Korean War measurements and the 1952 paper while they were being compiled. In response to Trotter's question in 1955 of which tibia measurement they had used, Gleser responded that "I believe that we used max length of the tibia – you'd better check it in our article however."[35]

On consulting the paper, Trotter would have confirmed that was the description. But it seems that the two still noticed problems with the measurements of not just the tibia, but other bones as well. In the summer of 1956, Trotter asked the Army to clarify which measurements the lab technicians had used. She received a response from Russell Newman

> that at least while I was in Japan, neither the 'anthropologist' nor the 'embalmer'... actually did the measuring; this was carried out by military laboratory technicians. I am enclosing some composite photographs that were taken by the identification laboratory to illustrate the techniques and their osteometric board.[36]

Photographs of several bones were included, and one depicted the measurement technique for left and right tibia "MAXIMUM LENGTH (TROTTER)" as taken on Korean War remains. The malleolus is clearly

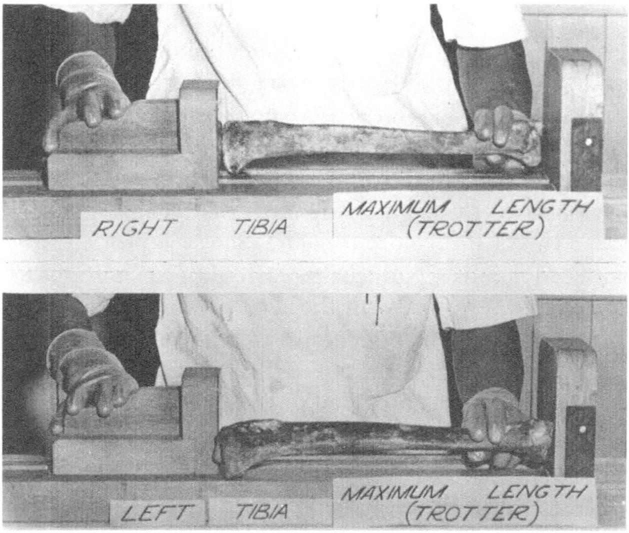

Composite photograph of measuring technique for the tibia in Kokura, Japan. VC170-i170264, Becker Medical Library, Washington University School of Medicine.

included in the measurement. Trotter saw and retained this image, so she knew that this was how the Korean War tibias were measured, and saw no reason to question that their standard measurement technique fit with her understanding of the description as well. This also, in clear visual terms, supports that, at this point in time anyway, Trotter believed this was the same manner in which she had measured the World War II tibias for the research project.

The problem became more obvious as the article preparations continued. In July of 1956, Gleser wrote to Trotter that

> there is something which puzzles me, however, about the tibia – fibula relation in these new samples. In all of our previous samples the fibula was slightly longer on the average than was tibm [maximum length of the tibia]. In these samples the reverse is true. Can you account for this? If the tibia were being measured in some way which gave a slightly larger value than previously, it would account for the fact that the stature appears shorter relative to it than in our previous sample. You will note this was true for the white sample also.[37]

With these words, Gleser directly pinpoints the ultimate problem and genuinely seeks answers. Trotter and Gleser were not attempting to conceal any personal fault, and they explicitly state this fact of the reversal of the tibia-fibula relationship in the 1958 publication. It seems that the two authors just never clarified what the original basis of the error was though. Gleser pointed to the various technicians who measured the Korean War remains, as opposed to one individual, as the likely source of the issue, since the tibia can be difficult to measure. She even proffered the possibility of running equations separately for each of the technicians to test their interobserver error.[38] Just as with the World War II data, even using the remains of individuals' whose identities were believed to never have been lost, "there is bound to be some error."[39] Trotter included these issues in numerous progress reports provided to the military. They further delved into potential explanatory theories of secular change, age-related changes in bone proportions, and population variations, for the tibia and other bones. Trotter sought references related to bone growth, and asked Stanley Garn if it is possible that the femur and tibia grow at different rates in relation to one another. Garn could only answer that the question did not appear to be answered in the literature.[40] Though she asked a lot of questions and investigated multiple possible causes, she never uncovered the root of the problem, and therefore never provided a possible solution.

Trotter and Gleser's comparison of World War II to Korean War data in the 1950s seems like it could have provided an ideal opportunity to expose and identify the tibia error. But their data was not as straight forward as the direct comparison of the Terry Collection in the 1990s. Jantz et al. remeasured the exact same tibias that Trotter had measured for her data. Such a revisit of the Terry Collection measurements would have benefitted Trotter, had she done it. But what Trotter and Gleser were comparing for the 1958 article were measurements of tibias of different men, taken by different technicians, at different times. And unlike the World War II project, the data was kept on transcribed IBM punchcards in Massachusetts, organized by Army scientists, and only provided in requested batches to Trotter and Gleser. As Gleser described the chaos, "I don't remember how we managed this by mail except to note that the actual data analysis was carried out by the army under my direction."[41]

The tibia was not the only complexity; there was other noise throughout the data that did not come just from Trotter's tibia mismeasurement. Additional problems were seen with other bones, particularly the femur, radius, and ulna, which attracted their attention as well, and possibly confounded the tibia issue. While preparing the Korean War comparisons, Trotter and Gleser were meticulous in their data scrubs. Conversion errors from centimeters to inches, interobserver error, measurement discrepancies, typos, machine errors, and transcription errors were common in the Korean War data. Gleser repeatedly found these specific problems in the punch card data, and requested edits, retabulations, and confirmation of very specific records from Russell Newman, who was handling the IBM punchcards in Massachusetts.[42] Newman, like Francis Randall in the 1940s, was an anthropologist employed by the US Quartermaster Corps' research branch. Trotter, Gleser, and Stewart had similar issues of professional trust and transparency with Newman as they had with Randall, so perhaps Trotter's problem was ultimately with those directing the Quartermaster research position, or with the department. Both Trotter and Newman seemed to have suspected the other of hoarding Korean War data that they felt they needed. When she realized Newman was withholding information from her, Trotter wrote to Stewart that "he will never forgive me for keeping the army data – not that he wanted them especially, but that he didn't win his point, and from a woman, too. Russell is a strange character."[43]

Trotter and Gleser also called into question which measurements were being used for other bones:

> I have been looking over our data again and have begun to wonder if by any chance the shorter rather than the maximum length of the femur may have been used by some of the labs who reported this data. The difference is not as gross as we find for the tibia, but it is suggestive in that the average femur length is a trifle short. What do you think?[44]

For these reasons, Trotter and Gleser felt they had been able to exercise greater control over the World War II project than they could for the Korean War project. Gleser's formulas also had found that the long bone measurements for the World War II set were more closely correlated with stature than the Korean War measurements were.[45] Trotter would advocate for preferentially using the World War II study for stature estimation, believing the Korean War data to be less reliable. In the 1958 publication, they made the tibia problem clear, but then dropped it: "the average length of the tibia in the present series is significantly longer than in the World War II series, whereas the average statures do not differ significantly."[46] Despite similar statures in both samples, World War II tibias were "shorter" due to the different measurement technique. At this point in time, there were other substantial errors seen in this extensive data, and apparently the tibia was lost in the mix. And after a lot of consideration, at some point they just abandoned the issue. They note the discrepancy in 1958 and leave it at that.

This underlying tibia problem went unperceived, or at the very least accepted as a minor issue in the data, for decades. But Trotter had received lots of attention from anthropologists on these stature publications in general. In 1969, she wrote to Stewart that "the chief trouble with stature estimation from length of an intact long limb bone… is that too much is expected of it—even by sophisticated workers in the field."[47] Many had written to her asking how to extrapolate her data for other populations, such as Asian females. Others wanted to use the formulas to extrapolate the unknown length of one bone from the known length of another bone combined with a known stature. Stewart, self-admittedly unfamiliar with the data and statistics, offered several questions and concerns that were unrelated to this error in the publication. He had reported stature with one standard deviation to the FBI in cases, telling agents that they could expect the estimates to be accurate within 1 or 2 inches.[48] Trotter then corrected him on the protocol of using two standard deviations, as reported in the 1958 paper, and to be more cautious in these expectations.[49] In one case, Stewart was concerned that the stature estimations from bone lengths deviated greatly from the victim's stature. Trotter told Stewart that maybe he had assumed the wrong race, and reminded him that

> we tend to expect too much precision for estimation of an individual stature and forget not only the broad range of statures but also that in a small number of cases the relationship between the actual stature and bone length is even more extreme than the S.D. implies.[50]

Other anthropologists using the formulas presented many opportunities for this error to be noticed. But it was not, even when it resulted in notable discrepancies in stature estimates compared to estimates derived from other bones. Research using Trotter and Gleser's 1952 formulas produced overestimations of stature when using the tibia. Jantz et al. (1995) observed that this effect on projects was noted without much comment in more relatively recent (1984 and 1992) projects. The problem had also been mentioned as early as 6 years after Trotter and Gleser's 1952 publication – by Santiago Genovés. In 1958, Genovés published a chapter in Spanish in a somewhat obscure book.[51] He summarized his 1958 findings in English in 1970:

> From a study of pre-Hispanic remains in the state of Oaxaca, I reached the conclusion (1958, p. 479) that 'the leg-thigh proportion was different, relative to those existing in Whites and Negroes, on account of a longer leg, or perhaps a shorter thigh, which is not surprising.'

> And I observed that the statures calculated from the tibia, using the statures formulated by Trotter and Gleser (1952), were much greater than those obtained for the femur, in the case of males the difference amounting to 11 cm.[52]

He also recognized that the radius and ulna produced much different stature estimates than did the humerus, highlighting a different problem which Stewart and St. Hoyme would later uncover. Like the researchers decades later, Genovés mentions this tibia discrepancy casually, and he attributes it to populational variation. So in response, he developed new formulas from an indigenous Mesoamerican sample, which were published in the *AJPA* in 1967.[53]

This does not seem to have attracted much attention at the time, perhaps because anthropologists' commitment to race-specific reference samples allowed the problem to masquerade as populational or racial variation. Also affecting the article's impact was that it first appeared in Spanish. In 1959, Trotter corresponded pleasantly with Genovés after conferring with Gleser (who was more or less fluent in Spanish) on his 1958 publication. She quoted Gleser as writing that, "'Dr. Genovés' suspicion that the Coixtlahuacans have longer tibiae, ulnae and radii (relative to stature) than American Whites is probably true, since such seemed to be the condition for the other groups we have studied'," referring to the 1958 Korean War samples of "Mongoloids, Mexicans, and Puerto Ricans."[54] Of course, these Trotter and Gleser (1958) tibia discrepancies between populations were affected by the very same 1952 tibia mismeasurement, and therefore White males varied just as much between 1952 and 1958 data. Gleser also commented that Genovés had made the error of using the maximum length femur formulas while actually measuring the bicondylar length. He therefore had incorrect results from the femur, which would make the difference in stature estimates from the femur and tibia smaller.

Trotter met Genovés in Mexico City at the American Anthropological Association conference in December 1959, at which point she and other present physical anthropologists (which included Stewart) must have been made aware of his research and results.[55] But this did not flag any wider concerns. Trotter was dismissive of Genovés in a 1969 letter to Stewart, in response to his question of her opinion of Genovés's new formulas for Mesoamericans. She cautioned Stewart to notice multiple inaccuracies in Genovés's paper, including his incorrect description of how Terry Collection cadaver heights were taken, and that he claimed "the maximum length of the tibia 'without the tuberosity' was measured...Genovés must be confusing the spine of the tibia with the tuberosity."[56] Indeed, it is highly unlikely that it was 'tuberosity' Genovés intended to write, but it is unclear if he meant that he excluded the spine or the malleolus. In any event, the discrepancy for tibias using Trotter and Gleser's 1952 formulas did affect research results enough to be remarked on in publication very early on, but did not attract further inquiry or investigation. And there seem to have been other problems with Genovés's work and references which warranted misgivings in his findings. Interestingly, Genovés may be better remembered for his 1973 "sex raft" social experiment on human violence, now depicted in a 2019 documentary, *The Raft*, by director Marcus Lindeen.

Perhaps the publication of raw data would have made the issue more obvious earlier. With new access to the original data, further typos and data errors continue to be uncovered today. Gleser admitted that the stature estimation publications did not include exhaustive tables and graphs for logistical reasons, and noted the diminishing usefulness relative to the cumbersome energy required.[57] Furthermore, the 1952 article was limited in page and figure length due to space constraints, and it was costly at the time for each individual table that was included.[58] While undertaking this research, Trotter and Gleser were distilling a mass of confusing and conflicting data into a constrained format.

Mistakes in scientific research are more common than one might expect. Scientific history is full of errors of varying types, origins, and magnitudes. David Salsburg outlines how errors have been inherent in science, because no matter how solid science is the abstract, it is always dependent on the fallible humans performing it, and the underlying expectations and biases of their time.[59] Even the best peer review prior to publication does not replicate methods or uncover all mistakes. Trotter and Gleser's papers have been in constant use and have now benefitted from extensive post-publication peer review. Most research papers do not receive the same scrutiny, over decades, that Trotter and Gleser's have, and for this reason many mistakes in scientific research, especially from the 1950s, would never be exposed.

Errors in themselves should not necessarily cause us to question the overall competence or integrity of a scientist. They are human, and even the best ones make honest mistakes in research design, interpretation, instrument calibration, or, as in Trotter's case, the recording of results and methods, even when this is due to some degree of negligence or lack of rigor.[60] These mistakes are distinguished from scientific misconduct, which involves deliberate dishonesty. But there is no evidence to believe Trotter or Gleser exhibited any intentional fabrication or distortion of data in order to alter their results (there would be no benefit in this). There is also no reason to believe that Trotter intentionally concealed the error. She was certainly willing to publish a corrigenda when the radius and ulna error was detected in 1976. Instead, it looks as though, despite noticing a problem, they never truly understood its basis. Indeed, they even highlighted the discrepancy in the 1958 paper, but without identifying the underlying cause. And users of their formulas did not notice the fundamental problem for decades, even though, or perhaps because, it was emphasized in the original paper. If anything, Trotter is guilty of self-deception; the problem was hiding in plain sight.

In the end, there is no one satisfying or conclusive answer for how Trotter was able to create and miss this error. I had very much hoped to have a eureka moment, discovering the exact process through which the error was made, but in that regard I am unsuccessful. There are, however, some mitigating factors to show that despite being a big mistake, it was most likely a genuine one that got lost in the extensive data across multiple references samples Trotter and Gleser were organizing. Even though guilty of error and perhaps negligence, Trotter should not be accused of scientific misconduct in relation to this. She certainly was not the only scientist to make an error in her work, and this is not likely to have been her only mistake in her entire career of research, though clearly it was her most well-known. What is left is a cautionary tale and a useful reminder that we are all fallible. Scientific research comes with a profound obligation to conduct careful, honest work.

NOTES

1 Letter, William S. Pollitzer to Trotter, October 9, 1974, series 3, box 4, folder 7, Mildred Trotter Papers, Becker Medical Library, Washington University School of Medicine.
2 Letter, Sherwood Washburn to Trotter, August 14, 1956, series 13, box 1, folder 8, Mildred Trotter Papers, Becker Medical Library, Washington University School of Medicine.
3 Mildred Trotter and Goldine C. Gleser, "Estimation of Stature from Long Bones of American Whites and Negroes," American Journal of Physical Anthropology 10, no. 4 (1952): 463–514, p. 473.
4 Mildred Trotter and Goldine C. Gleser, "A Re-evaluation of Estimation of Stature Based on Measurements of Stature Taken during Life and of Long Bones after Death," American Journal of Physical Anthropology 16, no. 1 (1958): 79–123, p. 82.
5 Mildred Trotter and Goldine C. Gleser, "A Re-evaluation of Estimation of Stature Based on Measurements of Stature Taken during Life and of Long Bones after Death," American Journal of Physical Anthropology 16, no. 1 (1958): 79–123, p. 88.
6 Mildred Trotter and Goldine C. Gleser, "A Re-evaluation of Estimation of Stature Based on Measurements of Stature Taken during Life and of Long Bones after Death," American Journal of Physical Anthropology 16, no. 1 (1958): 79–123, p. 93.

7 Richard L. Jantz, David R. Hunt, and Lee Meadows, "Maximum Length of the Tibia: How Did Trotter Measure It?," American Journal of Physical Anthropology 93 (1994): 525–528; and Richard L. Jantz, David R. Hunt, and Lee Meadows, "The Measure and Mismeasure of the Tibia: Implications for Stature Estimation," Journal of Forensic Sciences 40, no. 5 (1995): 758–761.

8 Emily K. Wilson, "Reanalysis of Korean War Anthropological Records to Support the Resolution of Cold Cases," Journal of Forensic Sciences 62, no. 5 (2017): 1127–1133.

9 Richard L. Jantz and Stephen D. Ousley, FORDISC 3 (Knoxville, TN: The University of Tennessee, 2005).

10 Jeffrey J. Lynch, Carrie Brown, Andrea Palmiotto, Heli Maijanen, and Franklin Damann, "Reanalysis of the Trotter Tibia Quandary and its Continued Effect on Stature Estimation of Past-Conflict Service Members," Journal of Forensic Sciences 64, no. 1 (2019): 171–174.

11 Richard L. Jantz, David R. Hunt, and Lee Meadows, "The Measure and Mismeasure of the Tibia: Implications for Stature Estimation." Journal of Forensic Sciences 40, no. 5 (1995): 758–761, p. 760.

12 Letter, Trotter to Suzanne Hyman, October 26, 1983, series 13, box 7, folder 3, Mildred Trotter Papers, Becker Medical Library, Washington University School of Medicine.

13 Frank Spencer, "The Rise of Academic Physical Anthropology in the United States (1880–1980): A Historical Overview," American Journal of Physical Anthropology 56, no. 4 (1981): 353–364, p. 360.

14 Phillip Tobias, Into the Past: A Memoir (Johannesburg: Picador Africa and Wits University Press, 2005), p. 101.

15 Richard L. Jantz, David R. Hunt, and Lee Meadows, "Maximum Length of the Tibia: How Did Trotter Measure It?" American Journal of Physical Anthropology 93 (1994): 525–528, p. 528.

16 Alěs Hrdlička, Practical Anthropometry, ed. T.D. Stewart, (Philadelphia, PA: The Wistar Institute of Anatomy and Biology, 1947); Rudolf Martin, Lehrbuch der Anthropologie, 2nd edition (Jena: Fischer, 1928).

17 See handwritten note card, no date, series 5, box 12, folder 5, Mildred Trotter Papers, Becker Medical Library, Washington University School of Medicine.

18 Mildred Trotter and Goldine C. Gleser, "Corrigenda to 'Estimation of Stature from Long Limb Bones of American Whites and Negroes', American Journal Physical Anthropology (1952)." American Journal of Physical Anthropology 47, no. 2 (1977): 355–356.

19 Letter, Trotter to Goldine Gleser, December 29, 1976, series 3, box 7, folder 20, Mildred Trotter Papers, Becker Medical Library, Washington University School of Medicine.

20 Letter, T.D. Stewart to Trotter, April 5, 1977, series 3, box 7, folder 20, Mildred Trotter Papers, Becker Medical Library, Washington University School of Medicine.
21 Letter, Goldine Gleser to Trotter, May 18, 1977, series 3, box 6, folder 6, Mildred Trotter Papers, Becker Medical Library, Washington University School of Medicine.
22 Letter, T.D. Stewart to Trotter, April 5, 1977, series 3, box 7, folder 20, Mildred Trotter Papers, Becker Medical Library, Washington University School of Medicine.
23 Document, "Quarterly Progress Report, Project No 7–64-12–004C," July 20, 1956, series 3, box 5, folder 1, Mildred Trotter Papers, Becker Medical Library, Washington University School of Medicine.
24 T. D. Stewart to Trotter, July 27, 1948, series 3, box 7, folder 17, Mildred Trotter Papers, Becker Medical Library, Washington University School of Medicine.
25 Letter, Trotter to W. M. Krogman, August 20, 1948, series 3, box 4, folder 23, Mildred Trotter Papers, Becker Medical Library, Washington University School of Medicine.
26 Letter, W.M. Krogman to Trotter, September 10, 1948, series 3, box 4, folder 17, Mildred Trotter Papers, Becker Medical Library, Washington University School of Medicine.
27 Letter, Trotter to T.D. Stewart, November 30, 1948, series 3, box 7, folder 17, Mildred Trotter Papers, Becker Medical Library, Washington University School of Medicine.
28 Letter, Trotter to T.D. Stewart, December 15, 1948, series 3, box 7, folder 17, Mildred Trotter Papers, Becker Medical Library, Washington University School of Medicine.
29 Letter, T.D. Stewart to Trotter, December 20, 1948, series 3, box 7, folder 17, Mildred Trotter Papers, Becker Medical Library, Washington University School of Medicine.
30 Douglas H. Ubelaker, "The Forensic Anthropology Legacy of T. Dale Stewart (1901–1997)," Journal of Forensic Sciences 45, no. 2 (2000): 245–252, p. 251.
31 Letter, Trotter to T.D. Stewart, November 17, 1953, series 13, box 6, folder 11, Mildred Trotter Papers, Becker Medical Library, Washington University School of Medicine.
32 Étienne Rollet, De la Mensuration des Os Longs des Membres (Lyon: Storck, 1888); Karl Pearson, "IV. Mathematical Contributions to the Theory of Evolution—V. On the Reconstruction of the Stature of Prehistoric Races." Philosophical Transactions of the Royal Society of London, Series A 192 (1899): 169–244.
33 Unpublished data for the tibia and fibula compiled by the author, in the manner of Wilson (2017) [note 8].

34 Letter, T.D. Stewart to Trotter, May 23, 1955, series 3, box 7, folder 19, Mildred Trotter Papers, Becker Medical Library, Washington University School of Medicine.
35 Letter, Goldine Gleser to Trotter, May 25, 1955, series 13, box 3, folder 5, Mildred Trotter Papers, Becker Medical Library, Washington University School of Medicine.
36 Letter, Russell Newman to Trotter, August 23, 1956, series 3, box 5, folder 2, Mildred Trotter Papers, Becker Medical Library, Washington University School of Medicine.
37 Letter, Goldine Gleser to Trotter, July 8, 1956, series 3, box 5, folder 2, Mildred Trotter Papers, Becker Medical Library, Washington University School of Medicine.
38 Letter, Goldine Gleser to Trotter, July 14, 1956, series 3, box 5, folder 1, Mildred Trotter Papers, Becker Medical Library, Washington University School of Medicine.
39 Letter, Trotter to T.D. Stewart, February 7, 1953, series 13, box 6, folder 11, Mildred Trotter Papers, Becker Medical Library, Washington University School of Medicine.
40 Letter, Trotter to Stanley Garn, November 26, 1956; and Letter, Stanley Garn to Trotter, November 28, 1956, series 3, box 5, folder 2, Mildred Trotter Papers, Becker Medical Library, Washington University School of Medicine.
41 Goldine C. Gleser, Getting It All (Seattle, WA: Keepsake Editions, 2000), p. 109.
42 See, for example, Letter, Goldine Gleser to Russell Newman, January 12, 1957 and Newman to Gleser, January 23, 1956, series 3, box 5, folder 2, Mildred Trotter Papers, Becker Medical Library, Washington University School of Medicine.
43 Letter, Trotter to T.D. Stewart, February 20, 1953, series 13, box 6, folder 11, Mildred Trotter Papers, Becker Medical Library, Washington University School of Medicine.
44 Letter, Goldine Gleser to Trotter, April 7, 1957, series 3, box 5, folder 2, Mildred Trotter Papers, Becker Medical Library, Washington University School of Medicine.
45 Letter, Goldine Gleser to Trotter, June 27, 1956, series 3, box 5, folder 2, Mildred Trotter Papers, Becker Medical Library, Washington University School of Medicine.
46 Mildred Trotter and Goldine C. Gleser, "A Re-evaluation of Estimation of Stature Based on Measurements of Stature Taken during Life and of Long Bones after Death." American Journal of Physical Anthropology 16, no. 1 (1958): 79–123, p. 93.
47 Letter, Trotter to T. Dale Stewart, March 19, 1969, series 3, box 7, folder 20, Mildred Trotter Papers, Becker Medical Library, Washington University School of Medicine.

48 Letter, T.D. Stewart to Trotter, October 10, 1958, series 13, box 6, folder 11, Mildred Trotter Papers, Becker Medical Library, Washington University School of Medicine.
49 Letter, Trotter to T.D. Stewart, October 13, 1958, series 13, box 6, folder 11, Mildred Trotter Papers, Becker Medical Library, Washington University School of Medicine.
50 Letter, Trotter to T.D. Stewart, October 6, 1958, series 13, box 6, folder 11, Mildred Trotter Papers, Becker Medical Library, Washington University School of Medicine.
51 Santiago Genovés, "Estudio de los Restos Óseos de Coixlahuaca, Oaxaca, México," in Miscellanea: Octogenario Dicata, Vol. I, ed. Paul Rivet (Mexico: Universidad Autónoma de México, 1958), 455–484.
52 Santiago Genovés, "Anthropometry of Late Prehistoric Human Remains," in Handbook of Middle American Indians, Vol 9: Physical Anthropology, eds. Robert Wauchope and T. Dale Stewart (Austin, TX: University of Texas Press, 1970): 35–49, p. 41.
53 Santiago Genovés, "Proportionality of the Long Bones and Their Relation to Stature among Mesoamericans," American Journal of Physical Anthropology 26, no. 1 (1967): 67–77.
54 Letter, Trotter to Santiago Genovés, January 27, 1959, series 13, box 3, folder 5, Mildred Trotter Papers, Becker Medical Library, Washington University School of Medicine.
55 Letter, Trotter to Santiago Genovés, January 7, 1960, series 13, box 3, folder 5, Mildred Trotter Papers, Becker Medical Library, Washington University School of Medicine.
56 Letter, Trotter to T. Dale Stewart, March 19, 1969, series 3, box 7, folder 20, Mildred Trotter Papers, Becker Medical Library, Washington University School of Medicine.
57 Letter, Goldine Gleser to T.D. Stewart, October 28, 1958, series 13, box 6, folder 11, Mildred Trotter Papers, Becker Medical Library, Washington University School of Medicine.
58 Letter, Russel Newman to Trotter, August 14, 1957, series 3, box 4, folder 28, Mildred Trotter Papers, Becker Medical Library, Washington University School of Medicine.
59 David S. Salsburg, Errors, Blunders, and Lies: How to Tell the Difference (CRC Press, 2017).
60 National Academy of Sciences, On Being a Scientist: A Guide to Responsible Conduct in Research (Washington, DC: National Academies Press, 2009).

CHAPTER 4

Life and Career

Trotter's work and research on the identification of World War II remains are what made her famous within anthropology, and her tibia mistake became somewhat infamous. But that time period was a relatively brief moment in the life of this woman, who was variably addressed as Dr. Trotter, Mildred, Millie/Milly, Aunt Mamie, and Trot. A former student would later describe that "the eponym [Trot] describes so very well her energy, enthusiasm and tempo of living."[1] Trotter was born on February 2, 1899 as the oldest of four children to parents James and Jennie (née Zimmerley). She grew up in the county where her family had lived and farmed since her grandparents had immigrated from Ireland (Robert Trotter) and England (Mildred Cotton).[2] Despite a Presbyterian upbringing, Trotter does not seem to have maintained an interest in organized religion or prayer in her adult life.[3] Trotter fondly described her childhood on a market garden farm outside a town named Monaca, about 30 miles northwest of Pittsburgh. During these years, Monaca had a population ranging from around 2,000 to 3,000. She playfully remembered farm life as excellent preparation for the scientific coursework, mental openness, and financial deprivation that she would experience in academic life.[4] She was able to roam open spaces and was unavoidably exposed to aspects of zoology and horticulture. She also enjoyed swimming in a nearby creek, which would become a lifelong activity, and took piano lessons. When young, she and her siblings rode a pony to school.[5]

Beaver County is in the far western side of the state, bordering Ohio. When her oral history interviewer in 1972 struggled to locate Monaca on her map, Trotter noted that it was probably too small of a town to appear. But Beaver Falls, the small town across the river from where Trotter went to high school, might appear. From sixth grade through high school Trotter lived weekdays with her mother's cousin, Sarah Bruce, in the town where she went to high school, Beaver.[6] This allowed her a better education than the one provided at the one-room country schoolhouse nearest to her family's farm. While in high school, her principal told her parents that home economics would be more "appropriate" than

DOI: 10.4324/9781003252818-4

Portrait of Trotter as an infant, ca. 1901. VC170-i170001, Becker Medical Library, Washington University School of Medicine.

a geometry course for Mildred.[7] She took geometry. Sarah Bruce claimed that Trotter would have the rest of her life to learn home economics.

Trotter's family and hometown always held a special place for her, and she continued to visit and remain in close contact with them. When young family members turned 16, she invited and paid for each of them to visit St. Louis.[8] Trotter encouraged one of her nieces, Nancy L. Trotter (daughter of Mildred's brother, Robert), to major in zoology and she later became an anatomy professor at Thomas Jefferson Medical College in Philadelphia.[9] Mildred and Nancy both shared an interest in swimming as well.[10] One of Trotter's great-grandnieces now has a doctorate in physical therapy, and the family is proud to boast three generations of women to be called "Doctor Trotter."[11] Many of her family members continue to operate a thriving dairy farm with Holsteins and prize-winning Guernsey cows, Trotacre Farm in Enon Valley. The Trotter family had been forced to sell the farm she grew up on in 1942 when the government decided to build in a synthetic rubber factory as part of the war effort and resettled nearby.[12] Her father, of whom Trotter was extremely proud and who always held an important position in her life, died in 1943.[13] And in 1955 Trotter returned home to help care for her

Portrait of Trotter as an adolescent, ca. 1913. VC170-i170003, Becker Medical Library, Washington University School of Medicine.

mother during her illness and subsequent death.[14]

After graduating from high school in 1916, Trotter chose to attend the same college that Sarah Bruce had before her and started at Mount Holyoke in Massachusetts.[15] Bruce had, however, left college prior to graduating when she married. Trotter decided to major in zoology after taking a course under Ann Haven Morgan her sophomore year. Zoology was a well-regarded subject at the school from which zoologist Cornelia Clapp, with PhDs from both Syracuse University and the University of Chicago, had only recently retired. Trotter also counted zoology professors Christianna Smith and A. Elizabeth Adams fondly as mentors. Smith, a Mount Holyoke alumna too, had a PhD from Columbia University and Adams a PhD from Yale. Trotter hung photographs of Morgan, Smith, and Adams in her office throughout her career.[16] Trotter claimed that the environment at Mount Holyoke and the mentorship from women meant that she "never thought, let alone worried, about being a woman in science."[17] In retrospect, maybe she should have. But these were meaningful years for Trotter, who, to describe her relationship to the school, said "it made me."[18]

The academics were vital to her positive experience, but so were the relationships and social opportunities Mount Holyoke provided. She remembered fondly getting extra snacks from President Mary Emma Woolley and one time that she stayed up all night with a classmate who cut bangs into Trotter's hair and jokingly called her 'Mildew'.[19] She and a small group of friends referred to themselves "the muses."[20] Her 1920 senior yearbook included a descriptive poem that even at this young age reflected both her humble demeanor and decisiveness. It read: "As sweet and guileless a maiden/ You simply never would find;/ yet she will never believe it, / for Trotter's 'made up her mind'."[21] This yearbook entry stated her majors as "Zoology and Physiology, Economics and Sociology." She spent the rest of her life active in the College's alumnae group, in recruitment activities, as a member and 1938–1940 president of the Mount Holyoke Club of St. Louis, and as a member of its Board of Trustees beginning in 1955.

Following graduation with an A.B. in 1920, Trotter was offered a teaching position at a high school in Pennsylvania with a salary of

$1,650.[22] She also received an offer from Associate Professor of Anatomy Charles H. Danforth at Washington University School of Medicine in St. Louis, Missouri to work as a research assistant for a salary of $1,000. Danforth had recently received funding for a project on hair growth and sought a research assistant. He had met with Christianna Smith at the Woods Hole Marine Biological Laboratory in Massachusetts that summer, who recommended Trotter for the position. Trotter had never heard of Washington University until this point.[23] She asked if the research could also count toward a master's degree, to which Danforth stated he was not sure. She accepted the assistantship offer only after she confirmed with the graduate school that she could simultaneously earn a master's degree, starting in the fall. Trotter later asked Danforth why he had not just told her it would certainly be possible to get graduate credit, and he replied, "I wanted to see how much gumption you had."[24] Trotter would never be accused of having too little "gumption," but this may have been one of the earlier occurrences of a pattern of men around Trotter assessing her for it or holding back opportunities to test her resolve, and sometimes even alleging that she had too much.

Trotter's first experiences in St. Louis were somewhat eye opening. She was mostly unaccustomed to cities after having only lived in rural Pennsylvania and a small college town in Massachusetts. The population of St. Louis in 1920 was nearly 800,000. She excitedly felt that this would be "an adventure. I might go swimming in the Mississippi or see Indians on the street in feathers."[25] Trotter arrived in St. Louis after a long, hot train ride along with two classmates from Mount Holyoke who were also starting assistantships at Washington University. She stayed temporarily at a boarding house where she had a sparse appetite, saw her first cockroaches, and was scandalized by an assigned roommate who read a paperback with content that was "not respectable."[26] She also discovered on the day after she first arrived that the house was not walking distance to the medical school. The entire experience certainly left a complicated impression on her, and the overall feeling is familiar to anyone who has followed their ambitions to an unfamiliar place, particularly on a tight budget. Even decades later, she remained protective of young women, often the children of colleagues or friends, who arrived at the university from far away.[27] Trotter soon moved to a women's and faculty dorm, McMillan Hall, where she would live for several years. The dorm maintained *in loco parentis* rules for its occupants, a somewhat common practice at the time in which a university would take on the legal and social role of a parent, usually to adult women. At McMillan Hall, women were forbidden to wear ankle socks or to smoke, and were required to wear skirts.[28] Interestingly, the building would much later come to house the anthropology department.

With her only other comparison for a city being Pittsburgh, Trotter felt St. Louis was slower paced and had a southern feel. She felt one popular leisure activity best described it: "I went to town nearly every Saturday afternoon for fun, with a friend or two, and we just ambled along the streets, and everybody else did."[29] The two things she remembered remarking on to herself at the time were the absence of "'keep off the grass' signs and the [inordinate] number of artificial limb stores located on Olive Street."[30] She would later be terrified to experience her first tornado in 1927, which left 76 people dead.[31] She also recalled that in her early years there, students and faculty alike dined together at the cafeteria most days.[32]

The anatomy faculty at the time consisted of six men. Even later in life, she claimed not to recall much daily difficulty encountered due to her gender from faculty or students during those early years as a student and instructor. Of course, this was an institution where, as of 1920, there were no women on the faculty and the medical school did not accept women as MD students until 1922. In 1921 the medical school installed only its second women's toilet between two buildings.[33] Trotter would not see any woman serve as a full professor at the medical school until she herself attained the position in 1946. And the only woman in a leadership position before that was pediatric pathologist Margaret Smith, who temporarily served from 1938 to 1939 as the unofficial acting Chair of Pathology after a colleague's death, only until she could be replaced.[34]

Trotter's master's advisor, Charles Danforth, had come to Washington University in 1908 for his PhD studies under Robert J. Terry, and graduated in 1912. In 1921, Danforth would leave Washington University for Stanford University. She and Danforth authored and coauthored numerous articles on related subjects before his departure. The first research projects they collaborated on at Washington University consisted of longitudinal observations of hair distribution and growth on different regions of bodies. Danforth had made observations of the body hair on nude male soldiers, which was initially part of a project encouraged in 1919 by Charles B. Davenport at Cold Spring Harbor Laboratory in New York. Trotter later made corresponding observations on nude female college students.[35] In another study, she looked for the incidence and appearance of hypertrichosis (excessive hair growth) on the faces of female college students, clinic patients, and family members of clinic patients.[36] Previous publications had made suppositional associations between hypertrichosis and insanity, and therefore, Trotter also included institutionalized psychiatric patients from the Kings Park Psychiatric Center in New York. This work, of course, found no correlation. In these projects, she measured the growth of hair on the bodies of orphans and nurses, and observed hair patterns on cadavers of men, women, and fetuses.[37] She also undertook longitudinal studies, directly and repeatedly observing hairs from pubic, armpit, and leg regions on women and girls in order to measure and describe growth patterns. To do this, she isolated individual hairs and marked them with tiny, permanent ink tattoos, measuring the lengths and widths weekly. A plastic surgeon at the medical school offered to remove the ink dots from any subject who wished, but apparently none took him up on the offer.[38]

The requirements of this research to have such close physical contact with women's and girls' bodies, and particularly with private regions of their bodies, explains Danforth's interest in specifically seeking a woman as an assistant researcher in the first place. The funding for her assistantship and Danforth's project came from the family of a patient who, along with two daughters, had hypertrichosis (excessive hair growth). This benefactor understood that little was known about the fundamentals of hair growth, and provided $5,000 to the University to help rectify this.[39] Danforth's biographer indicated that he had only taken on this project "reluctantly," for some unspecified reason, with a physician (Martin Engman) at Washington University when the funding was made available.[40] It was not possible to even begin to identify a cause or treatment for hypertrichosis, since scientists had not yet determined even basic principles about hair and hair growth. Danforth found it inappropriate or perhaps unallowable for himself, as a man, to undertake these observations of women's bodies. That is where Trotter's research started. Her work would ultimately be the first to determine the life cycle of hair follicles. She would maintain a conviction in the value of basic research for its own sake, without knowing in advance what the eventual applications of that research may be, throughout her career.[41]

Considering all of the people and bodies that Trotter would measure over several decades, it is interesting to note that she may have been a subject of morphological studies herself. For the first 2 years Trotter attended Mount Holyoke, the College maintained physical examination books (the practice dated from 1897 to 1917). These included "shadow pictures" which were often taken when a student entered as data collection for the purposes of student well-being.[42] In similar contexts, nude photographic studies were often used for assessment and correction of posture and overall physical condition.[43] As historian Margaret Lowe explains, such practices of measuring and monitoring college students' bodies were common at elite colleges as a method of gauging and proving the women's health within the perceived masculine environment of higher education.[44] More detailed anthropometric studies were also undertaken on college students during this time and published, including the works of anthropologist Morris Steggerda, to compare across populations, and sometimes for the purpose of supporting racial ideologies.[45]

Trotter's hair studies expanded on a broad method of anthropometric study that she may have been familiar with, and even subject to, before she might have recognized it as such.

Trotter completed her MS in 1921 and her PhD in 1924. When Danforth left for an associate professorship at Stanford in 1921, the hypertrichosis project funds were depleted. She had saved up money to take a 6-week course in embryology that summer at the University of Wisconsin, and was sad to return to St. Louis with Danforth gone.[46] She also made particular mention that Danforth brought another woman onto the anatomy staff the year after Trotter arrived, Beatrice Whiteside, whom he had met at the Woods Hole Marine Biological Laboratory.[47] Trotter's doctoral advisor shifted to the department head, Robert J. Terry, and her studies remained focused on hair. Trotter would continue to study hair throughout her career. She even had a method for receiving mailed hair samples internationally, which she confirmed with the postmaster of St. Louis: to label them "sample without commercial value" and leave them unsealed for inspection.[48]

Danforth also continued, separately, to research and publish on hair studies intermittently throughout his career, particularly as relates to heredity—the overarching theme of his research career. In 1925, Danforth published a series of articles on the topic of hair in the American Medical Association's *Archives of Dermatology and Syphilology*, which were compiled for a book, *Hair, with Special Reference to Hypertrichosis*. In his foreword, Danforth describes the book as the culmination of a study begun at Washington University, noting that the "principal results have been published by Trotter, Cady, and the author."[49] He went on to write that "it seemed desirable to bring together our own results and try to coordinate them with those of other workers." What follows is a literature review on hair growth and pathology, with occasional musings on possible research questions to be investigated. He recognized Trotter's contributions and cites Trotter more than any other author (including himself); and medical student Lee D. Cady seems to have coauthored only one article on hair, with Trotter.[50] He also sometimes describes details of Trotter's research, without directly citing her papers, such as her studies on the effect of shaving on hair growth.[51] Despite her continued research on the topic during this same time period, Trotter does not appear to have made any original contributions to this particular book, though she had also separately continued studies of hair. It is unclear why, aside from physical distance, the two never again collaborated after Danforth's move to California, at least for this book. But he also suspended research with another close colleague whom he had recruited to Washington University, biologist Edgar Allen.[52] Trotter kept a personal copy of his book which now resides in her archival collection, and she describes Danforth as "much loved" in his department.[53] She used her network to share the book (of which there were only 400 copies printed) among the much more numerous relevant researchers and clinicians.[54] And in 1927, as she continued her hair studies and reached out to him, Danforth reassured her that "you do not need fear 'encroaching on my field'."[55]

Trotter came to greatly admire her new advisor and lifetime mentor, Robert J. Terry, and decades later she would write his fond obituary in the *American Journal of Physical Anthropology (AJPA).* Terry was born in 1871 and grew up in Missouri. He attended Cornell University and then finished his MD at Missouri Medical College in 1895. In 1897, he studied for a year at the University of Edinburgh in Scotland and in 1903 at the University of Freiburg in Germany. From 1906 to 1907, he held a teaching fellowship at Harvard. Back in St. Louis, he became the head of the Washington University anatomy department where he would spend the remainder of his career. He alone among department heads at the University retained this position following the 1910 Flexner Report, which had prompted the restructuring of American medical education. She unwaveringly referred to him, publicly and privately, as "Dr. Terry." She remained in frequent contact with Terry and his adult children even after he moved to Massachusetts in retirement. Trotter held Terry in such regard that, despite an overfilled department after his retirement, she adamantly refused to occupy Terry's office while he was still alive.[56]

Throughout her tenure at Washington University, the anatomy department had three chairs. Terry was replaced by Edmund V. Cowdry in 1940. He was in turn replaced by Edward W. Dempsey in 1950. Trotter used an analogy to describe the administrative approaches of each of these men:

> my first chief, Dr. Robert J. Terry, told us what type and color of hat to buy. My next chief, Dr. Edmund V. Cowdry, didn't care about color and style as long as we had a hat. Dempsey, didn't care whether we had a hat or not.[57]

Trotter felt this was "a trend of the times. We've gone from a formal sort of academic life to one less formal."[58]

Upon graduating in 1924, Trotter held the temporary position of Instructor of Anatomy at Washington University, while organizing her next moves. She was nervous about her prospects, and began to reach out to colleagues and mentors, seeking advice and connections for options available to her to further her career.[59] She corresponded with Clark Wissler, then at the American Museum of Natural History in

Mildred Trotter with Charles H. Danforth, Robert J. Terry, E.V. Cowdry, and Edward W. Dempsey, ca. 1955. VC170-i170220, Becker Medical Library, Washington University School of Medicine.

New York. She sought Wissler's advice on how to plan for a new research opportunity she had heard of, the National Research Council (NRC) Fellowship.[60] She applied for and was awarded a 1-year anthropology fellowship to study hair. In letters of recommendation from the anatomy faculty, Trotter was described as "industrious, energetic, and resourceful," and later as "practical and business-like…self-reliant and unbiased," "possess[ing] an unusually quick and clear insight into problems, which she can discuss from many angles," and having "a good spirit of cooperation."[61] Because the laboratory at Washington University was more focused on physical anthropology and not particularly hair, and perhaps because he had studied for a year in Edinburgh, Terry encouraged Trotter to go to Oxford, where she ended up working with anatomist Arthur Thomson from 1925 to 1926.[62]

She left the US in June of 1925 and made it to Oxford in September, ready to start the next month. Trotter described herself as being "terribly homesick, not really homesick to be home."[63] She sought out the company of other women and Americans at the University, and even met the wife of the recently deceased, famed physician William Osler. Somerville College, one of the women's constituent colleges of Oxford, admitted Trotter as a member, and she could therefore use their dining hall, which was socially and financially good for her.[64] Trotter noted that there was only one woman on staff in the anatomy department, who was in charge of the women's gross anatomy laboratory; at that time men and women dissected on separate floors despite ample space to accommodate them

Portrait of Trotter, ca. 1925. VC170-i170014, Becker Medical Library, Washington University School of Medicine.

together. Trotter earned the nickname of "hothouse plant" for regularly using the small fireplace in her workspace at the museum (and presumably not for being overly delicate), and she was pleased to "learn how to punt on the Isis" (to boat in a flat-bottomed craft on the local name for the River Thames).[65]

Before it even began, her project was redesigned. As Trotter would later understand, "the trend of one's research can never be foreseen."[66] Despite her preferred interests, Thomson found her specific research proposal, in which she intended to study racial differences in hair, though excellently prepared, to be of a magnitude that would not feasible for a 1-year fellowship.[67] Her original, overambitious plan would have required the collection of hair from populations around the globe, as well as climate data. Such a collection and data did not already exist. Trotter was accepting of a shift in her project before she left for Oxford, noting that "although hair does interest me deeply, I am not partial to this subject and I am quite anxious to undertake an osteological study."[68] She asked Thomson to help her devise a new project, since her main goal was to undertake the fellowship at Oxford, whatever the research would be. Once she arrived, Thomson decided he would prefer for Trotter to work with a collection of Egyptian vertebrae that had been neglected. Though she was eager to start and would eventually come to prefer and build her career around osteology ("I discovered that I liked studying skeletons better than studying hair"), she was not necessarily pleased with this particular new plan.[69] The remains at Oxford were in such poor condition that she had to use much of her time simply performing conservation on them in order to get them in a condition that allowed for study.[70] Looking back decades later, Trotter did not believe this kind of treatment would have been subjected on a man in her situation. She notes in her oral history that a relative of Marshall Field from Chicago, Henry Field, was at also Oxford and "had things on a silver platter."[71] It seems she maintained an ongoing dislike for Field, a wealthy man who did not achieve much but enjoyed moderate professional success.

At the end of her NRC Fellowship, she and two history students took a canoe trip down the Thames to London, stopping to tour old churches along the way.[72] There Trotter spent 3 weeks at the Royal College of Surgeons under Sir Arthur Keith, met with several professors, and took measurements of more vertebral columns. She saw Prince Edward of Wales (briefly later King Edward VIII, and then Duke of Windsor) give a speech at the British Association for the Advancement of Science. She later could not recall the content of the talk, but simply wondered who must have written the speech for him.[73]

Trotter returned to Washington University as Assistant Professor in 1926, turning down an offer at Western Reserve University under anatomist T. Wingate Todd to undertake a year-long continuation of her NRC Fellowship. At a time when academic mentors would sometimes train women but would rarely, if ever, actually hire them as faculty at co-educational institutions, it seems that Terry was uncommon, at least in the case of Trotter.[74] She was only the third woman on the faculty at Washington University medical school, starting just 1 year after Beatrice Whiteside in anatomy and Ethel Ronzoni in the biochemistry department. Trotter's salary was $2,200. In 1926 she was accepted as a fellow of the American Association for the Advancement of Science. Trotter taught gross anatomy to medical students and undertook research, and soon also inherited an anatomy course for nurses from a more popular male physician, for which she made $400 in addition to her salary. A few weeks into this class, the Director of the School of Nursing complained to Terry about Trotter's blushing while she lectured. But the nursing department would quickly come to appreciate her teaching, and in 1935, they unsuccessfully tried to keep her as an instructor and advocated for a raise in her salary. Decades later, Trotter noted that she did, in fact, still blush while teaching.[75] And her blushing was not only connected to public speaking. A friend and colleague noted that she also "blushes furiously when she is praised."[76]

Trotter continued to publish on topics related to vertebral columns after her NRC Fellowship, but in the 1920s her principal research was still focused on hair. While still working on her PhD, Trotter had been the first to establish that women and men have the same amount of facial hair, it only differs by form (vellus vs. terminal).[77] Another aspect of her early research consisted of a series of controlled studies of the effects of shaving, temperature, sunburn, and other factors on hair growth, which had begun in 1923. She compared shaved and unshaved portions human skin and was the first to scientifically conclude that, contrary to the (still) popular myth, shaving does *not* make hair grow back faster or thicker.[78] She also looked at the effects on hair growth of exposure to petroleum jelly and sun, with similar negative results. Her first studies included women's legs, and some of the subjects were Trotter's friends. Trotter clearly enjoyed her ability to respond to long-held, though inaccurate, beliefs with new data to support her. She said that "the most fun for me occurred after I had presented the results at the annual meeting of the American Association of Anatomists."[79] Apparently Charles R. Stockard, head of anatomy at Cornell, stood up to refute her research, based only on his anecdote that his wife and daughter, early adopters of the bob haircut, were required to routinely shave the back of their necks to maintain the style.

After she presented a similar study of men's beards and shaving at the American Association for the Advancement of Science meeting in 1927, multiple news outlets published brief stories and opinions about the topic. Notable titles were "Bad News for Bald," and "Old Beard Yarn a Lot of Baloney," and "Growth of Man's Beard – Use of Razor has No Effect Says Woman Doctor."[80] The story even made it into the *Beaver County Times*, but without recognizing that Trotter was a local. Her previous publications and presentations on nearly identical studies with women's legs did not make it into popular news. These articles found it humorous to focus on a "woman doctor" having the intellectual authority to make determinations about men's beards. In response to Trotter's determination of cycles of growth and rest, one stated, "get some of your own [beard whiskers], woman, and see how much they rest."[81] Just as it was seen as appropriate (and unremarkable) for a woman to study women's leg hair growth, a woman was seen in this popular arena as being unqualified to study men's beard growth.

In 1927 and 1928, when Trotter's hair studies were receiving all this press, she also received encouragement from colleagues, offers to collect hair samples on her behalf, and professional queries on familial hair anomalies noticed by physicians. This also led to Trotter receiving a barrage of letters from strangers, many of which were steeped with emotion.[82] Men sought her advice on what, if not sun, shaving, or petroleum jelly, would help their head or beard hair grow. One local man detailed the high costs of a commercial hair treatment plan he was trying without seeing results, telling Trotter, "if I thought there might be an ultimate benefit I might persist, but if I discover that I am doomed inevitably to premature baldness (my age is 28) I can reconcile myself to a Stoic attitude."[83] Women, who worried about too much or too little hair, also requested her guidance on the best depilatory methods. Some even asked her opinion of their (sometimes expensive) hair growth or removal treatment attempts with commercial products. Some wrote to contradict her or question the scientific bases for the assertions made in the newspaper blurbs. One argumentative man from Saskatchewan, who was employed at an insurance agency, wrote, "it will, I fear, be necessary for you to 'show me' that my own experience in this matter has been a delusion… your findings to be of any value must, of course, be founded upon scientific data."[84]

Trotter frequently replied to earnest letters when she had information, suggestions, or even just personal sympathy to provide. Her work clearly filled an existing gap in professional and popular scientific knowledge, and she had established herself as an authority on hair growth. A decade later, Trotter discovered that a company was falsely claiming her professional endorsement of their hair removal method and incorrectly referencing her earlier academic papers. Despite a dismissive initial response from Lanzette Laboratories, Trotter persisted in demanding that her name and Washington University's name be removed.

> Certainly the implication is that I endorse the Lanzette Method. I have had not only letters but also telephone calls asking me about this which I should think would prove as embarrassing to you as it does to me… As the dean of our medical school has pointed out, our reports on research have not been made for commercial purposes.[85]

The company then relented.

In addition to studies of hair and vertebrae, in the 1930s and early 1940s Trotter's investigations broadened to include pelvic anatomy. This led to an appointment from 1943 to 1945 as a consultant for the US Public Health Service to study caudal anesthesia, particularly for use in surgeries or labor and delivery. Throughout these years, she was also teaching, sometimes a heavy load. She was the course master for anatomy and took the role seriously. When she discovered that the department chair, Cowdry, quietly planned to shift that role to a younger man whom she and others believed to be an inept teacher, she quickly addressed this

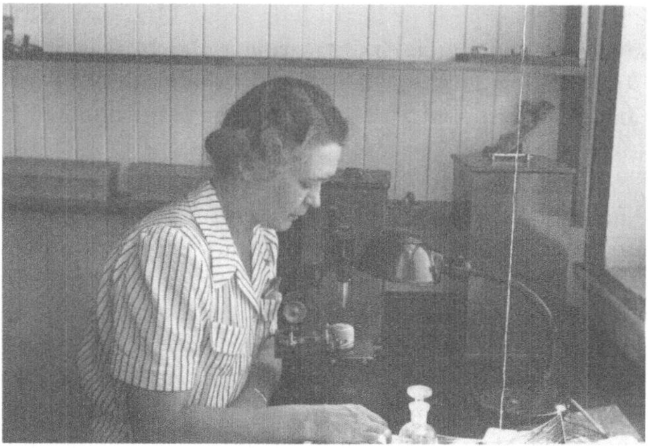

Mildred Trotter seated at a desk, using a microscope, July 1940. VC170-i170015, Becker Medical Library, Washington University School of Medicine.

directly and managed to keep her position.[86] A colleague would later jokingly refer to the anatomy staff as "Trotter's little empire."[87] She was promoted to associate professor and granted tenure in 1930. Though hair studies fell out of favor for her personally, she continued to work on these projects for pragmatic reasons: she could get hair samples easily and for free, they required no curation, and no animal care at a time when funding was so scarce after World War II.[88] Her studies of developmental changes in hair required only clippings from the children of her colleagues in St. Louis.[89] In 1935, she was offered a position to head the department of anatomy at the Woman's Medical College of Pennsylvania (now part of the Drexel University College of Medicine).[90] It was one of the few medical schools to educate women during the 19th century, before they were accepted at other universities, and it continued to maintain a faculty predominantly of women. She was offered a higher salary than she had at Washington University, and this would be closer to her hometown and family. Trotter, however, declined the opportunity and stayed in St. Louis.

With Robert J. Terry's retirement in 1941, Trotter took control of the curation and continued expansion of his assemblage of human skeletons for anatomical study, at the time known as the "Washington University Collection." Hunt and Albanese (2005) provide a comprehensive history of the collection.[91] Terry's intent was to systematically collect skeletons for anthropological research, a purpose that would become integral to the discipline of anthropology as it professionalized in the early 20th century. Around this same time, T. W. Todd at Western Reserve University also started a skeletal collection. Terry had made his first attempts to assemble a collection starting in 1898 and had instituted protocols for this purpose at Washington University by 1910. Terry had been directly inspired in his attempts by the earlier work of George S. Huntington at the College of Physicians and Surgeons in New York, among other foreign collectors.[92] Terry's and Todd's efforts were part of a wider movement across medical fields in the early 20th century to amass large reference collections of normal biological specimens with known and documented data for education and research purposes.[93] Terry and Todd were early adopters and also motivated other anthropologists to create skeletal collections, including William Montague Cobb at Howard University and Raymond A. Dart at the University of Witwatersrand.[94]

In addition to normal duties, Terry and staff (and later Trotter) would acquire, prepare, catalog, and curate these remains, making them available to internal and external researchers since at least 1920. The collection included not just the skeletal remains of these individuals but also related documentary antemortem and postmortem information, photographs, and plaster molds and casts of faces. When Terry had started the collection, Washington University received cadavers under the 1887 Anatomical Law of Missouri which allowed unclaimed bodies of dead individuals to be handed over to the state.[95] This meant that the Terry Collection was derived mainly from the bodies of indigent people and disproportionately represented Black males. When Trotter took over the "Washington University Collection," she renamed it the "Terry Collection" and actively sought to change the demographic content. Trotter endeavored to balance, as she saw it, the sex, age, and racial demographics of the individuals represented. This mostly consisted of adding more White females and younger individuals, and replacing earlier skeletons that were incomplete or had suffered from decades of student use with new ones. Trotter took deep satisfaction in her care for the collection and was once described as having "an almost affectionate regard for the skeletons she studies."[96]

Because the 1887 Anatomical Law (with its numerous subsequent revisions) was the only clear legal source of cadavers for medical schools at that time, and therefore, for this skeletal collection, the supply was insufficient to meet the demand. Fewer and fewer individuals died without being claimed, especially as religious and charitable organizations increasingly buried unclaimed remains. When bodies were available, they were too often unsuitable for study due to autopsies having already been performed. At the same time, enrollment in medical fields at schools was growing, along with the requirement for cadavers. Trotter served as president of the St. Louis Anatomical Board (1941–1948 and 1949–1967) and of the Missouri Anatomical Board (1957–1967). To meet the University's

Trotter measuring a femur with calipers, 1955. VC170-i170029, Becker Medical Library, Washington University School of Medicine.

need for cadavers for anatomical study, including for the skeletal collection, she campaigned to solve this problem through body donation, a practice which by this point only nine other states had adopted. This work resulted in the 1956 Missouri Uniform Anatomical Gift Act, which allowed individuals to donate their remains to specific institution types, such as hospitals, universities, and tissue banks. This made available a greater demographic variety for the skeletal collection, and greater availability of cadavers for gross anatomy courses.

Trotter wrote a letter to the editor in a local paper in 1957 noting the fact that one can now legally donate their body, and stressing the importance of anatomical study in medical education. She felt that "out of excessive delicacy" there had not been enough publicity on the practice, and drove the point home by stating that "such memorials today acquire all the greater significance for those who, after death, have made a last contribution to human betterment."[97] When asked in 1980 about her practical approach to such morbid subjects, Trotter is attributed to have said, "when you work with dead people you don't become calloused, but it becomes an interesting job," and that "the attitude of our culture toward death is silly. We all know we have to die."[98] But the decision to donate was still, of course, a complex one. In 1957, Terry was making plans to will his body to the medical school, but his adult children were less enthusiastic when he first sought their approval. Writing to Terry's daughter, Trotter wrote that she did not wish to persuade the family in any way, but that "many persons have said, if doctors and teachers don't will their bodies for dissection how can they expect others to do so."[99]

In April of 1956, Trotter also had a series of odd encounters with a man who misunderstood the new law. He wrote antagonistically to Trotter that after a visit where "as you well know we discussed the sale of a certain product, which you stated was not legal," he had later heard to the contrary that the University was offering $1,500 per cadaver.[100] He wanted to sell his and his wife's future cadavers to Washington University in order to pay off his debts. He later called to apologize for the confusion, since apparently the entire interaction started after a coworker had pranked him.

With her own retirement in 1967, Trotter was determined to find a secure and permanent home for the Terry Collection where it could be properly housed and available to researchers. The anatomy department had shifted its interests toward neuroanatomy and physiology, and that year was moving into a new building. In 1960, the anatomy department chair William Dempsey had off-handedly offered the collection to the University of Michigan. W. W. Howells had repeatedly proffered Harvard as an option for good home for the skeletal collection.[101] As she detailed in her 1981 obituary for Terry, Trotter had decided it was better to go not to a university, but to "some national institution, like the Smithsonian" which is "charter-bound" not to destroy or discard collections, and "where it would not only be preserved in perpetuity, but always available for research."[102] As she characterized conditions, university anatomy departments never have adequate space and funding, since the "collection of 1,728 disarticulated skeletons, [including] documentation, requires considerable responsibility."[103] She had also witnessed the unfortunate neglect and disorder of the Hamann-Todd Collection before it was rehoused at the Cleveland Museum of Natural History in the 1970s. This was not a fate she desired for Terry's painstakingly assembled collection.

She found it no trouble to convince Dempsey, now the Dean of the Washington University Medical School, and her trusted colleague and Curator at the Smithsonian's National Museum of Natural History, T. Dale Stewart, that this was the best choice. Stewart and Trotter had by this time maintained a decades-long professional relationship and friendship, including copious correspondence, as had Terry and Aleš Hrdlička (Stewart's predecessor at the Museum) before them.[104] Stewart had also grown up in Pennsylvania, earned a BA at George Washington University in 1927, and worked at the Museum under Hrdlička.[105] On Hrdlička's encouragement, he obtained an MD from Johns Hopkins University in 1931, though he never intended to practice medicine. He first married in 1932, remarried in 1952 after the death of his first wife, and had one daughter. He became curator of physical anthropology in 1943 after Hrdlička's death, the museum's director from 1962 to 1965, and retired in 1971, though he continued to be active.

The Terry Collection moved to DC in 1967 under the new physical anthropology curator, J. Lawrence Angel, at the Smithsonian's National Museum of Natural History. This included the skeletal remains of 1,728 individuals, records, photographs, and face masks made of the cadavers. Samples of hair and bone ash from Trotter's studies were included.[106] The original cabinets came with the Collection as well. Trotter had two face masks made of herself, one at age 25 and one at age 50, which she kept. As of 1980 these had been turned into bookends and were stored at her nephew's home in Pennsylvania.[107] The family remembers these odd items, which they never actually used or displayed as bookends, but cannot locate them today.[108]

Packing up the Collection had been estimated to take 6 days, but in the end was over budget by $1,049.07 (not including labor) and took 76 days. The Museum paid all costs. Angel had been surprised by this amount, which partly came from the fact that the bones were "wrapped individually, like china."[109] He would have to justify the price to the Museum, but, after all, the Collection would no longer have been valuable for research if it had arrived in poor condition.

Trotter had previous experience with the difficulty of shipping remains. Several Terry Collection crania were damaged in shipment following their loan to the National Museum of Natural History for a research project in 1955.[110] And transporting formalin-preserved skeletal remains to Western Reserve University had once resulted in the bags leaking in her car.[111] All parties were therefore interested in the Terry Collection arriving in perfect condition, and it did. Trotter was so pleased with the decision to transfer the Terry Collection that in 1978 she would decide to also transfer her research collection of macaque skeletons to the Museum (as an outright gift, since there were no legal strings attached to nonhuman remains).[112] She then sought to find a similar institution in the 1970s to entrust a collection of teratological human specimens (with congenital abnormalities), wondering if the museum associated with the Armed Forces Institute of Pathology (now the National Museum of Health and Medicine) would be interested.[113]

Two decades later, the arrangement for the Terry Collection was briefly in potential jeopardy. In 1985, Washington University anthropologist David L. Browman decided that the Collection should be returned to its original location, this time with the anthropology department.[114] Skeletal remains that had been removed from the main collection due to poor condition or incompleteness had stayed with the anthropology department, and he hoped to reunite them in St. Louis. Browman had just received unofficial word that a large endowment was set to arrive, and the anthropology department hoped to create a teaching museum based around the Terry Collection. He also seems to have mistakenly, but earnestly, believed that if the anthropology department (officially founded separately from sociology in 1968) had been equipped and able to curate the collection 1 year earlier in 1967, then the collection would still be at Washington University. This was contrary to Trotter's 1981 published explanation of her decision-making process. And 1985 was, notably, the same year that Trotter sustained an incapacitating stroke. The Museum was unwilling to return the Collection. Browman was aware that the Terry Collection was not transferred to the Museum as a gift, but as some form of loan, and tried to use this fact to rescind the agreement.

The Terry Collection was physically transferred to the Smithsonian in 1967 and categorized officially in 1968 not as a gift, but as a "deposit."[115] Earlier communications categorized this transfer as a "gift," a "permanent loan," or an "indefinite loan," but this was modified for legal purposes. The cadavers from which the skeletons were derived were assigned to Washington University by the Missouri State Anatomical Board, and ownership of the human remains could not legally be transferred and therefore must be recall-able by the state of Missouri or Washington University at any time.[116] Such an event was explicitly considered by all of the original parties involved to not be likely, but the contingency was a legal necessity.[117] "Deposit" was the term preferred by the Museum, because it denoted a status more stable than a loan or a transfer, while not being a gift.[118] This precise terminology was very important to Trotter. When, in 1982, J. Lawrence Angel offhandedly thanked Washington University for "giving" the Collection to the Museum in the acknowledgment section of a paper in the *AJPA*, Trotter demanded that Angel publish a correction to emphasize that this was not a gift.[119] She also reminded Angel of the legal status of the skeletons, and that the University had no intention to recall the skeletons unless the Smithsonian ever wished to discard them.

After what appears to have been an impassioned disagreement in 1985 on both sides, Browman discovered that the financial endowment would not actually come to the anthropology department after all, and so the dispute was moot. He notes that this type of financial instability is not unheard of in academic departments, but still laments that the Terry Collection was not returned to Washington University. He also described the flooding, damage to other collections, and other "space wars" plaguing the department around this same time. This substantiates what Trotter knew to be true in the 1960s about university finances, and which she had cogently documented in her biography of Terry in the *AJPA* in 1981. Luckily, her earlier efforts safeguarded the Terry Collection from an uncertain outcome, even after she was unable to personally intervene. Today the Robert J. Terry Anatomical Skeletal Collection is still housed at the National Museum of Natural History's Museum Support Center and has been an enduring resource for research and education. The Museum describes it as "the most intensively studied research collection in the Smithsonian Institution."[120]

Five years after Terry's retirement, after 16 years as an associate professor, Trotter became Professor of Gross Anatomy in 1946. She was the first woman to be full professor at the Washington University School of Medicine, a position she was only eventually granted after years of being passed over for promotion. She was unaware of, or oblivious to, being the first until years later when a new department head pointed this out to her.[121] Her salary was raised from $4,500 to $6,000 per year.[122] One colleague remembered that Trotter "had a lot of battles to get her promotions because she was a woman. She raised a lot of hell."[123] At a time when most men were promoted as a matter of course, she doubted this would ever have happened if she had not pointedly and directly asked for it after being intentionally overlooked.[124] As she stated, "I finally asked in what way I was deficient. They got me promoted."[125] The delay was unfortunate, because her work and teaching were by all known accounts unimpeachable. By this point, she had dozens of publications, her expertise had been sought by the US Public Health Service, and she was in charge of the department's growing skeletal collection. She had also served as the Anatomy Consultant for Washington University Mallinckrodt Institute of Radiology starting in 1948. During World War II, her teaching load had increased as new classes entered every 9 months. She even taught anatomy throughout the summer, at a time before the school had air conditioning, which was first added in 1957. And complaints that it was distressing to patients to accidentally see the medical students dissecting cadavers meant that windows could only be opened by 6 inches.[126]

As W. Maxwell Cowan, professor and head of the anatomy department from 1968 to 1980 described, "Mildred Trotter's teaching was exemplary for three reasons: it was rigorous, conscientious, and honest."[127] She taught more than 4,000 students during her decades at Washington University and, as one former student wrote, "Mildred carried the burden of teaching; she was the person who really taught us."[128] Two of her former students would later receive Nobel Prizes in medicine, Earl Wilbur Sutherland, Jr. (1971) and Daniel Nathans (1978). Nathans remembered Trotter as a "very vigorous teacher with just a tremendous enthusiasm."[129] For so many students, "Dr. Trotter was the first person who introduced us to the profession of medicine."[130] Another student remembered Trotter's address to new medical students on their first day: "this is the last day of being current in your professional lives.

There is always more to learn, and the trick is to control how far behind you get."[131] She seems to have truly found teaching to be an avocation, prioritized the students' learning, and respected their work and struggles. While accepting a new lecture series endowed by the University in her honor in 1975, Trotter thanked first and foremost her students. "I should say that those of you who were once my students have participated in my growth, also, and in ways that you little suspect.... I can assure you that there is no praise so sweet as the praise of one's former students.... My gratitude is heartfelt and carries my love to you."[132] Over time she even taught students from multiple generations of the same families.

Former students described her teaching style in a variety of conflicting ways, all of which portray a conscientious and effective educator. One student wrote that "Dr. Trotter has been called a phenomenon. Her ability to remain firm in her commitment to science while maintaining a softness about her that makes her appear fragile is disarming."[133] Another called her "a mother figure...Not that she was a pushover in class: She was tough, meticulous, exacting. Hands on her hips, she barked at students when she thought they needed a dressing down."[134] Another stated that "we admired and respected her and because, to an extent, we feared her."[135] Just as she was known for emphasizing the individuality and uniqueness of individual human bodies, she recognized the disparate needs of her various students. She encouraged students to pay attention to what was in front of them instead of memorizing textbooks. Like the anthropologist she was, Trotter trained her students to be consummate observers. One student remembers Trotter "for her incisive ability to size up people, and to teach according to their needs. Cockiness in her classroom was met with abrupt silence: shyness, with Dr. Trotter's own brand of understanding."[136] "When I first met Dr Trotter, [my] awe evoked fear...but as I grew to understand some of the many facets of her personality, I realized great warmth and affection behind her energy."[137] "'Trot' sees people as individuals, and accepts them and shares with them. If others do not agree with her, she gives them the respect she expects to receive for her own ideas."[138]

At least one former student's letters indicate a poorly hidden and longstanding infatuation with the professor.[139] He may not have been the only one; when an early, distant colleague of Trotter's was asked in his later oral history interview for any memories of her or her work, he mostly just remembered her as "a beauty."[140] Another former student sent Trotter a gift of gold earrings in the shape of the semicircular canal and cochlea of a left ear.[141] In a letter responding to a despondent student who had just failed his first year and was granted the rare permission to repeat it instead of being expelled, Trotter was firm, but encouraging. She detailed his poor performance in multiple courses and wrote, that his "final examination paper in anatomy was very disappointing," but that the instructors "have great confidence" in him and that she hopes he will "come back in September with a will to surmount every obstacle."[142] And despite her earlier refusal to tolerate foolishness in the classroom, someone in the class of 1960 apparently devised a fake student named Sam Farley, who failed exams, doctored course slides, wrote on blackboards, and graduated "sine laude," all of which amused Trotter and his story even made it into the local paper.[143] Trotter maintained her enthusiasm for teaching through her later years, the main difference was only that she required larger type on her lecture notes.[144]

Beyond teaching, Trotter's professional impact was extensive. But as one colleague noted, "you can't wring from her a list of achievements, even her friends have to look her up in 'Men of Science'."[145] In 1956, Trotter would become the very first woman to serve as President of the American Association of Physical Anthropologists (AAPA), as well as the first woman to receive the Wenner-Gren Foundation's Viking Fund Medal (preceding Margaret Mead by 1 year). Trotter produced over 100 scientific works across quite a diverse range of topics, and this publication record spanning the decades of her career shows general trends. Anthropologist Roy Peterson described them, somewhat florally, as "several themes, apparently unrelated yet interwoven" into a "tapestry" for which "the overall theme can be characterized as the structure of man."[146]

Her work started in the 1920s with studies of hair growth related to her master's and doctoral work, and the spine, in conjunction with her National Research Fellowship in England. This expanded in the 1930s to include pelvic anatomy and guinea pig models for hair growth. She soon abandoned live animal research due to the obligations involved in their care, with feeding, watering, and cleaning cages 7 days a week.[147] By the 1940s, in conjunction with her work for the Public Health Service, Trotter's research began to include specific studies of caudal anesthesia administration in addition to her hair research. After her identification efforts in Hawaii in the late 1940s, her work shifted to stature estimation and age-related stature and hair changes. She served as the anatomy consultant for Washington University's Mallinckrodt Institute of Radiology starting in 1948. From the late 1950s, she also began to study bone density and mineral content through various methods, which continued through the 1970s and began to include primate models. She received a $5,000 grant for her work in determining the organic and mineral content of bone in 1954 from Altrusa International. This funding partially supported her ongoing studies which contributed to the determination of the ratio of mineral to organic content of bone, through cremating bones in order to measure their ash weight compared to their unburnt weight.[148] Her contributions were even recognized in popular contexts; in 1955, she was named *St. Louis Globe-Democrat* Woman of Achievement in Science.

Trotter in her laboratory, June 13, 1972. VC170-i170037, Becker Medical Library, Washington University School of Medicine.

Trotter lamented the changes to anatomy instruction at the medical school over the years. Anatomy education hours had reduced over the course of her tenure from around 600 to 300 hours, and was covered within 1 year instead of 3.[149] She felt that if progress at other universities entailed forgoing dissection in favor of computers, film strips, and models, then she would prefer that Washington University lag behind instead.[150] Medical education had shifted to include microscopic anatomy, biochemistry, and physiology, with less focus on gross anatomy. She noted that "medicine has progressed, new subjects have been added," and gross anatomy has had to give – not because it has lost any of its important significance," but because there is increasingly more to learn.[151] She felt that not just physicians but also physical anthropologists did not receive enough education in anatomy.[152] In 1972, she even discouraged a college student from pursuing an anatomy PhD (as opposed to an MD), citing the general decline in anatomy education across medical schools.[153] Washington University had also physically changed since she had first arrived in 1920 and would have been unrecognizable to her. In her words, it had grown "'like Topsy' – without any plan."[154] Funding for research had also grown, which had been so rare in her earlier days. From witnessing all of these changes over the years, Trotter became reflective about the history of the anatomy department and the discipline of physical anthropology.

NOTES

1 No author, "A Tribute to Mildred Trotter, Ph.D.," *Outlook Magazine, Washington University School of Medicine* 12, no. 3 (Summer 1975): 15.

2 John Woolf Jordan, *Genealogical and Personal History of Beaver County, Pennsylvania*, Vol 2 (New York: Lewis Historical Publishing Company, 1914), 1093.

3 Letter, Trotter to Chuck Colbert, January 13, 1971, series 13, box 2, folder 5, Mildred Trotter Papers, Becker Medical Library, Washington University School of Medicine.

4 Mildred Trotter, interviewed by Estelle Brodman, May 19, 1972 and May 23, 1972, transcript, Becker Medical Library, Washington University School of Medicine.

5 Trotter, James. Interview by author. Phone conversation. December 18, 2020.

6 Letter, Trotter to Janet Bryan, November 22, 1978, series 3, box 6, folder 45, Mildred Trotter Papers, Becker Medical Library, Washington University School of Medicine.

7 Barbara Vancheri, "At 81, a County Native Goes Strong in the Lab," *Beaver County Times*, Wednesday, August 20, 1980, B-1.

8 Barbara Vancheri, "At 81, a County Native Goes Strong in the Lab," *Beaver County Times*, Wednesday, August 20, 1980, B-1.

9 No author,"Dr. Nancy L. Trotter," *The Times Online, Beaver County*, April 8, 2008, https://www.timesonline.com/article/20080408/news/304089888; Letter, Trotter to Nancy L. Trotter, February 17, 1969, series 13, box 7, folder 1, Mildred Trotter Papers, Becker Medical Library, Washington University School of Medicine.

10 Trotter, James. Interview by author. Phone conversation. December 18, 2020.

11 Trotter, David. Interview by author. Phone conversation. October 21, 2020.

12 Carol Ann Gregg, "Family Dairy Home to Top Producing Guernsey," *Lancaster Farming*, June 21, 2014.

13 Interview, James Trotter, December 18, 2020.

14 Letter, Trotter to T.D. Stewart, October 24, 1955, series 13, box 6, folder 11, Mildred Trotter Papers, Becker Medical Library, Washington University School of Medicine

15 Letter, Trotter to Janet Bryan, November 22, 1978, series 3, box 6, folder 45, Mildred Trotter Papers, Becker Medical Library, Washington University School of Medicine.

16 Marion Hunt, "Mildred Trotter: 'With Honor in Her Own Country'," *Outlook Magazine, Washington University School of Medicine* 17, no. 1 (Spring 1980): 8–13, p. 9.
17 Marion Hunt, "Mildred Trotter: 'With Honor in Her Own Country'," *Outlook Magazine, Washington University School of Medicine* 17, no. 1 (Spring 1980): 8–13, p. 9.
18 Marion Hunt, "Mildred Trotter: 'With Honor in Her Own Country'," *Outlook Magazine, Washington University School of Medicine* 17, no. 1 (Spring 1980): 8–13, p. 9.
19 This is handwritten as "Mildue." Letter, Trotter to Mrs. J.S. Brown (Esther), June 11, 1984, series 13, box 7, folder 4, Mildred Trotter Papers, Becker Medical Library, Washington University School of Medicine.
20 Letter, Lillian Hadsell to Trotter, September 11, 1929, series 2, box 3, folder 5, Mildred Trotter Papers, Becker Medical Library, Washington University School of Medicine.
21 Yearbook, *Llamarada*, 1920, p. 234, Class books, freshman handbooks, yearbooks, student handbooks, and alumnae registers, Mount Holyoke College Archives and Special Collections.
22 Draft, Trotter, "The Department of Anatomy in My Time," p. 1, no date, series 1, box 1, Mildred Trotter Papers, Becker Medical Library, Washington University School of Medicine.
23 Draft, Trotter, "The Department of Anatomy in My Time," p. 1, no date, series 1, box 1, Mildred Trotter Papers, Becker Medical Library, Washington University School of Medicine.
24 Mildred Trotter, interview by Estelle Brodman, May 19, 1972 and May 23, 1972, transcript, Becker Medical Library, Washington University School of Medicine.
25 Barbara Vancheri, "At 81, a County Native Goes Strong in the Lab," *Beaver County Times*, August 20, 1980, B-1.
26 Marion Hunt, "Mildred Trotter: 'With Honor in Her Own Country'," *Outlook Magazine, Washington University School of Medicine* 17, no. 1 (Spring 1980): 8–13, p. 9.; and Draft, Trotter, "The Department of Anatomy in My Time," no date, series 1, box 1, Mildred Trotter Papers, Becker Medical Library, Washington University School of Medicine.
27 Letter, Trotter to Wu Rukang, November 4, 1982, series 13, box 7, folder 11, Mildred Trotter Papers, Becker Medical Library, Washington University School of Medicine.
28 David L. Browman, *History of Anthropology at Washington University, St. Louis, 1905–2012* (St. Louis: Washington University, 2012), p. 4.

29 Mildred Trotter, interview by Estelle Brodman, May 19, 1972 and May 23, 1972, audio, Becker Medical Library, Washington University School of Medicine.
30 Mildred Trotter, interview by Estelle Brodman, May 19, 1972 and May 23, 1972, transcript and audio, Becker Medical Library, Washington University School of Medicine.
31 Draft, Trotter, "The Department of Anatomy in My Time," pp. 40–41, no date, series 1, box 1, Mildred Trotter Papers, Becker Medical Library, Washington University School of Medicine.
32 Mildred Trotter, interview by Estelle Brodman, May 19, 1972 and May 23, 1972, audio, Becker Medical Library, Washington University School of Medicine.
33 Draft, Trotter, "The Department of Anatomy in My Time," p. 7, no date, series 1, box 1, Mildred Trotter Papers, Becker Medical Library, Washington University School of Medicine.
34 Mildred Trotter, interview by Estelle Brodman, May 19, 1972 and May 23, 1972, transcript, Becker Medical Library, Washington University School of Medicine.
35 Charles H. Danforth and Mildred Trotter, "The Distribution of Body Hair in White Subjects," *American Journal of Physical Anthropology* 5, no. 3 (1922): 259–265.
36 Trotter and Charles H. Danforth, "The Incidence and Heredity of Facial Hypertrichosis in White Women," *American Journal of Physical Anthropology* 5, no. 4 (1922): 391–397.
37 Mildred Trotter, "Life Cycles of Hair in Selected Regions of the Body," *American Journal of Physical Anthropology* 7, no. 4 (1924): 427–437; and Mildred Trotter, "A Study of Facial Hair in the White and Negro Races." *Washington University Studies*, 9 (1922): 273–289.
38 Draft, Trotter, "The Department of Anatomy in My Time," p. 32, no date, series 1, box 1, Mildred Trotter Papers, Becker Medical Library, Washington University School of Medicine.
39 Mildred Trotter, interview by Estelle Brodman, May 19, 1972 and May 23, 1972, transcript, Becker Medical Library, Washington University School of Medicine.
40 Benjamin H Willier, *Charles Haskell Danforth, November 30, 1883- January 10, 1969* (Washington, DC: National Academy of Sciences, 1974), p. 24.
41 Mildred Trotter, interview by Estelle Brodman, May 19, 1972 and May 23, 1972, transcript, Becker Medical Library, Washington University School of Medicine.
42 Margaret Lowe, *Looking Good: College Women and Body Image, 1875–1930* (Baltimore: Johns Hopkins University Press, 2005), p. 170.

43 R. Marie Griffith, *Born Again Bodies: Flesh and Spirit in American Christianity* (Berkeley: University of California Press, 2004), p. 134.
44 Margaret Lowe, *Looking Good: College Women and Body Image, 1875–1930* (Baltimore: Johns Hopkins University Press, 2005), p. 170.
45 Morris Steggerda, Jocelyn Crane, Mary D. Steele, "One Hundred Measurements and Observations on One Hundred Smith College Students," *American Journal of Physical Anthropology* 13, no. 2 (1929): 189–254. See also Adelaide K. Bullen and Harriet L. Hardy, "Analysis of Body Build Photographs of 175 College Women," *American Journal of Physical Anthropology* 4, no. 1(1946): 37–68; and Faith Fairfield Gordon, "Physical Measurements of One Thousand Smith College Students," *American Journal of Public Health*, 20, no. 9 (1930): 963–968.
46 Draft, Trotter, "The Department of Anatomy in My Time," p. 19, no date, series 1, box 1, Mildred Trotter Papers, Becker Medical Library, Washington University School of Medicine.
47 Draft, Trotter, "The Department of Anatomy in My Time," pp. 24–25, no date, series 1, box 1, Mildred Trotter Papers, Becker Medical Library, Washington University School of Medicine.
48 Letter, A.J. Michener (Postmaster) to Trotter, January 25, 1931, series 2, box 3, folder 44, Mildred Trotter Papers, Becker Medical Library, Washington University School of Medicine.
49 Charles H. Danforth, *Hair, with Special Reference to Hypertrichosis* (Chicago: American Medical Association, 1925), no page (foreword).
50 Lee D. Cady and Mildred Trotter, "A Study of Ringed Hair," *Archives of Dermatology and Syphilology* 6, no. 3 (1922): 301–317.
51 See, for example, pp. 79–80.
52 Benjamin H Willier, *Charles Haskell Danforth, November 30, 1883–January 10, 1969* (Washington, DC: National Academy of Sciences, 1974), p. 24.
53 Book, series 2, subseries 3, box 17, folder 2, item 9, Lucile W. Ring Collection, St. Louis Mercantile Library; Mildred Trotter, interview by Estelle Brodman, May 19, 1972 and May 23, 1972, transcript, Becker Medical Library, Washington University School of Medicine.
Note: Somehow, I have now have Edgar Allen's copy.
54 Letter, Trotter to Richard S. Weiss, March 1, 1927, series 2, box 2, folder 19, Mildred Trotter Papers, Becker Medical Library, Washington University School of Medicine.
55 Letter, Charles H. Danforth to Trotter, July 12, 1927, series 2, box 2, folder 31, Mildred Trotter Papers, Becker Medical Library, Washington University School of Medicine.

56 Draft, Trotter, "The Department of Anatomy in My Time," pp. 58–9, no date, series 1, box 1, Mildred Trotter Papers, Becker Medical Library, Washington University School of Medicine.
57 Mildred Trotter, interview by Estelle Brodman, May 19, 1972 and May 23, 1972, transcript, Becker Medical Library, Washington University School of Medicine.
58 Mildred Trotter, interview by Estelle Brodman, May 19, 1972 and May 23, 1972, transcript, Becker Medical Library, Washington University School of Medicine.
59 Draft, Trotter, "The Department of Anatomy in My Time," pp. 22–23, no date, series 1, box 1, Mildred Trotter Papers, Becker Medical Library, Washington University School of Medicine.
60 Letter, Trotter To Clark Wissler, June 4, 1924, MSS.304, box 01, folder 096, Clark Wissler Collection, Ball State University, University Libraries, Archives and Special Collections, Muncie, IN.
61 Charles H. Danforth to Committee on Biological Fellowships, July 26, 1924, series 2, box 2, folder 31; and Letter, Unknown (filed under Danforth) to Board of Fellowships in the Biological Sciences, February 24, 1925, series 2, box 3, folder 30, Mildred Trotter Papers, Becker Medical Library, Washington University School of Medicine.
62 Mildred Trotter, interview by Estelle Brodman, May 19, 1972 and May 23, 1972, transcript, Becker Medical Library, Washington University School of Medicine.
63 Mildred Trotter, interview by Estelle Brodman, May 19, 1972 and May 23, 1972, transcript, Becker Medical Library, Washington University School of Medicine.
64 Draft, Trotter, "The Department of Anatomy in My Time," p. 33, no date, series 1, box 1, Mildred Trotter Papers, Becker Medical Library, Washington University School of Medicine.
65 Draft, Trotter, "The Department of Anatomy in My Time," p. 33, no date, series 1, box 1, Mildred Trotter Papers, Becker Medical Library, Washington University School of Medicine.
66 Letter, Trotter to Sherwood Washburn, September 16, 1957, series 13, box 8, folder 14, Mildred Trotter Papers, Becker Medical Library, Washington University School of Medicine.
67 Letter, Arthur Thomson to R.J. Terry, April 19, 1925, series 2, box 3, folder 45, Mildred Trotter Papers, Becker Medical Library, Washington University School of Medicine.
68 Letter, Trotter to Arthur Thomson, May 6, 1925, series 2, box 3, folder 45, Mildred Trotter Papers, Becker Medical Library, Washington University School of Medicine.
69 Marion Hunt, "Mildred Trotter: 'With Honor in Her Own Country'," *Outlook Magazine, Washington University School of Medicine* 17, no. 1 (Spring 1980): 8–13, p. 10.

70 Marion Hunt, "Mildred Trotter: 'With Honor in Her Own Country'," *Outlook Magazine, Washington University School of Medicine* 17, no. 1 (Spring 1980): 8–13, p. 10.
71 Mildred Trotter, interview by Estelle Brodman, May 19, 1972 and May 23, 1972, transcript, Becker Medical Library, Washington University School of Medicine.
72 Draft, Trotter, "The Department of Anatomy in My Time," p. 33, no date, series 1, box 1, Mildred Trotter Papers, Becker Medical Library, Washington University School of Medicine.
73 Draft, Trotter, "The Department of Anatomy in My Time," p. 34, no date, series 1, box 1, Mildred Trotter Papers, Becker Medical Library, Washington University School of Medicine.
74 Margaret W. Rossiter, *Women Scientists in America: Struggles and Strategies to 1940* (Baltimore: Johns Hopkins University Press, 1982), p. 185.
75 Draft, Trotter, "The Department of Anatomy in My Time," p. 26, 48, no date, series 1, box 1, Mildred Trotter Papers, Becker Medical Library, Washington University School of Medicine.
76 Adele Starbird, "The Dean Speaks Up: Solid Achievement Made by a Modest Woman," *St. Louis Post-Dispatch*, February 14, 1957, 5F.
77 Mildred Trotter, "A Study of Facial Hair in the White and Negro Races," *Washington University Studies* 9 (1921): 273–289.
78 Mildred Trotter, "The Resistance of Hair to Certain Supposed Growth Stimulants," Archives of Dermatology and Syphilology 7, no. 1 (1923): 93–98.
79 Draft, Trotter, "The Department of Anatomy in My Time," p. 31, no date, series 1, box 1, Mildred Trotter Papers, Becker Medical Library, Washington University School of Medicine.
80 Newspaper clippings, "Bad News for Bald," *Beaver County Times,* September 7, 1928; "Old Beard Yarn Lot of Baloney"; "Woman explodes theory about men's beards," *Reading Eagle*, December 27, 1927; "Growth of Man's Beard – Use of Razor Has No Effect Says Woman Doctor," *Montreal Gazette*, December 28, 1927, series 2, box 3, folders 6 and 7, Mildred Trotter Papers, Becker Medical Library, Washington University School of Medicine.
81 "Gleanings from the Press," *The Independent*, St Petersburg, FL, September 19, 1928.
82 Many examples are present in series 2, box 3, Mildred Trotter Papers, Becker Medical Library, Washington University School of Medicine.
83 Letter, W. Frank Swift to Trotter, May 21, 1929, series 2, box 3, folder 6, Mildred Trotter Papers, Becker Medical Library, Washington University School of Medicine.

84 Letter, J. J. Laddy to Trotter, January 3, 1928, series 2, box 3, folder 6, Mildred Trotter Papers, Becker Medical Library, Washington University School of Medicine.
85 Letter, Trotter to Hochbaum, June 10, 1938, series 2, box 3, folder 23, Mildred Trotter Papers, Becker Medical Library, Washington University School of Medicine.
86 Draft, Trotter, "The Department of Anatomy in My Time," pp. 44–45, no date, series 1, box 1, Mildred Trotter Papers, Becker Medical Library, Washington University School of Medicine.
87 Draft, Trotter, "The Department of Anatomy in My Time," p. 86, no date, series 1, box 1, Mildred Trotter Papers, Becker Medical Library, Washington University School of Medicine.
88 Marion Hunt, "Mildred Trotter: 'With Honor in Her Own Country'," *Outlook Magazine, Washington University School of Medicine* 17, no. 1 (Spring 1980): 8–13, p. 10.
89 Draft, Trotter, "The Department of Anatomy in My Time," 45–46, no date, series 1, box 1, Mildred Trotter Papers, Becker Medical Library, Washington University School of Medicine.
90 Marion Hunt, "Mildred Trotter: 'With Honor in Her Own Country'," *Outlook Magazine, Washington University School of Medicine* 17, no. 1 (Spring 1980): 8–13, p. 10.
91 David R. Hunt and John Albanese, "History and Demographic Composition of the Robert J. Terry Anatomical Collection," *American Journal of Physical Anthropology* 127 (2005): 406–417.
92 David R. Hunt and John Albanese, "History and Demographic Composition of the Robert J. Terry Anatomical Collection," *American Journal of Physical Anthropology* 127 (2005): 407.
93 Garland Allen, *Life Sciences in the Twentieth Century* (New York: Wiley, 1976).
94 Lesley Rankin-Hill and Michael L. Blakey, "W. Montague Cobb: Physical Anthropologist, Anatomist, and Activist," In *African American Pioneers in Anthropology*, ed. Faye V. Harrison and Ira E. Harrison (Urbana Champaign: University of Illinois Press, 1999), 101–136; Phillip Tobias, *Into the Past: A Memoir* (Johannesburg: Picador Africa and Wits University Press, 2005), p. 114.
95 M.D. Overholser, W.F. Alexander, and Mildred Trotter, "Can Missouri Schools Continue the Teaching of Human Anatomy Effectively?" *Mo Med* 53, no. 6 (1956):474–476, p. 475.
96 Mary Kimbrough, "Bone Detective," *The Everyday Magazine in the St. Louis Post-Dispatch*, May 8 1955, 1G.
97 Mildred Trotter and Edward W. Dempsey, "Letter to the Editor: A Service to Medicine," *St. Louis Post-Dispatch*, January 9, 1957, 2C.

98 Quoted in Jennifer Kramer, "Mildred Trotter," In *Notable Scientists from 1900 to the Present, Vol 5*, ed. Brigham Narins (Farmington Hills, MI: The Gale Group, 2001), 2252–2253. Original quotation source is not cited.

99 Letter, Trotter to Celeste (Forbes), February 7, 1957, series 13, box 7, folder 6, Mildred Trotter Papers, Becker Medical Library, Washington University School of Medicine.

100 Letter, James A. Brown to Trotter, no date (ca. April 24, 1956), series 13, box 2, folder 3, Mildred Trotter Papers, Becker Medical Library, Washington University School of Medicine.

101 Letter, W.W. Howells to Trotter, February 18, 1957, and letter, W.W. Howells to Trotter, August 29, 1966, series 13, box 4, folder 4, Mildred Trotter Papers, Becker Medical Library, Washington University School of Medicine.

102 Mildred Trotter, "Robert J. Terry, 1871–1966," *American Journal of Physical Anthropology* 56, no. 4 (1981): 503–508, p. 506.

103 Mildred Trotter, interview by Estelle Brodman, May 19, 1972 and May 23, 1972, transcript, Becker Medical Library, Washington University School of Medicine.

104 Mildred Trotter, interview by Estelle Brodman, May 19, 1972 and May 23, 1972, transcript, Becker Medical Library, Washington University School of Medicine.

105 See the Journal of Forensic Sciences Vol 45, Issue 2 articles devoted to Stewart, most notably Douglas Ubelaker, "The Forensic Anthropology Legacy of T. Dale Stewart (1901–1997)," *Journal of Forensic Sciences* 45, no. 2 (2000): 245–252.

106 David R. Hunt and John Albanese, "History and Demographic Composition of the Robert J. Terry Anatomical Collection," *American Journal of Physical Anthropology* 127 (2005): 406–417.

107 Letter, Trotter to Peggy C. Caldwell, October 17, 1980, series 13, box 7, folder 9, Mildred Trotter Papers, Becker Medical Library, Washington University School of Medicine.

108 Trotter, James. Interview by author. Phone conversation. December 18, 2020.

109 Letter, J. Lawrence Angel to Trotter, July 26, 1967, series 13, box 7, folder 7, Mildred Trotter Papers, Becker Medical Library, Washington University School of Medicine.

110 Letter, Trotter to T.D. Stewart, November 28, 1955, series 13, box 6, folder 11, Mildred Trotter Papers, Becker Medical Library, Washington University School of Medicine.

111 Letter, Trotter to Carl C. Francis, March 4, 1968, series 13, box 34, folder 4, Mildred Trotter Papers, Becker Medical Library, Washington University School of Medicine.

112 Letter, Thorington to Trotter, July 17, 1978, series 3, box 6, folder 47; and letter, Trotter to T.D. Stewart, February 27, 1978, series 13, box 6, folder 24, Mildred Trotter Papers, Becker Medical Library, Washington University School of Medicine.
113 Letter, Henry W. Edmonds to Trotter, December 22, 1970, series 13, box 3, folder 2, Mildred Trotter Papers, Becker Medical Library, Washington University School of Medicine.
114 David L. Browman, *History of Anthropology at Washington University, St. Louis, 1905–2012* (St. Louis: Washington University, 2012), pp. 60–61.
115 Memorandum, J. Lawrence Angel to the Registrar, October 7, 1968, series 7, box 25, folder 6, Mildred Trotter Papers, Becker Medical Library, Washington University School of Medicine.
116 Letter, Trotter to J. Lawrence Angel, April 12, 1967, series 13, box 7, folder 7, Mildred Trotter Papers, Becker Medical Library, Washington University School of Medicine.
117 Letter, W. Maxwell Cowan to J. Lawrence Angel, October 30, 1968, series 7, box 25, folder 6, Mildred Trotter Papers, Becker Medical Library, Washington University School of Medicine.
118 Letter, J. Lawrence Angel to Trotter, October 19, 1968, series 7, box 25, folder 6, Mildred Trotter Papers, Becker Medical Library, Washington University School of Medicine.
119 Letter, Trotter to J. Lawrence Angel, August 24, 1982, series 13, box 73, folder 11, Mildred Trotter Papers, Becker Medical Library, Washington University School of Medicine.
120 https://naturalhistory.si.edu/education/teaching-resources/written-bone/forensic-anthropology/skeletal-research-collections Accessed April 29, 2020.
121 Draft, Trotter, "The Department of Anatomy in My Time," p. 608, no date, series 1, box 1, Mildred Trotter Papers, Becker Medical Library, Washington University School of Medicine.
122 Draft, Trotter, "The Department of Anatomy in My Time," appendix 1, p. 2, no date, series 1, box 1, Mildred Trotter Papers, Becker Medical Library, Washington University School of Medicine.
123 John M McGuire, "Washington U. Professor Led Way in Identification," *St. Louis Post-Dispatch*, October 22 1986, 4F.
124 Letter, Trotter to Suzanne Hyman, October 26, 1983, series 13, box 7, folder 3, Mildred Trotter Papers, Becker Medical Library, Washington University School of Medicine.
125 Barbara Vancheri, "At 81, a County Native Goes Strong in the Lab," *Beaver County Times*, Wednesday, August 20, 1980, B-1.
126 Draft, Trotter, "The Department of Anatomy in My Time," p. 68, no date, series 1, box 1, Mildred Trotter Papers, Becker Medical Library, Washington University School of Medicine.

127 Marion Hunt, "Mildred Trotter: 'With Honor in Her Own Country'," *Outlook Magazine, Washington University School of Medicine* 17, no. 1 (Spring 1980): 8–13, p. 10.
128 Samuel B. Guze, interviewed by Marion Hunt, 1994, transcript, Becker Medical Library, Washington University School of Medicine.
129 Daniel Nathans, interviewed by Sondra Schlesinger and Dorothy A. Brockoff, May 4, 1979, transcript, Becker Medical Library, Washington University School of Medicine.
130 No author, "Lasting Lessons," *Washington University Magazine and Alumni News* 69, no. 2 (Summer 1999), 8.
131 Louis J. Rosenbaum, *Beware of GUS: Government-University Symbiosis* (self-published, 2010), p. 18.
132 No author, "A tribute to Mildred Trotter, Ph.D.," *Outlook Magazine, Washington University School of Medicine* 12, no. 3 (Summer 1975), p. 14.
133 No author, "A tribute to Mildred Trotter, Ph.D.," *Outlook Magazine, Washington University School of Medicine* 12, no. 3 (Summer 1975), p. 15.
134 Candace O'Connor, "First Class Teachers; Endowing Students with a love of Science: Mildred Trotter," *Outlook Magazine, Washington University School of Medicine* 40, no. 2 (Summer 2003), p. 13.
135 No author, "A tribute to Mildred Trotter, Ph.D.," *Outlook Magazine, Washington University School of Medicine* 12, no. 3 (Summer 1975): 15.
136 No author, "A tribute to Mildred Trotter, Ph.D.," *Outlook Magazine, Washington University School of Medicine* 12, no. 3 (Summer 1975): 15.
137 Twink Cherrick, "Named Lectureship, Portrait to Honor Anatomy Professor Mildred Trotter," *Washington University Record* (May 22, 1975): 4.
138 No author, "A tribute to Mildred Trotter, Ph.D.," *Outlook Magazine, Washington University School of Medicine* 12, no. 3 (Summer 1975): 15.
139 Several letters from Verne Goerger to Trotter, series 3, box 6, folder 7, Mildred Trotter Papers, Becker Medical Library, Washington University School of Medicine.
140 Andrew B. Jones, interview by Paul G. Anderson, October 10, 1980, transcript, Becker Medical Library, Washington University School of Medicine.
141 Letter, Trotter to M. Wharton Young, May 2, 1960, series 13, box 8, folder 17, Mildred Trotter Papers, Becker Medical Library, Washington University School of Medicine.

142 Letter, Trotter to Myron Susskind, June 15, 1928, series 2, box 3, folder 43, Mildred Trotter Papers, Becker Medical Library, Washington University School of Medicine.
143 Draft, Trotter, "The Department of Anatomy in My Time," p. 101, no date, series 1, box 1, Mildred Trotter Papers, Becker Medical Library, Washington University School of Medicine. Virginia Irwin, "Sam Farley, The Students' Friend," *St. Louis Post-Dispatch*, June 14, 1960, 3D.
144 Letter, T. Dale Stewart to Trotter, April 26, 1956, series 3, box 7, folder 19, Mildred Trotter Papers, Becker Medical Library, Washington University School of Medicine.
145 Adele Starbird, "The Dean Speaks Up: Solid Achievement Made by a Modest Woman," *St. Louis Post-Dispatch*, February 14, 1957, 5F.
146 Roy Peterson, quoted in Marion Hunt, "Mildred Trotter: 'With Honor in Her Own Country'," *Outlook Magazine, Washington University School of Medicine* 17, no. 1 (Spring 1980): 8–13, p. 11.
147 Draft, Trotter, "The Department of Anatomy in My Time," p. 42, no date, series 1, box 1, Mildred Trotter Papers, Becker Medical Library, Washington University School of Medicine.
148 See, for example, Trotter, Mildred, and Roy R. Peterson, "The Relationship of Ash Weight and Organic Weight of Human Skeletons," *Journal of Bone and Joint Surgery* 44, no. 4 (1962): 669–681.
149 Phillip Tobias, *Into the Past: A Memoir* (Johannesburg: Picador Africa and Wits University Press, 2005), 114; and Draft, Trotter, "The Department of Anatomy in My Time," p. 29, no date, series 1, box 1, Mildred Trotter Papers, Becker Medical Library, Washington University School of Medicine.
150 Mildred Trotter, interview by Estelle Brodman, May 19, 1972 and May 23, 1972, transcript, Becker Medical Library, Washington University School of Medicine.
151 Letter, Trotter to Dorothy Cross Jensen, March 8, 1955, series 13, box 4, folder 7, Mildred Trotter Papers, Becker Medical Library, Washington University School of Medicine.
152 Letter, Trotter to Sherwood Washburn, October 15, 1954, series 3, box 8, folder 18, Mildred Trotter Papers, Becker Medical Library, Washington University School of Medicine.
153 Letter, Trotter to Robert Headrick, September 27, 1972, series 13, box 3, folder 11, Mildred Trotter Papers, Becker Medical Library, Washington University School of Medicine.

154 Mildred Trotter, interview by Estelle Brodman, May 19, 1972 and May 23, 1972, transcript, Becker Medical Library, Washington University School of Medicine.
Note: This phrase refers to a character in *Uncle Tom's Cabin* - Topsy was a deprived and abused slave girl who did not know about her parents or the concept of God. She answered a question about who made her by stating, "I spect I grow'd. Don't think nobody never made me." Harriet Beecher Stowe 1852, *Uncle Tom's Cabin* (London: J. Cassell).

CHAPTER 5

Women in Early Physical Anthropology

Trotter can be accused of gaining an interest in the history of her field for the same reason she claimed anatomy chair E. V. Cowdry developed a late-in-life interest in gerontology: "because he was getting older."[1] With this historical interest, Trotter decided to personally document many of her own experiences. Around 1978 she wrote, though never published, "The Department of Anatomy in My Time," which is included in her archival materials at Washington University. With this draft, she provided her own narrative, and sometimes a counternarrative, recounting not only her own career but also the people, buildings, and activities of the entire department. She provided basic details on every staff member, visiting professor, and key administrative worker. She gave particular attention to women on staff and described the 1978 department as having "a sprinkling of women."[2]

Trotter apparently never learned to type, which turned out to be "a blessing in disguise – more than once it saved me, the only other woman around, from being called on to help the secretary when the load was too heavy or when she was ill."[3] Trotter had at least two much-trusted personal secretaries over time, Carol P. Keller and Patricia M. Ronan. Trotter described her own experiences and career trajectory alongside the developments within the department, and the appendices provide her salaries and course loads by academic year throughout her career. In another endeavor to document the history of anthropology, in 1981 Trotter assembled a biographical history of Robert J. Terry and the Terry Collection of human skeletons, which was published in the *American Journal of Physical Anthropology (AJPA)*.[4]

At landmark anniversaries of the founding of the American Association of Physical Anthropologists (AAPA), Trotter found herself involved in organizing the documentation and presentation of historical material. She arranged, during her AAPA presidency, a celebration of the Association's 25th year, including a historical note on the first meeting, which was published in the *AJPA* in 1956. As the 50th meeting

DOI: 10.4324/9781003252818-5

approached, Trotter's known interest in history was rewarded by being unwittingly announced as the chairman of a new "History and Honors" committee of the AAPA in 1977. When she worried to Stewart, "am I to blame for what I did in 1956?" he instead responded, "why don't people who think up these chores do them themselves?"[5] The attempts at compiling a history of the association and celebration continued haphazardly over the next few years, without gaining much traction. Trotter attempted to get responses and interest from AAPA members, but found support, in the form of both finances and time, to be completely lacking. She, Stewart, and Sherwood Washburn shared various ideas for marking the anniversary. She thought it would be beneficial to entice the five founding members out of the 84 who were still living to come to the meeting and be, in her words, "on exhibit."[6] Stewart and Trotter hoped to make a translation and update to Juan Comas's 1969 history of the AAPA, but this would not be accomplished until 2005.[7] Stewart also wanted the Association to start officially tracking each member's professional status, and perhaps co-locate the scattered records held and inconsistently retained by various officers throughout the decades. But these attempts were unsuccessful. The next year she officially and unapologetically resigned from the committee position that she had never formally agreed to take in the first place.[8] She continued to advocate for the cause of historical research, however, telling the incoming AAPA president that "I would hope that we would keep with our yen for history as 'extracurricular' activities."[9]

In April of 1978, historian and archivist G. E. Erikson, who had worked with the American Association of Anatomists (AAA), agreed to assist in assembling historical information on the AAPA.[10] Erikson shared Trotter's dismay at the AAPA's purported interest in history, but complete lack of resources allocated to the project. By October of that year he abandoned the work, noting that such computerized databasing and research took money and time, not just a nonchalant assignment to "a willing victim."[11] Anthropologist Frank Spencer took on the role eagerly, having recently completed his dissertation on a history of Ales Hrdlička.[12] Spencer sought input from anthropologists on which subjects would be of greatest interest, and his first publication on the topic appeared in the *AJPA* in 1981, "The Rise of Academic Physical Anthropology in the United States (1880–1980): A Historical Overview." He and Trotter also corresponded regarding how to investigate women's contributions to the field specifically.[13]

Partly due to her own later realizations of gender disparities and her status as a founding member, Trotter was particularly interested in documenting the historically often minimized roles of women. In her "Department of Anatomy in My Time" draft, she included an accounting of the students entering their first year of medical school by decade. In the 1920s, 4.2% were women, 6.6% in the 1930s, 8.8% in the 1940s, 3.9% in the 1950s, 10.3% in the 1960s, and an average of 18% between 1970 and 1977.[14] She noted that Estelle Brodman arrived at Washington University as a historian of medicine in 1961 and contributed greatly to the preservation of the school's history, including the establishment of the medical archives, and her interview for Trotter's 1972 oral history.[15]

Despite her memory of clearly sexist structures throughout her career, Trotter admits to not fully recognizing them at the time. Trotter explains her earlier obliviousness to her experiences of sexism with her later interest in "women's lib" that, "I really don't think I started out with that [point of view]," but that "all these things developed that in me."[16] She certainly noticed that women were not offered the same opportunities as men. As early as 1933, she wrote to encourage one young woman finishing her PhD, "since women in this field are so few and so scattered."[17] But she, like most others, did not at the time always have the terminology or frame of reference to directly address it. This later recognition came with some concrete actions on her part, including her mentoring of women and her AAPA historical notes, but her explicit and more public responses really started in the 1970s. In conversations and interviews, she noted certain experiences and specifically labeled some as examples of "sex discrimination." Her 1972 oral history shows her to be quite plain-spoken on the subject, even exasperated by the extent of it. In 1978, she wrote that "in recent years I have become very conscious of the subdued role women have been forced to play."[18] But she was also careful

Women at the Washington University School of Medicine, 1939. Trotter is in the middle row, third from the left. VC170-i170261, Becker Medical Library, Washington University School of Medicine.

to dismiss the categorization of all of her experiences and treatment as being directly related to her gender.

In a letter to Stewart during planning for the 50th annual meeting, Trotter wondered, "why were you surprised to note that I gave a paper before Section H in New York in Dec 1928? I gave my first paper before Section H in Boston in 1922, following a request from Hooton ('Your work on hair is important')."[19] Hooton then repeatedly referred researchers to her as the known expert in hair studies.[20] But Trotter also went on to tell Stewart that "your question about my attending the meeting *following* the Section H program when the AAPA was founded amazes me. Of course I wasn't there – I was a female... and if by some wild chance I had been present, Hrdlička would probably have named me secretary (the job normally given to females.)"[21] It seems as though some of the moments that were obvious and sometimes painful to Trotter had been completely invisible to even her closest male colleague.

Trotter first began to firmly refer to herself as a feminist in the 1960s. In a 1965 letter to a former student from Makere University in Uganda, Trotter wrote that "I am especially interested in girls because I am a feminist. Your wife is a nurse. I hope your daughter will become a doctor."[22] Responses to her feminism varied. She and W. Montague Cobb were in agreement on the topic.[23] But at least one former student wrote that "you may be a feminist with good reason, but you are more important a LADY."[24] He went on to state that "to me that is one of the highest classes possible," and despite her explanations to him of her sexist treatment in salary and promotion, he argued that feminism was women asking for "special," not equal, rights.[25] Her reaction to these comments is unknown; her responses to these letters are not present in her archival collection, though she appears to have had ongoing and cordial communication with him. When writing to a colleague in 1970, Trotter noted that women were becoming better represented in some ways, but "this doesn't mean that I won't try to be aggressive on behalf of women."[26]

At the same time, the AAPA's interests in its history were developing, the AAA was beginning to take an active interest in tracking the status of women in the field. In 1977, a committee was appointed to address the lack of representation and recognition of women and "minorities" in the AAA, and whether they lagged behind other similar organizations.[27] Trotter later wrote to Frank Spencer in 1979 along these same lines,

> I would suggest that the history of the A.A.P.A. be examined to show whether the A.A.P.A. has been a leader among organiztions in the reception of women members or has it just gone along with the trend of increasing (under pressure?) the mebership of women.[28]

In the 1970s and early 1980s, she compiled listings of historical and contemporary women who were members of the AAPA in the since the 1930s.[29]

Though Trotter took some issue with their treatment of women, the AAPA and AAA were her home organizations throughout her career. The American Academy of Forensic Sciences had added a physical anthropology section in 1972, spearheaded by Ellis Kerley and Clyde Snow, but I have no specific record of Trotter attending any of their meetings. Even when she received an award from the Academy in 1982, it was accepted on her behalf by Michael Finnegan due to her absence.[30] The previous winners of the recently established section award were Kerley, Stewart, and, jointly with her that year, Krogman. Of course, she was already a member of both the AAA and AAPAs, whose early conferences were both often held in conjunction with the American Association for the Advancement of Science meetings, and she felt that "the best way I know to bring on an early death is two meetings in succession."[31] Trotter further expressed in 1978 that she hoped a colleague would not abandon the AAPA meetings for the American Academy of Forensic Sciences conference, which she felt "may be more fun but at the same time probably less scientific."[32]

In 1978, Trotter expressed that she supported the Equal Rights Amendment, which would guarantee equal legal rights to all people regardless of 'sex'.[33] At that time, it had been passed by Congress and awaited ratification by the states, under an extended deadline. The proposed amendment remains, to this day, unratified. Not much other evidence of her political life is present, but she noted in her oral history that, when questioned by some of her students in Uganda, she confirmed she had voted for John F. Kennedy for US President.[34]

Trotter was able to contribute to legal cases concerning sex and gender discrimination though, as is indirectly linked to height. In 1973, she provided expert testimony on the distribution of body sizes in men and women for a court case in Cleveland which contended that height and weight minimum requirements (68 inches and 150 pounds) for employment as police officers represented hiring discrimination.[35] A federal district court agreed that these requirements conflicted with the Equal Protections Clause of the 14th Amendment, which was first successfully used in reference specifically to gender discrimination only 2 years prior, in 1971.[36] The court found that the height and weight minimums disproportionately excluded women while having no direct connection to job performance.

A similar legal opportunity arose in 1976. Trotter was enlisted to take body measurements of several men and one woman pilot for a case in which a woman was denied a job as a pilot with Ozark Airlines in St. Louis, due to its height requirement.[37] The regional airline employed 380 pilots, all men. In this case, reasonable justification was found for having a minimum height requirement, though the company was made to change this minimum from 67 to 65 inches.[38] Unfortunately, the pilot who started the case was 62 inches tall, and she was therefore still denied a job, despite having experienced no physical limitations in performing her duties, and there being no Federal Aviation Administration height requirement.[39] It may have been quite satisfying for Trotter to have her scientific data and expertise at least help in reducing officially sanctioned sexism in American workplaces which she had witnessed throughout her own career. Trotter and her oral history interviewer agreed on at least one change that had occurred over time: that in 1972 "places that still discriminate do it with embarrassment, when before they just took the practice for granted."[40]

Trotter, as a woman in science in the early 20th century, has been called "a rare bird."[41] But this concept of a small few 'exceptional' women in White male-dominated fields reinforces the myth that merit alone has been the basis by which women and marginalized people have been systemically excluded and diminished in science. This narrative falsely implies that women as a whole were not as capable or functional as men – except for those few rarae aves who were able to succeed. It is not simply the competence of an individual that affects career opportunities and outcomes though but also variable privilege and underlying structural prejudices, which often have the effect of reinforcing and exacerbating inequities. I do not intend to ignore the impressive individual achievements of specific women such as Trotter but rather to put this common and sometimes unintentionally demeaning attitude in a more careful perspective. In an attempt to fulfill Trotter's interest in investigating the history of physical anthropology, as it includes the roles and experiences of women, what follows is an accounting of some of the women (and later, other marginalized people) contemporary with Trotter. In compiling this information, I situate modern women in anthropology within a deeper historical context. This exposes commonalities experienced by women in physical anthropology, and can fill in some of the lacunae left in Trotter's own accounts.

An earlier version of these two, paired chapters appeared in the *American Journal of Physical Anthropology*, and is expanded here.[42]

CONTEMPORARY WOMEN

Despite continued gender disparities in the discipline and a clear interest in promoting equity, there is little documentation of the historical experiences of women in anthropology. Recently, Turner, Bernstein, and Taylor (2018) compiled data on these disparities specifically for biological anthropology and emphasized the considerable interest within the field in better understanding and addressing these inequities.[43] In the absence of demographic surveys of AAPA members, which did not begin until 1996, there remains minimal information on the early experiences of women in anthropology from which to provide historical context to current conditions. Presenting existing documentation of treatment based on gender for each of these early AAPA members, in some cases firsthand, provides an indirect, and admittedly incomplete, retrospective member survey.

This work is necessarily limited by the surviving historical documentation. My sources include oral histories, biographies, newspaper interviews, magazine articles, archival sources, contemporary academic and popular literature, and historical reviews. I will briefly introduce each of these early members, as well as a few others who were active during this period but were not members, with basic biographical details necessary mainly for context. The purpose of this is not to provide a comprehensive index of women and their careers, and undoubtedly there are many women who contributed to the field who are unfortunately left out of this discussion. More substantial biographies for some of these women are presented elsewhere, many of which are referenced in this text. The individuals discussed here represent the majority of women professionally active in physical anthropology in the first decade of the AAPA. These experiences, therefore, mainly represent those of the few women who were able to successfully navigate a career, even if only temporarily.

Historian Margaret W. Rossiter's 1982 compendium of historical data on women in scientific fields prior to 1940 indicates that disparities evident in early physical anthropology were common in most scientific fields at the time, to varying degrees.[44] Although analogous data on the membership of other scientific associations has not been assembled, the AAPA's early representation of women was in line with a sister organization, the AAA. In 1945, the AAA had at least 65 members who were women (8%) out of the 810 total members.[45] I determined this by assessing first names on the 1945 AAA membership list. This method certainly misses women who provided only initials or whose names were not conventionally female, therefore I consider this a minimum number. Today, women represent 41% of AAA members.[46] Insufficient comparative historical data is currently available with which to systematically compare physical anthropology during this time to other disciplines regarding particular details and experiences, but I attempt to provide context from other fields where possible. Conversely, in some instances where detail is lacking for anthropology specifically, I draw on research from other fields.

After introducing the women in this chapter, I will then provide accounts of their individual experiences related to their gender in the next chapter, and identify shared patterns of those experiences, in order to situate women within the early years of the discipline of physical anthropology. These commonalities in experiences include receiving social and financial discouragement at all stages of education, gaining entrance into professional work by studying women and children, serving in temporary and lower paid positions, working within the federal government or military, disappearing from professional spheres early in their careers, finding their work subsumed under that of their male colleagues, facing discrimination in pay and promotion, experiencing additional limitations to their career if they married or had families, often internalizing and outwardly downplaying their own experiences of sexism.

This compilation of historical patterns shows that women's experiences in anthropology today, though certainly distinct and in many ways improved, are similar to those experienced at the inception of the AAPA. The low number of women itself was not the crux of the problem since women now represent a majority while still facing disparities. A historical perspective shows that the bases of these inequities are longstanding, even if they manifest somewhat differently today. While these chapters focus on a specific and significant period in the history of American physical anthropology, further research is merited on the intervening decades to better understand the complexities of women's experiences within the field throughout time. This pattern may look somewhat different for women today, and more optimistic, than it did for early women who were AAPA members, but the roots of these modern disparities were in place from the very beginnings of the discipline. Examining the persistence of gender inequality in anthropology and the sciences may provide a new lens through which to understand and improve the current state of the field.

With the founding of the AAPA in 1929, Aleš Hrdlička wrote, "Resolved: I. That there should be, and hereby is, founded an organization of American and allied scientific men and women active or interested in physical anthropology, to be known as the American Association of Physical Anthropologists."[47] At that time, "women" meant only two people, and by 1940 at least 14. Out of the 84 founding members of the AAPA, the women were Trotter and Ruth Otis Sawtell Wallis (1895–1978).[48] Unfortunately I have not found correspondence between these two women or any other information linking them professionally or socially. Wallis had earned an AB at Radcliffe in 1919, where she acted in plays, served as Editor-in-Chief for the Radcliffe News, and had a short story selected for publication in a compilation of "The Best College Short Stories, 1917–1918."[49] After graduation, she spent a year working as the editor of a factory newspaper for an optical company in Massachusetts. When she decided to start a graduate degree in anthropology at Radcliffe, Hooton and A. M. Tozzer reluctantly took her on as a student.[50] She completed her AM in 1923 at Radcliffe where she also worked at the Peabody Museum. Wallis received a Traveling Fellowship in Science from Radcliffe from 1923 to 1925. As part of this funding, she undertook fieldwork excavating prehistoric human remains in the French Pyrenees along with writer and journalist Ida Treat and her then-husband Paul Vaillant-Couterier.[51] Wallis would publish their findings in both scholarly and popular formats, including a book coauthored with Treat titled *Primitive Hearths of the Pyrenees*.[52]

Wallis completed her PhD in 1929 under Boas at Columbia University. Boas had chosen her as a research assistant because, according to her, he needed someone to measure women and children on a particular immigration study – apparently, the Sicilian men would not have allowed a man to measure their wives.[53] Her doctoral research focused on bone development, which continued when she started as an assistant professor at the University of Iowa in 1930. So, not only was she one of only two women who were founding members of the AAPA, but one of only six (along with five men) who were trained or functioning specifically as physical anthropologists, instead of as anatomists or physicians.[54] In 1931, she met and married cultural anthropologist Wilson D. Wallis, a widower and father of two young children. At this point, her career trajectory became more inconsistent and she experienced intermittent unemployment. She taught sociology at Hamline University in Minnesota while her husband worked at the nearby University of Minnesota until she was fired from the position in 1935. Wallis then worked as a consultant for the Works Progress Administration from 1935 to 1937 and for the Bureau of Home Economics of the USDA from 1937 to 1938 gathering the data that led to the standardization of children's clothing sizes.[55] During the 1930s, she also presented and published on topics critical of eugenicist concepts of racial purity.[56] Due to her reduced opportunities as a woman married to an academic, for nearly two decades she worked mainly in collaboration with her husband on sociocultural anthropology topics. She undertook ethnological research on Canadian Indians in conjunction with her husband in the 1950s. When he retired, Wallis took a teaching position at Annhurst College, where she would later retire as their first professor emerita.[57] Wallis and her husband financed at least one former Minnesota student's graduate work at Radcliffe. For repayment, they asked only that the woman similarly assist another student in the future.[58] Later in life she wrote a biography of her husband but declined to work on her own autobiography.[59]

Wallis disappeared from the AAPA membership list by 1940. But while in 1930 there were only two women members, by 1940 there were 14 women out of the 144 total.[60] One of the more prominent within physical anthropology was Alice Brues (1913–2007). Brues completed an AB at Bryn Mawr in 1933 and in 1940 was the only Radcliffe PhD graduate under Hooton at Harvard. She worked first as a research assistant at the

Peabody Museum and with Hooton on anthropometric data used for military uniform and equipment design, as an assistant statistician for the Air Force, and as a consultant for MIT during World War II. She finally secured joint positions at the University of Oklahoma Medical School (1946–1965) and Stovall Museum (1956–1965).[61] During this time, she began innovative work with computer simulated modeling for evolutionary theories.[62] From 1965 to 1984, she was a professor at the University of Colorado at Boulder. Her most famous work was on the frequencies of ABO blood group types and recognizing variable forms of syphilis in paleopathology.[63] She was the second woman to serve as president of the AAPA, 14 years after Trotter, from 1971 to 1973. Of 47 total AAPA presidents, only 9 have been women (19.1%). The discipline's gender ratio is changing, along with attitudes, and four of the more recent presidents have been women (2012–2020).

Another member of the AAPA, Edith Boyd (1895–1977), completed an MD, following in the footsteps of her father, at Johns Hopkins in 1921. After residencies in San Francisco and at Stanford, she finished a fellowship in pediatrics at the Mayo Clinic and remained in Minnesota for 16 years at working through the University of Minnesota and the Minnesota Institute of Child Welfare on fetal and child growth and development. From 1946 to 1969, she held various positions at the University of Colorado Medical School, where she established and undertook a massive longitudinal study on human growth and development.

Other members of the AAPA in 1940 held a variety of positions. Ruth Clarke MacDuffie Mackaye completed an AM at Radcliffe in 1920, and became chair of anthropology at Vassar.[64] Helen Lucerne Dawson completed her PhD at Washington University in 1932 and her dissertation, like Trotter's, focused on hair growth using guinea pigs.[65] She worked briefly in 1936 at Hooton's statistical and anthropometric laboratory, and held positions at the University of Iowa for the remainder of her career.[66] Stella M. A. Leche Deignan (1901–1993) completed a PhD at Tulane in 1932 and became an assistant professor there, later directing and organizing the Medical Science Information Exchange of the National Research Council, which would become the Smithsonian Biological Information Exchange.[67] Though not on the 1940 AAPA membership list, Isabel Gordon Carter completed her PhD in 1928 at Columbia under Boas on the effects of inbreeding on populational variation, as determined from measurements of children.[68] She was on the faculty of Social Work at the University of Pennsylvania from 1933 to 1962, and had served as a White House advisor to the Commission on Children and Youth, as well as the DC Economic Board of Opportunity.[69] Another student of Boas, Eleanor (née Phelps) Hunt, finished an AB at Barnard in 1923 and a PhD in anthropology at Columbia in 1932, and worked with a variety of government agencies, including the Public Health Service, on extensive child health and development projects.[70] Carolyn Adler Lewis finished a PhD at Columbia in 1936, but disappears from anthropology listings and publications soon after (and she was never a member of the AAPA). Ruth De Witt Pearl was the daughter of biologist and later President of the AAPA, Raymond Pearl, with whom she published in the early 1930s. She completed a BA at Wellesley and in 1940 she was listed as an assistant in the Department of Biology at Johns Hopkins.[71] A Mrs. Rosanna Duncan Sanderson worked as a voluntary researcher at the American Museum of Natural History in New York and later compiled data on American maritime shipping history.[72] Helen Thompson Woolley (1874–1947) was listed as a member, though her education and career were entirely in psychology.[73] I mistakenly excluded Woolley from the 2019 *AJPA* article listing of 14 women who were members, while at the same time including non-member Carter. So, despite this very unfortunate error, the math was still right. For two other women, listed as Mrs. Emily Graham of Englewood, NJ and Mrs. John Jay Whitehead of New York, I have not been able to locate further information on their education or careers.

Charlotte Gower (1902–1982), like many of these women, had left little trace beyond her mention in the literature and her brief membership in the AAPA. This prompted anthropologist Maria Lepowsky (2000) to seek more information. Gower completed a BA at Smith College and PhD at the University of Chicago under Fay-Cooper Cole in 1928. After graduating, she taught at the University of Wisconsin. Both Chicago and Wisconsin rejected her dissertation for publication, despite positive reviews. Subsequent to these rejections, her dissertation was lost for decades, and only published in 1971 when a carbon copy was located.[74] After suspicions arose of an affair between Gower and a male colleague, Gower was fired from the University of Wisconsin (and not the colleague), and she took an offer at Lingnan University in China in 1938. She spoke Cantonese and worked as a nurse/pharmacist during bombing and Japanese occupation. In 1942, during the occupation, she was imprisoned in Hong Kong. On her return to the US, she became the director of training for the Marine Corps women's reserve. She married in 1947, the same year that she joined the CIA.[75] Despite evidence to the contrary, and similar to many others, Gower claimed to have experienced no negative effects during her career due to being a woman.

One other woman who was not an anthropologist and entered academia decades later than the women above, but whose name is inextricably linked to Trotter's, was Goldine Cohnberg Gleser (1915–2004). Gleser (named for her grandmother, Goldie) grew up in St. Louis and enjoyed a vivacious young adulthood spent traveling in Mexico, where she became fluent in Spanish and turned down a marriage proposal.[76] On returning to Missouri, she hitchhiked to New York to visit a friend.

Though her parents discouraged her, Gleser was awarded a partial scholarship to Washington University during the Depression and earned an AB in 1935. She went on to complete an AM in mathematics there in 1936. Her first choice had been physics, but she was told they did not want any women.[77] That same year she would also marry. In 1937, she left her PhD program in math, all but dissertation complete, when the department pulled her funding, citing that her husband should be supporting her.[78] Gleser had three children and, once the youngest was 2 years old, she felt that "my family came first, but I had no desire to be just a housewife. I knew I needed to find more ways to direct my energy or I would be miserable."[79] She later switched tracks to earn a PhD in psychology in 1950 since she had found math to be too esoteric.[80] She eventually became director of the Psychology Division of the Department of Psychiatry at the University of Cincinnati College of Medicine and held visiting professorships at Stanford and at Macquarie University in Australia. Her later research focused on post-traumatic psychological effects. Her history of at least 124 publications is almost exclusively on psychology topics, including the widely used Gottschalk-Gleser verbal content psychological test.[81] The only exceptions in her publications are very few articles and books where her primary (though not exclusive) contribution was statistics. One of her most well-known of these collaborations was her work with Mildred Trotter on stature estimation equations in the 1950s. In 2000, she published her autobiography, optimistically titled *Getting It All*.[82]

NOTES

1 Mildred Trotter, interview by Estelle Brodman, May 19, 1972 and May 23, 1972, transcript, Becker Medical Library, Washington University School of Medicine.

2 Draft, Trotter, "The Department of Anatomy in My Time," p. 12, no date, series 1, box 1, Mildred Trotter Papers, Becker Medical Library, Washington University School of Medicine.

3 Draft, Trotter, "The Department of Anatomy in My Time," p. 7, no date, series 1, box 1, Mildred Trotter Papers, Becker Medical Library, Washington University School of Medicine.

4 Mildred Trotter, "Robert J. Terry, 1871–1966," *American Journal of Physical Anthropology* 56, no. 4 (1981): 503–508.

5 Letter, Trotter to T.D. Stewart, May 16, 1977; and Letter, T.D. Stewart to Trotter, May 20, 1977, series 13, box 1, folder 5, Mildred Trotter Papers, Becker Medical Library, Washington University School of Medicine.

6 Letter, Trotter to William S. Pollitzer, July 20, 1979, series 3, box 4, folder 7, Mildred Trotter Papers, Becker Medical Library, Washington University School of Medicine.
7 Letter, T.D. Stewart to Trotter, May 20, 1977, series 13, box 1, folder 5, Mildred Trotter Papers, Becker Medical Library, Washington University School of Medicine.
8 Letter, Trotter to James A. Gavan, November 20, 1978, series 13, box 1, folder 5, Mildred Trotter Papers, Becker Medical Library, Washington University School of Medicine.
9 Letter, Trotter to William S. Pollitzer, July 20, 1979, series 3, box 4, folder 7, Mildred Trotter Papers, Becker Medical Library, Washington University School of Medicine.
10 Letter, Trotter to G.E. Erikson, April 18, 1978, series 3, box 5, folder 47, Mildred Trotter Papers, Becker Medical Library, Washington University School of Medicine.
11 Letter, G.E. Erikson to Trotter, October 24, 1978, series 13, box 1, folder 5, Mildred Trotter Papers, Becker Medical Library, Washington University School of Medicine.
12 No author, "Obituary of Frank Spencer," *History of Anthropology Newsletter* 26, no. 1 (June 1999):18.
13 Letter, Frank Spencer to Trotter, October 26, 1979, series 3, box 7, folder 14, Mildred Trotter Papers, Becker Medical Library, Washington University School of Medicine.
14 Draft, Trotter, "The Department of Anatomy in My Time," p. 7, no date, series 1, box 1, Mildred Trotter Papers, Becker Medical Library, Washington University School of Medicine.
15 Draft, Trotter, "The Department of Anatomy in My Time," p. 104, no date, series 1, box 1, Mildred Trotter Papers, Becker Medical Library, Washington University School of Medicine.
16 Mildred Trotter, interview by Estelle Brodman, May 19, 1972 and May 23, 1972, audio, Becker Medical Library, Washington University School of Medicine.
17 Letter, Esther L. Boyer to Totter, January 25, 1933 (with handwritten draft of response from Trotter), series 2, box 2, folder 45, Mildred Trotter Papers, Becker Medical Library, Washington University School of Medicine.
18 Letter, Trotter to Janet Bryan, November 22, 1978, series 3, box 6, folder 45, Mildred Trotter Papers, Becker Medical Library, Washington University School of Medicine.
19 Letter, Trotter to T.D. Stewart, September 28, 1979, series 13, box 6, folder 12, Mildred Trotter Papers, Becker Medical Library, Washington University School of Medicine. Trotter notes that her paper was added too late to be included in the printed program.

20 Letter, Howard L. Barlow to Trotter, July 13, 1927, series 3, box 3, folder 15; and Letter, Walter Landauer to Trotter, January 5, 1926, series 3, box 3, folder 21, Mildred Trotter Papers, Becker Medical Library, Washington University School of Medicine.
21 Letter, Trotter to T.D. Stewart, September 28, 1979, series 13, box 6, folder 12, Mildred Trotter Papers, Becker Medical Library, Washington University School of Medicine.
22 Letter, Trotter to Isaac Gatumbi, July 13, 1965, series 13, box 3, folder 6, Mildred Trotter Papers, Becker Medical Library, Washington University School of Medicine.
23 Letter, Trotter to W. Montague Cobb, April 19, 1960, series 13, box 2, folder 4, Mildred Trotter Papers, Becker Medical Library, Washington University School of Medicine.
24 Letter, Verne Goerger to Trotter, July 14, 1983, series 3, box 6, folder 7, Mildred Trotter Papers, Becker Medical Library, Washington University School of Medicine.
25 Letter, Verne Goerger to Trotter, August 10, 1983, series 3, box 6, folder 7, Mildred Trotter Papers, Becker Medical Library, Washington University School of Medicine.
26 Letter, Trotter to Elizabeth Moyer, April 20, 1970, series 13, box 4, folder 15, Mildred Trotter Papers, Becker Medical Library, Washington University School of Medicine.
27 Letter, Helen A. Padykula to Carmine Clemente, April 5, 1977, series 3, box 8, folder 39, Mildred Trotter Papers, Becker Medical Library, Washington University School of Medicine.
28 Letter, Trotter to Frank Spencer, November 26, 1979, series 3, box 7, folder 14, Mildred Trotter Papers, Becker Medical Library, Washington University School of Medicine.
29 Letter, Trotter to Elizabeth Moyer, April 20, 1970, series 13, box 4, folder 15; and letter, Trotter to T.D. Stewart, January 23, 1980, series 13, box 3, folder 12, Mildred Trotter Papers, Becker Medical Library, Washington University School of Medicine.
30 Letter, Michael Finnegan to Trotter, February 26, 1982, series 3, box 4, folder 4, Mildred Trotter Papers, Becker Medical Library, Washington University School of Medicine.
31 Letter, Trotter to T.D. Stewart, April 20, 1957, series 13, box 6, folder 11, Mildred Trotter Papers, Becker Medical Library, Washington University School of Medicine.
32 Letter, Trotter to Louise M. Robbins, May 10, 1978, series 13, box 6, folder 3, Mildred Trotter Papers, Becker Medical Library, Washington University School of Medicine.
33 Letter, Trotter to Louise M. Robbins, November 10, 1978, series 13, box 6, folder 3, Mildred Trotter Papers, Becker Medical Library, Washington University School of Medicine.

34 Mildred Trotter, interview by Estelle Brodman, May 19, 1972 and May 23, 1972, audio, Becker Medical Library, Washington University School of Medicine.
35 Elizabeth A. Smith et al., v. City of East Cleveland et al., United States District Court, N. D. Ohio, E. D. September 6, 1973.
36 Walter Karabian, "The Equal Rights Amendment: The Contribution of Our Generation of Americans, *Pepperdine Law Review* 1, no. 3 (1974): 327–354, p. 345.
37 Letter, Donald J. Meyer to Trotter, March 15, 1976 , series 3, box 5, folder 13; and letter, Susan Spiegel to Trotter, March 17, 1976, series 3, box 3, folder 13, Mildred Trotter Papers, Becker Medical Library, Washington University School of Medicine.
38 "Boyd v. Ozark Air Lines, Inc.," *US District Court for the Eastern District of Missouri* 419 F. Supp. 1061 (E.D. Mo. 1976), August 23, 1976.
39 Victor Volland, "Woman Pilot Unhappy with Ruling on Height," St. Louis Post-Dispatch, August 25, 1976, 16A.
40 Estelle Brodman quote, in Mildred Trotter, interview by Estelle Brodman, May 19, 1972 and May 23, 1972, transcript, Becker Medical Library, Washington University School of Medicine.
41 For example, Williams, Robert C. *The Forensic Historian: Using Science to Reexamine the Past* (New York: Routledge, 2013), p. xi.
42 Emily K. Wilson, "Women's Experiences in Early Physical Anthropology," *American Journal of Physical Anthropology*, 170 (2019): 308–318.
43 Trudy R. Turner, et al., "Participation, Representation, and Shared Experiences of Women Scholars in Biological Anthropology," *American Journal of Physical Anthropology* 165 (2018): 126–157.
44 Margaret W. Rossiter, *Women Scientists in America: Struggles and Strategies to 1940* (Baltimore, MD: Johns Hopkins University Press, 1982).
45 "Proceedings of the American Association of Anatomists," *The Anatomical Record*, 92, no. 3 (1945): 305–358.
46 American Association of Anatomists, "2018 Year in Review: Building upon the Present, Preparing for the Future," 2018, https://www.anatomy.org/uploads/4/6/5/1/46517773/2018_yir_final_web_-_ao.pdf.
47 Aleš Hrdlička, "American Association of Physical Anthropologists," *Science* 69 (1929): 304–305.
48 "Meeting of the American Association of Physical Anthropologists," *American Journal of Physical Anthropology* 14, no. 2 (1930): 321–329.
49 *The Radcliffe News* 5, no. 5. 26 (October 1917): 8; *The Radcliffe News* 5, no. 27 (May 10, 1918): 4; Ruth Otis Sawtell, "The Way of Peace," in *The Best College Short Stories, 1917–1918*, Henry T. Schnittkind, ed. (Boston, MA: The Stratford Company, 1919).

50 June M. Collins, "Ruth Sawtell Wallis 1895–1978," *American Anthropologist* 81, no. 1 (1979): 85–87, p. 85.
51 June M. Collins, "Ruth Sawtell Wallis 1895–1978," *American Anthropologist* 81, no. 1 (1979): 85–87, p. 85.
52 Ruth Otis Sawtell and Ida Treat, *Primitive Hearths in the Pyrenees* (New York: D Appleton, 1927).
53 Patricia Case, "Ruth Sawtell Wallis (1895–1978)," in *Women Anthropologists: Selected Biographies*, ed. Ute Gacs, Aisha Khan, Jerri McIntyre, Ruth Weinberg (Urbana Champaign: University of Illinois Press, 1988), 362.
54 Frank Spencer, "The Rise of Academic Physical Anthropology in the United States (1880–1980): A Historical Overview," *American Journal of Physical Anthropology* 56, no. 4 (1981): 353–364, p. 360.
55 Patricia Case, "Ruth Sawtell Wallis (1895–1978)," in *Women Anthropologists: Selected Biographies*, ed. Ute Gacs, Aisha Khan, Jerri McIntyre, Ruth Weinberg (Urbana Champaign: University of Illinois Press, 1988), 362.
56 Mary Lucas Powell, Della Collins Cook, Georgieann Bogdan, Jane E. Buikstra, Mario M. Castro, Patrick D. Horne, David R. Hunt, Richard T. Koritzer, Sheila Ferraz Mendonqa de Souza, Mary Kay Sandford, Laurie Saunders, Glaucia Aparecida Malerba Sene, Lynne Sullivan, and John J. Swetnam, "Invisible hands: Women in Bioarchaeology," in *Bioarchaeology: The Contextual Analysis of Human Remains*, ed. Jane Buikstra and Lane Beck (Routledge, 2017): 131–194.
57 Marilyn Ogilvie and Joy Harvey, The Biographical Dictionary of Women in Science: Pioneering Lives from Ancient Times to the Mid-20th Century (Routledge, 2003), p. 1343.
58 Jennifer Cash, "Biographies: Elizabeth Florence Colson," posted May 1998, http://www.indiana.edu/~wanthro/theory_pages/Colson.htm.
59 June M. Collins, "Ruth Sawtell Wallis 1895–1978," *American Anthropologist* 81, no. 1 (1979): 85–87, p. 86.
60 "Proceedings of the Eleventh Annual Meeting of the American Association of Physical Anthropologists," *American Journal of Physical Anthropology* 27, no. 2 (1940): 1–21.
61 Mary K Sandford, Lynn Kilgore, Diane L France, "Alice Mossie Brues (1913–2007)," in *The Global History of Paleopathology: Pioneers and Prospects*, eds. Jane Buikstra and Charlotte Roberts (Oxford: Oxford University Press, 2012), 156–161.
62 Darna L. Dufour, "Alice Mossie Brues (1913–)," in *Women Anthropologists: Selected Biographies*, ed. Ute Gacs, Aisha Khan, Jerri McIntyre, Ruth Weinberg (Urbana Champaign: University of Illinois Press, 1988).

63 Mary K Sandford, Lynn Kilgore, Diane L France, "Alice Mossie Brues (1913–2007)," in *The Global History of Paleopathology: Pioneers and Prospects*, eds. Jane Buikstra and Charlotte Roberts (Oxford: Oxford University Press, 2012), pp. 156–161.
64 *International Directory of Anthropologists* (Washington, D.C.: National Research Council, 1940).
65 Mildred Trotter and Helen L. Dawson, "The Hair of French Canadians," *American Journal of Physical Anthropology* 18, no. 3 (1934): 443–456.
66 David L. Browman and Stephen Williams, *Anthropology at Harvard: A Biographical History, 1970–1940* (Cambridge, MA: Harvard University Press, 2013), p. 406.
67 Herbert Friedmann, "In Memoriam: Herbert Girton Deignan," *The Auk* 87 (1970): 16.
68 Isabel Gordon Carter, "Reduction of Variability in an Inbred Population," *American Journal of Physical Anthropology* 11, no. 3 (1928): 457–471.
69 Almanac, University of Pennsylvania 35, no. 4 (September 13, 1988), 2.
70 *International Directory of Anthropologists* (Washington, D.C.: National Research Council, 1940).
71 *International Directory of Anthropologists* (Washington, D.C.: National Research Council, 1940).
72 *International Directory of Anthropologists* (Washington, D.C.: National Research Council, 1940); and The G. W. Blunt White Library, Mystic Seaport, Collection of Rosanna Duncan Sanderson, Manuscripts Collection 273.
73 Katharine S. Milar, "Breaking the Silence: Helen Bradford Thompson Woolley," in *The Life Cycle of Psychological Ideas*, ed. Thomas C. Dalton, Rand B. Evans (Boston, MA: Springer, 2005), 301–328.
74 Maria Lepowsky, "Charlotte Gower and the Subterranean History of Anthropology," in *Excluded Ancestors, Inventible Traditions: Essays toward a More Inclusive History of Anthropology*, ed. Richard Handler (Madison: University of Wisconsin Press, 2000), p. 152.
75 Maria Lepowsky, "Charlotte Gower and the Subterranean History of Anthropology," in *Excluded Ancestors, Inventible Traditions: Essays toward a More Inclusive History of Anthropology*, ed. Richard Handler (Madison: University of Wisconsin Press, 2000), p. 163.
76 Goldine C. Gleser, *Getting It All* (Seattle, WA: Keepsake Editions, 2000).
77 Goldine C. Gleser, *Getting It All* (Seattle, WA: Keepsake Editions, 2000), p. 54.

78 Goldine C. Gleser, *Getting It All* (Seattle, WA: Keepsake Editions, 2000), p. 66.
79 Goldine C. Gleser, *Getting It All* (Seattle, WA: Keepsake Editions, 2000), p. 88.
80 Alan F. Friedman and William N. Dember, "Obituaries: Goldine Gleser (1915–2004)," *American Psychologist* 61, no. 6 (2006): 636.
81 Louis August Gottschalk and Goldine C. Gleser, *The Measurement of Psychological States through the Content Analysis of Verbal Behavior* (University of California Press, 1969).
82 Goldine C. Gleser, *Getting It All* (Seattle, WA: Keepsake Editions, 2000).

CHAPTER 6

Women's Experiences

While the women introduced in the last chapter had extremely varied and in some cases successful careers, many of their experiences as women were similar. Trotter's own experiences were depressingly typical for women during this time. Many women received discouragement at all stages of their education, and sometimes avoided this temporarily by matriculating at women's colleges. They were often from wealthy or otherwise supportive families who could support them instead of depending on scholarships, and all of these early women who were American Association of Physical Anthropologists (AAPA) members were White. In many instances, their entrance into professional work was facilitated by being brought on to study women, children, or social spaces where male professors felt they were unable to use White men. Partly as a result, they also often worked in child and development studies throughout their careers. Another common entrée into professional anthropology was through government or military employment. Many found themselves in temporary and lower paid positions. Others could never get a foothold and seem to have disappeared from the record in what should have been their early career. Even when they were active in the field, their work was sometimes subsumed under their male colleagues or husbands. They experienced demonstrable disparities in hiring, pay, and promotions. Few married, and those who did experienced damage and limitations to their careers, especially if their husband was an academic. Even fewer of these women had children, and none of them were openly gay. Many internalized and outwardly downplayed, discounted, or denied their own blatant experiences of sexism at the time, only publicly recognizing their differential treatment later in life, if ever. The following are accounts of women's individual experiences within these shared patterns, and the associations of those same experiences to their modern reverberations.

Most of these women have documented experiences of discouragement starting very early in their education from the would-be mentors who surrounded them, directly related to their gender. While in high school, Trotter's principal had stated that home economics would be

DOI: 10.4324/9781003252818-6

more "appropriate" than a geometry course.[1] When Wallis decided to start a graduate degree in anthropology at Radcliffe, Hooton and A. M. Tozzer patronizingly cautioned her that women usually abandoned their work when they married, but they would help her out if she was truly serious.[2] Alice Brues, in addressing her experiences in the almost exclusively male field of physical anthropology, downplayed the influence of sexism even late in life, stating that "people were not so painfully conscious of those things as they are now."[3] Coming, as she was, from a prominent academic family in Boston, Brues stated that she felt that getting a PhD "seemed natural." But, while doing her PhD coursework, she was not allowed in the lecture room and had to instead sit in the open door to audit Hooton's classes at Harvard in order to get credit from Radcliffe.[4] Her father, a professor of entomology at Harvard, had to speak to Hooton on her behalf in order to gain permission to take the course even in this manner.[5]

Another student of anthropology at Radcliffe, Doris Zemurray Stone, later noted that "never did I attend a class at Harvard Yard... Yet I owe most of my education to the Harvard professors who deigned to teach at Radcliffe. I use the word 'deign' because some teachers actually *refused* to be associated with the training of women students."[6] Stone also recounted an experience with Hooton that "I was advised against studying for a PhD. Women simply weren't encouraged to go that far, *particularly* in anthropology . . . . One of my former professors ... thought little came from educating females because they soon grew up and were married."[7] Stone did not pursue a graduate degree, though she did remain active in archaeology and ethnology.[8] Women who did pursue a graduate degree at Radcliffe often stopped with the AM, and if they did get a PhD, it was at another institution, and often decades later.[9] The single exception was Brues.

Most of these women, including Trotter, completed their undergraduate work, and sometimes master's degrees, at women's colleges including Radcliffe, Mount Holyoke, Barnard, and Smith. These environments may have insulated them from certain forms of sexism, and may have provided an opportunity at a young age to thrive outside of the confines of academic environments which gave preferential treatment to male students. Women's colleges also provided them with mentors who were women, which was not typically the case at co-educational institutions. Quality mentorship opportunities have more recently been shown to positively shape careers for women, and women particularly benefit from quality mentorship by women.[10] Women's colleges did not have large research grant funds or graduate programs in the early 20th century though, and many ambitious women would eventually need to look elsewhere.[11] Furthermore, even women's colleges during this time period are documented to have preferentially hired men, especially at higher ranks and often explicitly, reducing the available posts for graduates who were women.[12] Trotter also recognized what is now the well-established phenomenon of mentors more commonly choosing proteges who are like themselves, particularly in terms of race and gender.[13] She noticed that Washington University anatomy chair Edward Dempsey had taken a particular liking to a younger male colleague named Alexander Duncan Chiquoine, III because he "fancied that he had looked like Duncan when he was Duncan's age."[14]

The discrimination against women did not come only in the form of discouragement but also through funding across scientific disciplines.[15] Based only on their limited biographical information, most or perhaps all of these women in anthropology seem to have come from relatively financially secure family backgrounds. But students who were women were repeatedly warned of their poor job prospects, and this fact was even used as a justification to limit the opportunities and monetary awards presented to them. The University of Chicago advertised an award by unapologetically stating, "as there are at present open to women relatively few professional positions in anthropology, the number of scholarships granted to women should be limited."[16] Stone remembered when she was 18 years old overhearing a scientist visiting from the Smithsonian "expound[ing] on the advisability of accepting only men in the field, especially in tropical regions" due to women's supposed maternal obligations.[17] This distinguished visitor went on to dismiss the comments of one woman in the room (the wife of an archaeologist) who noted her healthy pregnancies and childcare in the field. These demeaning attitudes and practices toward women only served to reinforce existing biases and disparities, effectively limiting women's opportunities.[18] At Berkeley, Kroeber commented that he didn't like to admit women because he didn't think they would find jobs. He also did not want women on summer fieldwork because he felt "they were not interested in archaeology, but only in male archaeologists."[19] Considering the sexual harassment and assault particularly to women in the field documented more recently by Clancy et al.[20] this scenario not only misrepresented the dynamic but demonstrated that such concerns may have posed even bigger barriers to women seeking these types of research projects.

At this point in time, physical anthropology was strongly linked to anatomy, and few people were trained specifically in physical anthropology. Anatomy and physical anthropology remain closely linked in training and employment today; and 27% of women surveyed as part of the AAPA Committee on Diversity Women's Initiative work in departments other than anthropology.[21] At the founding of the AAPA, only 4 out of 84 members (5%) held PhDs in physical anthropology; by 1943 that number was 21 out of 176 (12%).[22] Opportunities to be formally trained were increasing for physical anthropology as a distinct field (as opposed to anatomy or other subfields of anthropology). But while few graduated in physical anthropology specifically, fewer women were educated in physical anthropology relative to men. Even so, more women were educated than were actually able to maintain a career.

Boas was the mentor for the plurality of these early AAPA members who were women. Of his seven PhD students at Columbia in physical anthropology specifically, four were women (Wallis, Lewis, Hunt, and Carter). Wallis was able to stay in academia, albeit intermittently; Hunt was able to create a career in government-funded projects; Carter built a career in social work; and Lewis never developed a professional career in anthropology. Of the three men who graduated under Boas, one was a prolific publisher who worked on federal public health projects (Marcus Goldstein); one had a successful career at the American Museum of Natural History before dying prematurely in his 30s (Louis R. Sullivan); and one was prominent anthropologist Ashley Montagu.[23] At the University of Chicago, Gower's mentor was Fay-Cooper Cole, who had been a cultural anthropology PhD student under Boas. Gower was, in 1928, the first woman to earn a PhD in anthropology at the University, and by 1940, the University of Chicago had graduated 27 men and only 2 women in anthropology.[24] At Harvard, Hooton mentored at least 21 PhD students in physical anthropology from 1926 to 1951, the majority of whom had successful careers.[25] Only one of these students, Brues, was a woman. The remaining early AAPA members with doctorates had studied anatomy at medical schools (Trotter, Dawson, and Leche Deignan) or held an MD (Boyd).

Even when women continued their education despite overtly sexist treatment and financial discouragement, a degree did not result in equal access to professional opportunities. This pattern continues today, where increasing numbers of PhD graduates are women, yet they are still underrepresented in academia.[26] By 1984, women were earning around 50% of the PhDs in anthropology.[27] In the 1998 AAPA Membership Survey, women represented a greater proportion of PhD recipients than men (64.6%), but a smaller proportion of individuals attaining tenure-track jobs (54.5%), obtaining tenure (53.6%), and promoting to full professor (31.7%).[28] As of 2014, women hold only 54.5% of tenure-track positions and 38% of full professorships despite the relatively higher proportion of women within the field for decades.[29]

In her extensive and engrossing 1982 study on women in science in the early 20th century, Margaret W. Rossiter compiled comprehensive data on women's involvement in American institutions. While each scientific field was unique in its specific treatment of women, anthropology shared in the general patterns of other disciplines at the time. Women represented 30% of US PhDs in anthropology (all subfields) from 1920 to

1938, which constituted the highest proportion of women holding doctorates in any scientific field.[30] But by 1938, there were 225 men (89%) and only 29 women (11%) actively working as anthropologists.[31] Only 17 women held academic faculty positions in anthropology departments.[32] Across scientific fields in 1938, women represented an average of 13% of PhD holders but an average of 7% of the active scientific professionals.[33] Women were systematically underrepresented in employment in scientific fields relative to their numbers of PhD graduates. More scientists and institutions were willing to train women than would actually hire them at coeducational universities or other permanent positions after they finished the degree. A similar pattern has persisted, with disproportionate numbers of women prematurely "leaking" out of the pipeline at all points along their career,[34] and advancing more slowly than men in academia.[35] This is also documented specifically in anthropology.[36]

Women were overrepresented relative to the number of PhD graduates from 1920 to 1938 in one aspect though: National Research Council Fellowships in anthropology (39%). Rossiter determined that this was partially an intentional decision by senior anthropologists to give women provisional posts, while men were afforded more career-track and permanent opportunities.[37] Trotter was one of these recipients from 1925 to 1926. Among these AAPA members, women educated in anatomy and medicine (Trotter, Boyd, Dawson, and Leche Deignan) were more likely to find faculty positions at medical schools than were women educated in anthropology.

One common opportunity for women was in government-funded projects, particularly on children's development. This may have been due to the perception of women as acceptable and appropriate researchers for women and children's studies (and therefore as less acceptable researchers for other studies). World War II also opened up federal funding for many anthropometric and other projects. Trotter worked with the US Public Health Service and the World War II identification of remains,[38] Wallis worked with the Works Progress Administration and the USDA on data used for children's clothing sizes,[39] Brues assisted in military equipment design,[40] Boyd committed her career to the study of fetal and child growth through numerous funding bodies,[41] Ruth Clarke MacDuffie Mackaye contributed to the body measurements behind women's military uniforms, and Eleanor P. Hunt served with the Children's Bureau of the Department of Health, Education, and Welfare.[42] Carter's career began with taking measurements of children and later focused on social work, particularly involving children.[43] Trotter's 1932 recommendation for Dawson's unsuccessful National Research Council Fellowship application specifically noted that the measurements of women and children for this particular study could only be accomplished by a woman and would otherwise have to be omitted from the project.[44]

A common opportunity involved participation in the research projects of more senior male anthropologists. A pattern existed of White male academics only choosing women and people of color as assistants for specific projects when they believed such assistants were required in order to have socially appropriate access to their preferred human subjects. Charles Danforth sought a woman as an assistant to expand his studies of male hair growth, choosing Trotter to make observations related to women's face and body hair growth for what would become her master's thesis.[45] Boas chose Wallis as a research assistant because he needed someone to measure women and children on a particular immigration study.[46] Hooton sought a Black woman, Caroline Bond Day, to study "racial mixture" in a population.[47] Though unrelated to access to research subjects, faculty members who are men continue to train and employ fewer women than do faculty members who are women.[48]

While these projects provided opportunities for women's advancement, some senior male colleagues also exploited women's labor and took credit for their work. Women were particularly prevalent in roles such as "assistant," "researcher," and "lecturer," which freed up men's time for other work.[49] Many of these anthropologists held temporary or low-level positions for a large portion of their careers – a pattern which remains disproportionately true for women in academia today.[50] Earnest Hooton at Harvard was explicit, even self-congratulatory, about his exploitation of a student's work in 1930:

> A Harvard instructor who teaches Radcliffe classes can select from his more promising pupils the most splendidly equipped and competent research assistants and super-secretaries to be found. These female aids are more patient, more conscientious, more accurate, and more loyal, than young men of comparable status are. They take better care of you and they do not immediately think that they know more than you do.... A perspicacious professor... can often manage to get these brainy Radcliffe graduates to do almost all of the harder work. Thereby he can enormously increase his scientific output.[51]

Rossiter expanded on the "Matthew Effect" – that a well-known researcher will get more or exclusive credit compared to a less well-known researcher for the same or less work.[52] She determined that this phenomenon plays out in gendered ways and demonstrated a well-documented bias against recognizing the accomplishments of women and instead attributing them to men. Rossiter provides abundant examples of cases where women have been given less credit, forgotten, mistaken for men or for their husbands, or have gone unrecognized for their contributions to even major scientific findings. More recent analyses of conference participation have shown a continued, demonstrable bias toward under-representation and under-recognition of the contributions of women relative to men in anthropology.[53] Rossiter's "Matilda Effect" is evident for these anthropologists. Edith Boyd's work was described in her own obituary in a way that subsumed it under her male colleague's, as "Richard Scammon's opus magnum."[54] Boyd was, however, the primary contributor and first author on their manuscript on human growth. Ruth Sawtell Wallis worked on sociocultural anthropology projects with her husband while employment prospects for herself were slim. Though neither Wallis may not have described their collaboration exactly in this way, his biographer described that Ruth was "an anthropologist of proven stature" who "assist[ed]" her husband with his field work, just as his first wife apparently had before her.[55]

Goldine Gleser's contribution to the Gottschalk-Gleser test was dismissively described by Gottschalk:

> I should, here, give some acknowledgment to a person I met at the University of Cincinnati, Goldine C. Gleser who had specialized in measurement psychology. She had a doctorate degree, a PhD. She had also been a math major. She helped me, in some aspect, on the statistical side of doing some of the problems to be solved in developing a measurement tool for detecting and assessing the magnitude of various psychobiological states.[56]

Despite this lukewarm comment which mischaracterized her experience and contributions, her involvement in the development and application of this test was substantial, and they were co-authors on two books. It should also be mentioned here that Gottschalk and Gleser were both equally named in investigations of the University of Cincinnati Total Body Irradiation experiments led by Eugene Saenger from 1960 to 1971. The two undertook psychological testing of cognitive impairment on patients who were given large, nontherapeutic doses of radiation without consent in order to hypothetically test physiological reactions to nuclear warfare. Another psychologist, Lee Cronbach, praised Gleser's contributions and expertise on their collaborative work, explaining that she was able to develop a mathematical formula that he and another colleague could both use, despite their deep theoretical divide.[57] The other colleague was Jane Loevinger, who was denied a faculty appointment at Washington University because her husband was on the faculty of the chemistry department.[58]

If Gleser's contributions to her co-authored works with Trotter are any indication, her role in publications was essential. Gleser was a true collaborator on their stature estimation publications, not simply a statistical technician brought on to develop formulas. Unfortunately, in approving the 1952 stature estimation publication, Trotter had to ask the Army to correct Gleser's name from the odd error of "Robert J. Gleser" (so close to "Robert J. Terry").[59] In their extensive correspondence, Trotter and Gleser volley questions about the data, the organizational structure, and the wording of the content. Gleser identifies bad or confusing data to be checked and she improvised solutions to problems and questions that arose for her in looking over their work.[60] Gleser came up with concrete plans for testing her questions and concerns with results, at a time when each IBM run took money out of their funding and hours of her time to prepare. The two women were also supportive of each other and shared some personal details of their lives, Gleser once writing friendly words of encouragement to Trotter during a stressful period of manuscript preparations: "don't fret too much. Just stay calm, cool, and collected."[61] Gleser had to fit her Army-funded trips to St. Louis into her busy schedule, which in addition to her work also included home requirements typical of wives and mothers (but not husbands and fathers) at the time. She once wrote to Trotter in regard to planning a visit that "we are going on a two-week vacation on the 21st, so I'm not anxious to come there, as I have to get everyone's clothes ready and packed."[62] The two were well-teamed for this project and seemed to mostly maintain a friendly and collegial relationship that centered on their work, most often closing their letters to each other with 'Love' and 'Affectionately'.

Though some aspects of sexism are more subversive than others, many of these sexist conditions were not especially well hidden. Trotter witnessed and was subjected to discriminatory practices in hiring, promotion, and salary levels at Washington University. With specific reference to Trotter, a male colleague noted that "in those days there was great prejudice about females, on the faculty even ... Everybody who was a female was put down."[63] Trotter noted that she only saw one woman serve in a leadership role at the Washington University medical school. Pediatric pathologist Margaret Smith, a fellow Pennsylvania native and Mount Holyoke graduate, was temporarily the unofficial acting Chair of Pathology before she could be replaced.[64] In a newspaper article discussing the shortage of scientists, one male anatomist (and former student of Trotter's) "credits women scientists with a good deal of the inspiration for his career," noting Trotter in particular. He went on to claim that "there is ample opportunity for women in science... although as in all other fields, men of equal ability usually get preference."[65] Trotter witnessed a particularly and atypically candid comment from a surgeon at the University: when asked why he was so upset with the number of women applicants for academic positions, he responded "Nothing. Frankly, I don't want the competition." And when a woman student in pathology at Washington University was struggling financially to finish her degree, the dean advised her to "dig down in the family stock."[66]

Trotter once told a colleague that as a woman, "it has not been my privilege to plan very far ahead; rather I had to watch for an opportunity and make the most of it."[67] In 1941, an intelligent and charismatic anatomist who had been with the University since 1928, Gordon H. Scott, had privately asked the department chair who replaced Terry, Edmund Vincent Cowdry, if he could take over the Gross Anatomy course when Terry retired. This plan was not formally announced, but Scott had happily informed Trotter she could expect to change to teaching histology, and that the small anatomical museum teaching specimens Terry had painstakingly procured would be removed. Trotter was infuriated by this plan and felt that Scott was not experienced enough, having only taught anatomy once for a class of nursing students at the University of Minnesota and being unfamiliar with some standard anatomical terminology.[68] She decided shortly after, despite the hesitancy of friends and a colleague, that she had "nothing to lose." She asked Cowdry to come to her office and, as she put it, "put all my cards on the table."[69] Faced with a direct inquiry, Cowdry acquiesced and made Trotter the new course master. Scott left St. Louis the next year, in 1941, with him and Trotter on good terms. This critical point would lead the way to her becoming Professor of Gross Anatomy in 1946. Years later, Trotter realized that she was the first woman to be full professor at the Washington University School of Medicine. Such lags in promotion are still evident in women's career trajectories compared to men's in science more recently.[70] This also includes the common practice of "promoting" women to positions of increased responsibility, without corresponding increased compensation.

The sexism Trotter experienced was also obvious in direct financial terms. Women in science were routinely and intentionally paid less than men in the early 20th century.[71] During her oral history, the interviewer asked if men in the department were paid more than her. Trotter's response: "Of course, Estelle, they were paid a lot more." As an example, Trotter explains that when she took an unpaid leave of absence from 1948 to 1949 to work in Hawaii (during which time she was compensated by the Army), the department chair, Cowdry, not only declined her recommendation of a woman (Elizabeth Moyer from Boston University) as a temporary replacement but actually hired a man for 6 months to whom they paid Trotter's full annual salary.[72] At another point, she was offered to write a nursing textbook. Though she supported the purpose and certainly could have used the supplement to her income, she did not accept the offer on the advice she received from a colleague that “it may add to your income, Trotter, but it won’t help your scientific prestige.”[73]

Later, Cowdry would apparently complain often and widely about the poor pensions at Washington University, particularly for himself and another male professor. As Trotter remarked, then “I wonder how he thought it was for me?”[74] Not only was the pension system insufficient at the time, but Trotter’s relatively low salary over decades, some of which Cowdry himself was directly responsible for, compounded this problem for her. Trotter’s oral history interviewer remarked at how surprising this fact was because in the 1970s Cowdry appeared to support ‘women’s lib’. But as of the 1940s, the anatomy department chair followed the standards of the time in regard to professional treatment of women. In a newspaper article on Trotter in 1980, the author wrote that Trotter’s salary was approximately 40% of her male counterparts’.[75] This may have been the case, particularly when accounting for rank and workload. The clearest evidence I have found demonstrates a substantial discrepancy, though not as stark. Trotter’s self-reported salary in the 1940 US Census as the senior Associate Professor on the faculty was $3,210; more junior Associate Professor Gordon H. Scott (PhD 1926, University of Minnesota) reported a salary of $4,300.[76] Sometime in the late 1950s, the new chair, Dempsey, became aware of this ongoing disparity and raised her salary by $1,000 a year until her mandatory retirement in 1967. Though she had “become accustomed to the slight,” the unnecessary specifier of “Gross” was then also removed from her title.[77] She retired with a salary of $19,000. But that was not enough to make up for the decades of lost income and savings.

Many women in science in the early 20th century internalized and accepted the sexist conditions they operated under, and some even opted not to (at least publicly) acknowledge them.[78] Alice Brues refuted any recognition of differential treatment due to her gender,[79] as did Charlotte Gower.[80] In a 1977 oral history interview, a woman who was a medical student at Washington University while Trotter served on the faculty felt the same, and even went so far as to say that women who do claim to have experienced sexism are incorrect. “There was no prejudice whatsoever. There was no pressure from anyone about anything... I have no patience with some of these women that I have had contact with who go around with chips on their shoulders. I never had any problems.”[81] Elizabeth Crosby, a renowned neuroanatomist, claimed even in later life, after having been passed over for promotions and having to hide her personal relationship with a colleague, fellow neuroanatomist Tryphena Humphrey, to not have noticed any differential treatment. Women in science more recently have been documented to not report harassment and discrimination due to valid concerns of inaction and retaliation.[82] Perhaps similar concerns contributed to these attitudes for earlier women in anthropology.

This coping method of stoicism and approach of working harder sometimes served individual women relatively better, but in the end led more to exploitation than to equality and did not effect a change in the status quo for women as a whole.[83] Though sometimes counterproductive, this method was also clearly Trotter's take on how to confront sexism throughout many stages of her career. Former students noticed that she held all students to high standards but held women to higher standards. Due to her own treatment in academia, both positive and negative, Trotter often sought to mentor young women in her field. She remained active in recruiting and mentoring activities for Mount Holyoke for many years. Washington University students appreciated the presence of a woman in the anatomy department, one stated that, "only two women were in my class in 1952, and it was a great model to see a woman in a position of leadership."[84] A medical school graduate from 1959 remembered that Trotter took all of the students who were women out for a picnic, and there were so few that they could all fit in her car.[85] She further recounted that "no one ever wanted to be found by Dr. Trotter not to be doing one's best. I think this was especially true of the women." Other former students noticed that she held all students to high standards but held women to higher standards. A male student even recognized that "if the student happens to be a woman, then the standards are even higher because I suspect 'Trot' believes that the capabilities and obligations of the woman are greater than those of the opposite sex."[86] Another former student recalled Trotter's hospitality toward women but also felt that Trotter did not specifically seek out each student who was a woman to mentor. As the student stated: "if you think because, both being women, that she would have been more embracing of some of us, I didn't truly feel that she was."[87] This treatment also extended to her personal life and family. She was encouraging of one of her nieces, Nancy Trotter, in becoming an anatomy professor but also held young girls to different standards than boys. One of her nephews, James Trotter, remembers that she seemed to favor the boys in the family and was much stricter with her sisters and nieces and softer on her brother and nephews.[88]

Trotter later recognized that this was her strategy in response to knowing that women would experience greater struggles than men, noting later in life that "the only way of combatting that [gender discrimination] is to be so darn good."[89] Trotter's advice may have provided her students with realistic expectations. But this approach, particularly when adopted by mentors who were women, actually discouraged some later women from pursuing careers in science that had been modeled by the previous generation as unduly demanding, isolating, and restrictive to women's personal lives.[90] Gleser somewhat more encouragingly advised, writing in 2001,

> to those women who are still struggling to balance a marriage, children, and a career I can only say what I tell my female students - there is more time than you think to fit it all in. Don't be afraid to prioritize one or the other at a particular time.[91]

Ruth Sawtell Wallis also recognized gender-based disparities later in her career. She contributed to an increasingly common practice for physical and forensic anthropologists today – authoring fictional novels imbued with familiar professional details (this includes Kathy Reichs, Thomas Holland, and a woman who goes by the nom de plume Lucy Park Hunter). Among other novels, Wallis wrote *Blood from a Stone* (1945) in which the protagonist is a young archaeologist in the French Pyrenees, and elements seem to be borrowed directly from her fieldwork experiences as recounted in *Primitive Hearths in the Pyrenees* (1927).[92] While recovering from an illness in 1940, Wallis began to write her first novel, *Too Many Bones*.[93] The plot was based around a young woman who was an anthropologist working at a museum in a small Midwestern town. Further parallels to Wallis's own life appear, such as reference to the protagonist's recent graduation from a women's college ("Edgewood"), which is paired with a nearby men's college ("Oldwick") (i.e., Radcliffe and Harvard). Similar details are consistent with Wallis's own geographical and institutional background, though one hopes the criminal dramatics were not. From this semi-autobiographical account, we can partially extrapolate Wallis's own experiences and observations as a woman in anthropology. The lead character, Kay Ellis, is accidentally hired as an assistant when her abbreviated name ("K. Ellis") is mistaken for a man's in a letter of reference. Her salary, which was "awfully good for a girl, but not quite as high as a man can usually get," is reduced by a third once she arrives and the error is noticed.[94] The museum director explains that "I want you also to know that your work is satisfactory. I have no fault to find with you. But it has been suggested that the higher figure is somewhat out of proportion to your needs in this town. A young woman, I believe, does not have expenses commensurate with those of a man."[95] Ellis works under a renowned male curator with a well-documented skeletal collection from the Carpathians, who takes a romantic interest in her. Without giving away the delightful ending, cracking the case depends on Ellis's knowledge of comparative osteology. This interestingly involves the maceration of a chimpanzee cadaver in order to access the bones, which Wallis had previously done at Radcliffe.[96] Our protagonist then leaves town, and her love interest, to instead pursue a PhD in New York after heeding another character's advice that "no woman should permit her happiness to depend upon a man."[97]

Wallis's former professor, Hooton, also undertook his own version of literary pursuit. A selection of his poetry and cartoons was assembled and posthumously published in 1961 under the title *Subverse*. His biographers explained in 1995 that "some of these verses were included in his scholarly texts, some found their way into his popular works, and others were used to enliven his classroom lectures and the lectures he was invited to give at conventions and conferences," and that the poems had somehow been "likened to the work of Ogden Nash."[98] Hooton seems to have intended most of these poems to be humorous. Like the work of Wallis, it presumably also speaks directly to the mindset of the author. In one particularly relevant poem, "Advice to a Gifted Female," Hooton wrote:

> For God's sake, Lydia, be chary / Of conversations literary; / For when you try to show your culture / To some bald academic vulture, / Your half-wit dicta fail to please — / Far better to display your knees. / And your gluteus maximus / More likely will attract the cuss / Than the ideas that you strain / Out of the quagmire of your brain. / You'll not impress men with your clarity / On hemispheric solidarity, / Unless the views that you expose/ Are what you have beneath your clothes. / Why do you keep on talking physics / When all you know is aphrodisics? / The functions of the female kind / Involve the body, not the mind; / Women are the superior sex / below and not above their necks; / So stop your feeble cogitation/ And use your carnal education.[99]

It is no coincidence that the author of this poem discouraged young women, including Wallis and Stone, from pursuing careers and education in anthropology. I do not know what audiences he presented this poem in front of, but certainly this attitude informed his interactions with women, and particularly with women who were his students.

In a 1944 interview, Hooton also claimed (one assumes only half facetiously) that the US needed a woman President because "woman's reproductive apparatus is so complicated that all the rest of her needs to be simple... and great statesmanship requires simplicity," and a "transparency of character" that is "more common in women than in men."[100] Of course, Hooton, like anyone, was not one-dimensional, and also had encouraged Trotter in some way by valuing her hair research in the 1920s, an act which stuck positively with Trotter for decades. Her first impressions of him were not entirely flattering though: "the man I met coming down the hall was wearing thick glasses and a drab, shabby lab coat full of holes and tears and was so unprepossessing in appearance that I thought he must be a diener [a morgue attendant]," before he introduced himself.[101] Hooton had also taken several AM students who were women and one PhD student who was a woman. But the loathsome words above are Hooton's, and he chose to record and share them in a poem.

On a personal level, these early women in anthropology had further commonalities. Few of these women were married, fewer had children, none were divorced, and none were openly gay. Those who did marry most often found their work subsumed by their husbands, their jobs threatened or nonexistent due to discriminatory "antinepotism" laws, which served almost exclusively to prohibit wives from employment at the same institutions as husbands.[102] As archaeologist Doris Zemurray Stone (AB Radcliffe 1930) later described her approach, "though not a feminist in an active sense, I was... determined to follow a profession in spite of marriage and family."[103] This implies that, unlike for men, marriage and family were seen as incompatible with an academic career. This tendency has lessened but continues today. Recent research shows that women's academic careers are more negatively affected by family concerns than are men's; relatively fewer women are at the highest ranks, and they are much less likely than men to be married or to have children.[104] This has more recently been documented specifically in fieldwork-based anthropology.[105]

Ruth Sawtell Wallis found that after marrying her career options became more limited and dependent on her husband's location. Perhaps her two new stepchildren added further limitations. Her biographer and former student recounted that Wallis believed her undeserved firing from the University of Minnesota in 1935 to be due to "envy over the dual income" of the couple during the Depression, typical of academic antinepotism rules at the time.[106] Responses could be more immediately damaging; at the University of Wisconsin Gower lost her position as Assistant Professor resulting from suspicions of a relationship with a fellow anthropologist.[107] One professor at Washington University who was contemporary with Trotter, Beatrice Whiteside, married in secret because married women were not allowed to be employed on the medical school faculty.[108] In 1951, Trotter wrote to a fellow member of the Mount Holyoke Club of St. Louis that a newcomer to the city who had a master's degree in zoology from the University "has one baby and is expecting another but even so I think that our club should make some effort to have her know that we would welcome her."[109] Apparently, the woman's personal situation, for whatever specific reasons, made her much less likely for membership. In 1957, anatomist William Strauss, Jr. lamented the disappointing loss of a promising graduate student who was a woman who "decided to get married and throw in the academic sponge, settling for a M.A. I am, of course, disappointed; but I scarcely have any right to expect that anthropology could compete with the biological urge."[110] In the very same letter, he instead recommended a married man with a young child in response to Trotter's query for an available anatomist. Though Strauss was sympathetic to the student's situation, he blamed the woman, while being apparently oblivious to the institutionalized constraints and sexism that made these life choices come in conflict with academia for women but not for men.

When later Nobel Prize recipients Gerty and Carl Cori came to Washington University, Carl recalled that "the [University's] only stipulation when I came" in 1931 "was that she was not to have a high salaried position."[111] This was apparently preferable to their previous situation at another institution, which would not offer her an official position at all. But at the University, Gerty was considered a secondary hire, she was paid less, and she was conveniently not given a full professorship until the year they were jointly awarded, along with Bernardo A. Houssay, the Nobel Prize in 1947. Following their award, it was Carl, not Gerty, who was courted by numerous other universities. Carl also described, somewhat enviously, that Gerty did not have a teaching position or administrative duties, so she was able to work longer hours in the actual laboratory performing the experiments.[112] He does not address what disproportionate effect this must then have had on their respective contributions to their collective prize-winning work, though they both recognized a close and entangled collaboration. Nor does he, enviously or otherwise, mention any additional, unshared obligations she may have had due to their child, born in 1936, or all of the laboratory cleaning duties Gerty had to perform which Carl did not.[113]

Though she entered professional anthropology later than the women primarily discussed here, Bernice Kaplan also experienced this bias. She was converted to a part time position at a greatly reduced salary at Wayne State due to their antinepotism rule. But when Kaplan soon received a full time offer at the University of Michigan, Wayne State suddenly decided that the rule no longer applied to her. Her husband, fellow anthropologist Gabriel Lasker, also noted several additional restrictions to her career related to her gender: that she was "chiefly responsible for raising our family," that her "research interests have been somewhat opportunistic, since she has been with me wherever I've gone," and furthermore that "much of [Kaplan's] academic work is credited to others such as her students and myself."[114]

Despite the title of her autobiography, *Getting It All*, Goldine Gleser's career was hampered and slowed due to her marriage, having children, and the attitudes of those around her toward working mothers. Before she had children, Gleser lost PhD funding for her first degree in math within a year of marrying her husband, Sol, in 1936 when the department believed that he, a civil engineer, should support her.[115] Without this financial support, she had to quit. She was also forced to quit a job as a statistician when she became pregnant because, as she recalled, "women were *protected from* work during pregnancy" [my emphasis].[116] She struggled to find paying projects while her three children were young and sometimes aided her husband on his difficult projects, or took on part-time appointments. This persisted despite access to childcare by living next door to Gleser's parents and the ability to afford some in-home household help. Gleser eventually earned her PhD while caring for three small children and teaching math courses on the side for income. As she said, "with the children no longer needing my personal attention, I finally felt free to work full-time starting in the autumn of 1963," which was 13 years after finishing her doctorate.[117]

Gleser attributed some of her long-term success to her choice of spouse. She described that Sol "was knowledgeable and liberal-minded; someone I could admire and with whom I could share ideas."[118] But she also had to leave a faculty position at Washington University when Sol found a job in Cincinnati, where it took her 2 years to secure another faculty appointment.[119] Another 2 years later, and only following the previous failure of an external hire who was a man after less than a year in the post, Gleser became the head of the Psychology Division of the Department of Psychiatry at the University of Cincinnati College of Medicine.[120] When, in 1979, she was chosen to receive a local award for distinguished scientific achievement, she felt that "it made all the struggle seem worthwhile. In particular, it made me feel that I had personally accomplished enough to merit acclamation rather than just being a helpmate to my many male partners."[121]

In her personal life though, Gleser also experienced some unfortunate internalized misogyny. Though she already had two sons, she was at first scared to raise her daughter because "I had never identified with women… I always wanted something different, something more."[122] She had felt some degree of distance from, and perhaps even contempt for, most other women's experiences. This also may have reflected her somewhat conflicted relationship with her own more traditional mother as an ambitious young woman. She was relieved to later discover this fear was unfounded.

In addition to their actual personal lives, how these women were portrayed and chose to present themselves was much more important than it was for men. In laudatory moments, language to describe women was often highly gendered. In a short memorial address at Gerty Cori's funeral in 1957, Houssay described her as "highly cultured, gentle and modest" woman who "never flagged in the fulfillment of her duties as a wife, mother and scientist, the triple crown that adorned her life."[123] For some inexplicable reason, although ostensibly to exemplify her complete attention to any one specific task at hand, a male colleague used 158 words of Edith Boyd's 1,005 word memorial in the Anatomical Record to detail an inadvertently sexual joke she had once made to him.[124]

When presenting Trotter's prestigious selection as Viking Fund Medalist and as President of the American Association of Physical Anthropologists in 1956, the AAPA Chairman of the Awards Committee, Charles W. Goff, specifically noted that the committee had broken tradition to choose its first "lady," and that she had excelled in a field dominated by men. He jokingly declined to mention her year of birth, so as to not reveal her age. I have seen no mention of male presidents' ages in announcement speeches anyway, and no attempt on Trotter's part to ever hide her age. The chairman went on to state that "one of the things that impresses everyone is her capacity to remain so feminine in spite of the tough type of work in which she has been engaged. That may account, in part, for her successes."[125] Trotter had received an earlier draft of this speech, to which she made edits, and she also specifically asked Stewart to covertly request changes on her behalf, with "no 'lovely lady' stuff."[126] These recommended edits were apparently ignored.

At a seminar she organized with T. Dale Stewart in 1968, she was introduced as "the charming Dr. Trotter."[127] Prior to the seminar, Stewart noted privately that "you may be the only female present, but doubtless you are used to that."[128] A 1980 news story about her stated that she traded "life behind an apron for life behind a lab coat."[129] Irritatingly, this otherwise complimentary article appeared directly above another titled "Beneath the Anger are Their Unfulfilled Needs" in the "Working Woman" section. It presents a fictionalized vignette that describes and justifies a man's insecurities and emotional demands surrounding his wife's new employment and reduced house work. He states that "I don't really need a home-cooked meal every night, but I sure do need to know you're thinking about me while I eat a sandwich alone."[130]

Another article on Trotter has the title of "Feminine Bone Detective" and describes her as "soft-spoken and exceedingly gracious in manner and appearance."[131] Yet another calls her a "white-haired, brown-eyed, ultra-feminine professor of gross anatomy" who does her work "as casually as a secretary," while being "modest and self-effacing," and is an "enthusiastic conversationalist on every subject except herself. That's where she clams up – in a ladylike way, of course."[132] The author condescendingly describes that she even "works as long of hours as any man on the faculty," but still makes time for her students.[133] An article in this very same newspaper 3 years later details the work of T. Dale Stewart, presents none of these physical descriptions or commentary on his masculinity, and exclusively discusses his professional work.[134] One former student remembered Trotter as "a breath of loveliness in an environment of dead bodies," "a teacher you could become closer to than some of the tough, steely guys on the faculty," and "a mother figure" to many.[135] Despite that description, a friend and former student noted in her eulogy that "I don't believe there was a maternal bone in Trot's body, but she was a very caring person."[136] It is impossible to imagine any man, especially one of Trotter's professional standing, receiving such extensively gendered and patronizing language, across so many contexts, spanning decades of his illustrious career.

To a degree much greater than for men, personality and demeanor mattered for women in academia. Being perceived as feminine, to maintain cultural feminine ideals, and particularly to be modest and humble, was a requirement. As Rossiter explains, a woman who "mastered the art of subduing her own personality while under adverse conditions" in order to be an "assimilator" was more likely to succeed.[137] They were sometimes, at least in the cases of Trotter and neuroanatomist Tryphena Humphrey at the University of Pittsburgh and despite their actual roles, compared to and even overtly called, *mothers* in the classroom.[138] The perception of women as performing second-rate compared to their male counterparts persisted despite the quantifiable fact that, compared to their male counterparts, women were actually over-qualified and higher-performing, while their time and energies were exploited and they were being judged according to unreasonable social standards. To be perceived as equal to men, women had to be better, while at the same time performing femininity by acting "like a woman." But even when women were perceived as 'equally' competent, this did not result in equal pay, treatment, or opportunities.

Trotter, at least in some ways, also contributed to this undercurrent of expectations for women's roles. She served as a judge for the 1957 Miss Missouri competition of the Miss America beauty pageant. She was invited by a former student who was the pageant judges' committee chairman.[139] They clearly had an ongoing friendship, since Trotter and her apartment mate had previously thrown a bridal shower for his wife, whose older sister had also been a student of Trotter's.[140] Trotter and Adele Starbird, Dean of Women at Washington University, were two of the nine judges. The program consisted of "an evening gown competition, an aquacade and water ballet, swim suit competition, a dinner, a talent stage show presentation, coronation, and a formal reception and ball," and one portion of the prize consisted of a $1,000 "scholarship."[141] It is unclear what Trotter's and Starbird's ultimate or personal motivations for doing this were, but in 1945 this had been the first pageant to offer academic scholarships to winners, and organizers attempted to bill it as a 'scholarship competition', which may have had some influence on their interpretation of the task.[142] Interestingly though, the winner that year, Sara Cooper, daughter of Cardinals baseball player Walker Cooper, does not appear to have gone to university at that time or after. She was a 20-year-old flight attendant for Ozark Airlines when she married her father's teammate, Don Blasingame, in 1960.[143] Starbird wrote about her judging experience in an article for the local newspaper 1 week after the event. She provided basic details of the pageant day, including the content of the interview questions which were pre-determined by a committee, which "ranged from husbands, television, food, old age and juvenile delinquency to evening gowns."[144] The young women's favorite topic was their gowns, and Starbird was startled that most of the contestants' responses to the most sought-after qualities in a husband focused on patience and consideration. Starbird ended her otherwise quite neutral article by asking, "What effect does such a contest have upon the personality of the participants? That question has been put to me by thoughtful people. It's a good question."[145]

To maintain a view of women as feminine and inferior to men, they were often excluded from aspects of academia that were seen as characteristically masculine. When women were allowed to even attend professional meetings, they were sometimes unwelcome, by the content or by non-invitation, to participate in many formal and informal banquets, dinners, and other events. Margaret Rossiter provided the example of the American Chemical Society's evening "smokers," where academics smoked cigars and networked, speaking freely with each other.[146] Smoking was seen as a distinctly masculine activity, so even when a woman stated that she wished to come and smoke, she could still be excluded in the first half of the 20th century. These proscriptions on social events often kept women from interacting with the majority of their colleagues in the beneficial ways that their male peers could.

At least one woman though, Lucile St. Hoyme, smoked, and one time she surprised Trotter's secretary by smoking a pipe while working with the Terry Collection.[147] In 1948, older and more established in her career, it was at a smoker event that Trotter met a young soldier who was helping to recruit an anthropologist to go to Hawaii. And after Trotter had been unsuccessful through other channels, it was only after attending that cocktail party in November of 1948, where she could have casual access to the Commanding General, that she was able to gain military approvals for her stature estimation research. Unfortunately, academic conferences across disciplines, though open to men and women alike, continue to maintain climates that discourage women's participation through incivility, sexism, and exclusionary treatment,[148] as well as sexual harassment.[149] Promisingly, some social events are now specifically aimed at encouraging inclusion, such as the American Academy of Forensic Sciences Anthropology Section's unofficial LGBTQIA+ Community and Allies night.

Physical anthropology had those types of male-exclusive events, at least early in its history. In 1956, when Trotter was elected President of the AAPA, she decided, with the encouragement of T. Dale Stewart, to prepare a historical note for the flagship journal.[150] After actually seeing a draft, Stewart advised her against publishing this paper at all – but if she must, to rewrite it, shorten it, put it in a footnote, or at least remove the letters from individuals that she intended to include.[151] She presented and published all of it. Her "Note on the History of the American Association of Physical Anthropologists" starts with a fond description of the founding of the AAPA under Aleš Hrdlička out of the American Anatomical Association, and descriptions of early meetings, starting in 1930. She specifically notes that there were only two women among the founding members. She then included selected "recollections" she had solicited from founding members and presented them without comment. Most items were mildly interesting and pleasantly humanizing, and at first it is difficult to see what Stewart found so potentially damaging.

Trotter included one anthropologist's recollection that recounts a humorous and embarrassing moment for Hrdlička that demonstrates a dismissive attitude toward a woman when he felt challenged, due to a lack of his own knowledge on a topic. Edith Boyd spoke at the third AAPA meeting about statistical "probable errors" in her anthropometric studies. Not understanding the definition of what are now often called "standard errors," and being notoriously anti-statistics, Hrdlička claimed, "that illustrates exactly what I have been thinking and saying about the uselessness of statistics. Even Doctor Boyd admits that there are probable errors in her work."[152] Separately, Hrdlička had in 1934 also recommended that Trotter exclude the section providing statistics from an article draft he reviewed.[153]

But in addition to a few possibly unflattering details throughout the historical note, Adolph Schultz's recollection describes an unmistakable boys club. Before the official banquet, a young Schultz was invited to a hotel room filled with anatomists and a "huge bucket of moonshine" during prohibition.[154] When Schultz tipsily got up (at the urging of a superior) to give an impromptu speech at the banquet intended to draw connections between the anatomists and anthropologists, he told a series of anecdotes. One was the time he and George Corner alone chloroformed a camel at 5 am for a research project at Johns Hopkins. This story is potentially humorous and likely gives a good perspective on the founding meetings. But it also points out circumstances that women were certainly not welcome to join – meeting alone with a man in the middle of the night to acquire an anatomical specimen, drinking with men in a hotel room at a conference, and even the banquet itself. In her historical outline, Trotter specifically notes that the first business meeting was "open to all members," but she was not able say the same for all events that year, including the 1930 banquet.[155] She could not provide her own personal memories of the events because she was not allowed in the very talk during the first meeting that established the association, of which she was a founding member and now President.[156] Apparently women were, however, implicitly expected to contribute to decorations and preparations for these events because Trotter once wrote to Sherwood Washburn's wife, lauding that, "observation through the years has shown me that the key person for such accomplishment is the wife of the chief. I salute you."[157] If that was the case, it is unclear whether Trotter performed these additional, non-professional duties during her Presidency or let them fall by the wayside.

TROTTER'S PERSONAL LIFE

Trotter once wrote, concerning the difficulties of being a woman in physical anthropology, that she had an overall "lack of women friends related to the school," and early on "the wives were stand-offish, perhaps because what we had in common was their husbands."[158] But even with the wives of colleagues, Trotter did maintain some positive relationships, including with Sharon S. McKern (wife of Thomas), who wrote after her husband's death that Trotter was the only person to say Sharon had courage or fortitude; "so few know what to say in a condolence letter – you knew exactly what I needed to hear."[159] In this letter and in many letters to friends and some close colleagues, Trotter often signed off with a friendly 'Love'. She must have cherished the friendships she did have with women in her personal and professional lives. Trotter's friends in St. Louis included Mabel E. Boss, Evelyn Damond, Gertrude Hance, Adele Starbird, and Marjorie Mullins.

Mabel Boss worked at the St. Louis Department of Education and as a school principal from 1930 to 1976; she had an MS from the University of Minnesota in 1925.[160] She accompanied Trotter for 3 months in 1963 during her work in Uganda.[161] Boss is mentioned in passing in some of Trotter's correspondence in the early 1960s. When Boss retired in 1976, she returned to Minnesota.[162]

Evelyn Damond and Trotter were longtime symphony companions.[163] Gertrude Hance was a medical illustrator and modeler employed at the medical school, and Trotter described her as "my first friend in St. Louis."[164] Adele Starbird was the Dean of Women at Washington University from 1931 to 1959 and had previously taught French at the Mary Institute. Starbird's popular newspaper column in the *St. Louis Post-Dispatch*, "The Dean Speaks Up," included occasional mentions of Trotter, Mullins, and Boss. Starbird compiled essays from these articles for her 1977 book, *Many Strings to My Lute*.[165] Trotter also maintained

Mildred Trotter and two friends (labeled "Marjorie" and "Cathe") in Hungry Jack Lake, Minnesota. VC170-i170260, Becker Medical Library, Washington University School of Medicine.

contact with several Mount Holyoke classmates and colleagues around the world and commonly shared hotels at annual conferences with fellow alumna and anatomist Elizabeth Moyer.

Marjorie Deupree Mullins graduated with an AB from Ouachita Baptist College in Arkansas in 1916 and a PhD from the University of Toulouse, France in 1927. She produced several publications related to French-language education. Mullins served as Dean of Women at Mary-Hardin Baylor College (the women's college associated with Baylor at the time) in Texas until she moved to St. Louis to teach at a local private girls' school, the Mary Institute in 1941.[166] She retired as the head of the modern languages department in 1971.

In 1968 and 1969, Mullins and Trotter spent summer vacations in the Caribbean.[167] In 1970, Mullins traveled with Trotter to Russia for a meeting of the International Congress of Anatomists and attempted to learn some Russian words in preparation.[168] In 1973, she and Trotter went on a Christmas vacation to Florida.[169] Trotter wrote candidly to Mullins lamenting and joking about the trivial, but uncomfortable, difficulties of her travels while in Tel Aviv and Antarctica. Robert J. Terry wrote directly to Mullins in 1961, thanking her for her congratulations at his 90th birthday celebration, and applauding her for her recent award from the French Consul.[170] She had been awarded the Order of the Academic Palms and then received the first sabbatical granted from the Mary Institute to study modern literature at the Sorbonne in Paris.[171] In a letter to Trotter, one colleague referred to Mullins as "your companion friend."[172] In 1981, Trotter and Mullins were joint donors in a memorial tribute to the Missouri Botanical Garden.[173] Mullins was listed as Trotter's emergency contact in her 1975–1984 passports. While she was in the hospital, Trotter and her nephew visited Mullins, who told him that "getting old is not for sissies."[174] When Mullins died at the Bethesda-Dilworth nursing home in 1989, she willed her body to the Washington University School of Medicine.[175]

Along with sexism, Trotter had witnessed homophobia in academia, though she never specifically addressed it. Historian Ann Karus Meeropol detailed the career of Mary Emma Woolley as the 11th president of Trotter's alma mater, Mount Holyoke, and her controversial 1937 replacement with the college's first male president.[176] Woolley, the daughter of Congregationalist reverend and women's suffragist J. J. Woolley, graduated with the first class of women allowed to attend Brown University. She was recruited in 1895 to teach at Wellesley College in the history department, where she would soon become full professor. In 1899, she turned down an offer for the Dean of the Women's College at Brown and became the President of Mount Holyoke, where she would stay for the remainder of her career. Woolley's leadership and influence was admired and respected at the college. She improved the quality and compensation of faculty, ended the domestic work program required of students, improved admissions requirements, and increased the school's endowment tenfold. Her longtime partnership with a former Wellesley student, Jeannette Augustus Marks, had been a poorly kept secret on campus and was mostly considered unremarkable. But this became a subject of public controversy when Woolley planned to retire. The majority-male board of trustees at that time was transparent in their preference for a man to replace her, and to "change the culture established by Woolley over 36 years as president."[177] Despite the board's mandate to select a woman and a vocal faculty demand to continue with a woman in leadership, the board sought to reduce their perceived inferiority of a woman's school by placing a man in the position. They furthermore made clear their distaste for her personal life and noted their plan to get a "normal family in the president's house."[178]

Trotter involved herself in the controversy because, after all, this was the institution which she described as having "made me."[179] She wrote to the President of the Board in 1935, during the search: "As an alumna of Mount Holyoke College, I am deeply interested in the choice of Mount Holyoke's next president, and am convinced that the president of Mount Holyoke should be a woman."[180] Ignoring the preferences of faculty, alumnae, and students, the board selected the first man in the college's more than 100 year history – an underqualified associate professor of English literature from Yale with some unknown prior controversy, Roswell G. Ham. A photograph of him in the Mount Holyoke archives posing with the presidents and deans from the Seven Sisters women's colleges in 1948 or 1949 shows him as one of three men in a group of 12.[181]

Trotter may have observed the success of a semi-openly gay woman as president during her undergraduate years at Mount Holyoke. But she would certainly have learned from Woolley's later treatment that in addition to the prejudices she experienced by simply being a woman, to expose your private life was a threat to your career and reputation, as well as a threat to the careers of the women who would come after you. When in 1978 a biography was published, *Miss Marks and Miss Woolley* by Anna Mary Wells, Trotter was initially worried to read anything in which "Miss Woolley would be considered in any derogatory way."[182] In the end, she did read and enjoy the book. In Trotter's words, the author "treated the problem in a restrained, sympathetic, and dignified" way, and Trotter was pleased to personally know many of the "characters."[183] Other women are now known to have concealed their sexual orientation and private lives during this time, including neuroanatomists and partners Elizabeth Crosby and Tryphena Humphrey. But while successful male anthropologists and other academics surrounding Trotter openly had multiple divorces, children, and conflicts with colleagues, you simply did not typically see even mundane details exposed from the lives of successful women during her time. Any details of a personal life at all, and especially of gay relationships in the cases of both women and men, usually had to be vaguely concealed or entirely suppressed.

Trotter embodied this cautiousness in regard to her own personal life. She chose to be somewhat covert about her private life in general and about at least one long-term relationship in specific. Trotter shared apartments with a woman named Alice Louise Minton for at least 28 years, beginning while in her early thirties or before. Minton is mentioned in Trotter's correspondence with several people, including Robert J. Terry, Goldine Gleser, Oliver Duggins, and William H. Danforth. The references to Minton in these letters describe only a friend and apartment mate. Of course, her correspondence archived at Washington University consists almost exclusively of professional materials. Personal details are limited, and certainly this accounting does not include any correspondence she might have considered to be private and did not save for the sake of posterity. Trotter referred to other handwritten letters to Minton, but these are, unsurprisingly, not saved in her professional archival materials. The very few preserved exceptions were typed by Trotter's secretary (which Trotter explicitly noted in these letters) for various reasons, and may therefore contain details that are less personal.[184] Two people living in the same apartment would also naturally produce less written correspondence.

Trotter stated that in the 1940s she "shared a small apartment in the building on the corner of Union and Washington Avenues with a Mary Institute teacher."[185] On a military form in 1949, Trotter listed her forwarding address as her own, "530N. Union Blvd.," in care of "Miss Louise Minton."[186] The apartment number was once listed as G21 in Trotter's archival materials. This does not correspond to the current numbering system, but the building has units ranging from studios to three bedrooms and is just under 2 miles away from the medical school. In letters, Trotter describes repeated, multiple weeks-long summer vacations with Minton and refers to her as "Miss Minton" and "Julep" (as in 'mint julep').[187] Minton had likely also been part of Trotter's group of friends, which included several teachers. In 1955, Marjorie Mullins (driving) and Louise Minton (passenger) were in a minor car crash together. The accident was noted in the local newspaper, which listed Minton as residing at the Union Boulevard apartment, where she lived with Trotter.[188]

Analysis of census records provides additional insight. In the 1930 Census, the entry for a "Louise L. Minton" (likely a recording error), a 32-year-old teacher, was listed directly next to "Mildred B. Trotter" as "boarders" in Washington University's McMillan Hall.[189] Trotter had no middle name or middle initial,[190] but she occasionally listed "Bruce" when it was required, which was her maternal grandmother's maiden name. The Mary Institute was a private girls' school operated by Washington University until 1949, which would explain Minton living in University housing. Trotter later noted that she made many friends from her time at McMillan Hall, including several Mary Institute teachers.[191] Though Trotter and Minton were part of a large circle of friends with this dormitory or the Mary Institute in common, I did not also see other names that I recognize as Trotter's friends on this exact same 1930 census sheet. Ten years later, the 1940 census listed Trotter with only one other occupant of her apartment on North Union Street, "Alice Louise Minton." According to the census, Minton was born around 1895 (she was actually born in 1892), and was employed as a school teacher.[192] Minton had graduated from a St. Louis high school in 1908.[193] Both women were listed as having lived at that same address in 1935 as well.

In answer to the 1940 Census form prompt, "Relationship of this person to the head of household [Trotter]," the census enumerator wrote code "6" and "partner." Code 6 in the 1940 Census "Instructions for General Population Coding" indicated a "lodger, roomer, boarder, or partner, (wife, son, or daughter of a lodger, boarder, etc.)."[194] Instructions state that if a description is not provided, the census enumerator may determine the probable relationship. So it is unclear who selected this term – Trotter, Minton, or the enumerator. But, despite the option of using "roomer" or "boarder," Minton's entry is clearly listed as "partner." The 1940 Census defined the term "partner" as "two or more persons who are not related by blood or marriage [who] share a common dwelling unit as partners."[195] This is, of course, a circular definition. I have not found a clear history of the etymology and social usage of the term "partner" at the time, but the US Census was not likely using slang or wording unfamiliar in common parlance. Dictionary entries list definitions such as "financial partner," "spouse," "cohabitant in romantic relationship," "dancers," and "team players." In this census context though, one logical and relevant option from the Oxford English Dictionary is "person who is linked by marriage to another, a spouse; a member of a couple who live together or are habitual companions; a lover."[196] This definition's earliest documented use was in 1667, is still today a commonly understood definition of the word, and is a reasonable one in this context.

In 1958, Trotter wrote to Goldine Gleser that Minton had retired and moved to Santa Fe, and that she had not "gotten used to living alone" since moving to a new apartment building in St. Louis, the Montclair.[197] Minton's brother, Charles E. Minton, was an attorney who became the Executive Director for the New Mexico Commission on Indian Affairs, and Minton left to join him in Santa Fe.[198] Finances may have played a part in the women's shared housing over the years, as Trotter noted that "I do not recall that I was perturbed by the economies that it was necessary to practice (for example, I never paid more than $70.00 per month rent, including all utilities, until 1958)," which was the year Minton moved away.[199]

Trotter's new apartment, at 18 South Kingshighway, was about half a mile away from the medical school. It was less than a block away from the building where Marjorie Mullins, Mabel Boss, and other friends lived. In 1961, Trotter had planned to spend August with Minton in New Mexico but was unable to leave Washington University after the Chair of Anatomy became ill.[200] In reference to another possible visit to Santa Fe around Christmas 1964 with Mabel Boss, Trotter wrote to a colleague that she would see "my friend with whom I shared an apartment for so many years."[201] In 1969, she visited Minton, whom she described to a friend as being "my longtime apartment-mate, who is somewhat older than I am and quite feeble. Her spirit is marvelous and I'm very glad I went."[202] She also wrote to Minton about a possible visit in 1971.[203] When Minton died in July 1973, Trotter was listed as one of several heirs to her estate, and hers is the only name that does not appear to be family.[204]

I cannot reliably speculate on the exact nature of Trotter's relationship with Minton or anyone else. I do not want to draw any definite conclusions about Trotter's personal life exclusively from such indirect sources, but I also do not want to be obtuse. Trotter shared what appears to be at least one extremely close relationship in her life, whatever particular shape it took. I have seen no private association of Trotter with any one specific man, outside of relationships with friendly colleagues and former students.

If anyone suspected that Trotter was concealing or suppressing her sexual orientation, or any specific partnership with a woman, I have found no record of it. Colleagues seem to have known that, at the very least, she had close friendships. A friend and former student, Ann Randolph Flipse Gerber, described Trotter's thoughts and knowledge as being openly available to students. But at the same time, she found Trotter to be a "very private, somewhat shy person" in other aspects of her life.[205] In correspondence, Trotter regularly asks after the health and families of even purely professional contacts. She provides small details of her health and overall wellbeing, but very few personal details to even fewer correspondents. That Trotter's friend Mabel Boss traveled with her to Uganda in 1963 was actually published in the local paper,[206] but I have found no record of Trotter's many trips accompanied by Minton (or later with Mullins for that matter) ever appearing in public forums. In an article from the *St. Louis Dispatch* in 1955, the author described Trotter as being uninterested, even "anguish[ed]," to talk about herself, unless it pertained to her work.[207] Perhaps this was self-preservation, and possibly contrary to her nature in other aspects of her life. The article went into some broad detail on Trotter's home and her personal interests, even her exact address. Although Minton lived with Trotter at this time, no mention is made of her existence, or of an apartment mate at all. In her draft publication of "The Department of Anatomy in My Time," Trotter repeatedly names several non-professional friends who seemingly would have had much less impact on her life, but she never once refers to Minton specifically by name.

In addition to the extensive homophobia of society and academia, Trotter's consultations with the Army were notably undertaken during a heightened time of persecution during the 1940s and 1950s now known as the "Lavender Scare," an official campaign orchestrated by Senator Joseph McCarthy to remove gay people from federal positions, which paralleled the "Red Scare."[208] Census data, including Trotter's listing as a "partner" with Minton in 1940, were not yet legally protected under the 72-year rule for public release of records. Though *public* disclosure of the data was officially (though not legally) prohibited at that time, the federal government had previously been allowed to use census data for several purposes, such as to track military draft evasion.[209] The Second War Powers Act of 1941 officially repealed the confidentiality of census records for federal use, until it was restored in 1947. Even if this is an incorrect impression garnered only from indirect sources, the potential stakes at the time for Trotter's discretion in how her personal life was even perceived cannot be overstated.

NOTES

1 Barbara Vancheri, "At 81, a County Native Goes Strong in the Lab," *Beaver County Times*, Wednesday, August 20, 1980, B-1.
2 June M. Collins, "Ruth Sawtell Wallis 1895–1978," *American Anthropologist* 81, no. 1 (1979): 85–87. p. 85.
3 Darna L. Dufour, "Alice Mossie Brues (1913–)," in *Women Anthropologists: Selected Biographies*, ed. Ute Gacs, Aisha Khan, Jerri McIntyre, Ruth Weinberg (Urbana Champaign: University of Illinois Press, 1988), p. 23.
4 Gabriel W. Lasker, *Happenings and Hearsay: Experiences of a Biological Anthropologist* (Detroit, MI: Wayne State University Press, 1999), p. 56.
5 Joseph T. Hefner, *The Statistical Determination of Ancestry Using Cranial Nonmetric Traits* (Doctoral dissertation, University of Florida, 2007), p. 32.
6 Doris Stone, "A Fair Period for a Field Study," *The Radcliffe Quarterly* 66, no. 3 (1980): 20–22, p. 21.
7 Doris Stone, "A Fair Period for a Field Study," *The Radcliffe Quarterly* 66, no. 3 (1980): 20–22, p. 21. Attributed to Hooton in David L. Browman and Stephen Williams, *Anthropology at Harvard: A Biographical History, 1970–1940* (Cambridge, MA: Harvard University Press, 2013), p. 406.
8 E. Wyllys Andrews and Frederick W. Lange, "In Memoriam: Doris Zemurray Stone, 1909–1994," *Ancient Mesoamaerica* 6 (1995): 95–99.
9 David L. Browman and Stephen Williams, *Anthropology at Harvard: A Biographical History, 1970–1940* (Cambridge, MA: Harvard University Press, 2013), p. 401.
10 Trudy R. Turner, et al., "Participation, Representation, and Shared Experiences of Women Scholars in Biological Anthropology," *American Journal of Physical Anthropology* 165 (2018): 126–157; and Penelope Lockwood, "Someone Like Me Can Be Successful": Do College Students Need Same-gender Role Models?," *Psychology of Women Quarterly* 30, no. 1 (2000): 36–46.
11 Margaret W. Rossiter, *Women Scientists in America: Struggles and Strategies to 1940* (Baltimore, MD: Johns Hopkins University Press, 1982), pp. 174–175.
12 Margaret W. Rossiter, *Women Scientists in America: Struggles and Strategies to 1940* (Baltimore, MD: Johns Hopkins University Press, 1982), pp. 176–178.
13 George F. Dreher and Taylor H. Cox Jr., "Race, Gender, and Opportunity: A Study of Compensation Attainment and the Establishment of Mentoring Relationships," *Journal of Applied Psychology* 81, no. 3 (1996): 297–308.

14 Draft, Trotter, "The Department of Anatomy in My Time," p. 86, no date, series 1, box 1, Mildred Trotter Papers, Becker Medical Library, Washington University School of Medicine.
15 Maria Lepowsky, "Charlotte Gower and the Subterranean History of Anthropology," in *Excluded Ancestors, Inventible Traditions: Essays Toward a More Inclusive History of Anthropology*, ed. Richard Handler (Madison: University of Wisconsin Press, 2000), pp. 131–132.
16 Faye-Cooper Cole, Roland B. Dixon, and Alfred V. Kidder, "Anthropological Notes and News," *American Anthropologist* 31, no. 3 (1929), 565–578, pp. 571–572.
17 Doris Stone, "A Fair Period for a Field Study," *The Radcliffe Quarterly* 66, no. 3 (1980): 20–22. p. 20.
18 Margaret W. Rossiter, *Women Scientists in America: Struggles and Strategies to 1940* (Baltimore, MD: Johns Hopkins University Press, 1982), p. 271.
19 Oral history, cited in Maria Lepowsky, "Charlotte Gower and the Subterranean History of Anthropology," in *Excluded Ancestors, Inventible Traditions: Essays toward a More Inclusive History of Anthropology*, ed. Richard Handler (Madison: University of Wisconsin Press, 2000), p. 131.
20 Kathryn B. Clancy, Robin G. Nelson, Julienne N Rutherford, and Katie Hinde, "Survey of Academic Field Experiences (SAFE): Trainees Report Harassment and Assault," *PLoS One* 9, no. 7 (2014): e102172.
21 Trudy R. Turner, et al., "Participation, Representation, and Shared Experiences of Women Scholars in Biological Anthropology," *American Journal of Physical Anthropology* 165 (2018): 126–157.
22 Frank Spencer, "The Rise of Academic Physical Anthropology in the United States (1880–1980): A Historical Overview," *American Journal of Physical Anthropology* 56, no. 4 (1981): 353–364, p. 360.
23 Michael A. Little, "Franz Boas's Place in American Physical Anthropology and Its Institutions," In *Histories of American Physical Anthropology in the Twentieth Century*, ed. Michael A. Little and Kenneth A. R. Kennedy (Lanham, MD: Lexington Books, 2010), 58–85, p. 66
24 Maria Lepowsky, "Charlotte Gower and the Subterranean History of Anthropology," in *Excluded Ancestors, Inventible Traditions: Essays toward a More Inclusive History of Anthropology*, ed. Richard Handler (Madison: University of Wisconsin Press, 2000), pp. 130–131.
25 Frank Spencer, "The Rise of Academic Physical Anthropology in the United States (1880–1980): A Historical Overview," *American Journal of Physical Anthropology* 56, no. 4 (1981): 353–364, p. 361.

26 Donna J. Nelson and Diana C. Rogers, *A National Analysis of Diversity in Science and Engineering Faculties at Research Universities* (Washington, DC: National Organization for Women, 2003).
27 David B. Givens and Timothy Jablonski, "1996 AAA Survey of Departments," *American Anthropological Association Guide 1996–1997* (Arlington, VA: American Anthropological Association, 1996).
28 Trudy R. Turner, "Changes in Biological Anthropology: Results of the 1998 American Association of Physical Anthropologists Membership Survey," *American Journal of Physical Anthropology* 118, no. 2 (2002): 111–116.
29 Susan C. Antón, Ripan S. Malhi, and Agustín Fuentes, "Race and Diversity in US Biological Anthropology: A Decade of AAPA Initiatives," *American Journal of Physical Anthropology* 165 (2018): 158–180, p. 161.
30 Margaret W. Rossiter, *Women Scientists in America: Struggles and Strategies to 1940* (Baltimore, MD: Johns Hopkins University Press, 1982), p. 270.
31 Margaret W. Rossiter, *Women Scientists in America: Struggles and Strategies to 1940* (Baltimore, MD: Johns Hopkins University Press, 1982), pp. 134, 136.
32 Margaret W. Rossiter, *Women Scientists in America: Struggles and Strategies to 1940* (Baltimore, MD: Johns Hopkins University Press, 1982), p. 173.
33 Margaret W. Rossiter, *Women Scientists in America: Struggles and Strategies to 1940* (Baltimore, MD: Johns Hopkins University Press, 1982), p. 136.
34 Joe Alper and Ann Gibbons, "The Pipeline is Leaking Women All the Way Along," *Science*, 260, no. 5106 (1993): 409–412.
35 Stephen Kulis, Diane Sicotte, and Shawn Collins, "More than a Pipeline Problem: Labor Supply Constraints and Gender Stratification across Academic Science Disciplines," *Research in Higher Education* 43, no. 6 (2002): 657–691.
36 Trudy R. Turner, et al., "Participation, Representation, and Shared Experiences of Women Scholars in Biological Anthropology," *American Journal of Physical Anthropology* 165 (2018): 126–157.
37 Margaret W. Rossiter, *Women Scientists in America: Struggles and Strategies to 1940* (Baltimore, MD: Johns Hopkins University Press, 1982), pp. 270–272.
38 Mildred Trotter, interview by Estelle Brodman, May 19, 1972 and May 23, 1972, transcript, Becker Medical Library, Washington University School of Medicine.

39 Patricia Case, "Ruth Sawtell Wallis (1895–1978)," in *Women Anthropologists: Selected Biographies*, ed. Ute Gacs, Aisha Khan, Jerri McIntyre, Ruth Weinberg (Urbana Champaign: University of Illinois Press, 1988).

40 Mary K Sandford, Lynn Kilgore, Diane L France, "Alice Mossie Brues (1913–2007)," in *The Global History of Paleopathology: Pioneers and Prospects*, eds. Jane Buikstra and Charlotte Roberts (Oxford: Oxford University Press, 2012), pp. 156–161.

41 Stuart W. Smith, "Edith Boyd (1895–1977)," *The Anatomical Record* 198, no. 2 (1980): 301–303.

42 *International Directory of Anthropologists* (Washington, DC: National Research Council, 1940).

43 Isabel Gordon Carter, "Reduction of Variability in an Inbred Population," *American Journal of Physical Anthropology* 11, no. 3 (1928): 457–471; Almanac, University of Pennsylvania 35, no. 4 (September 13, 1988), 2.

44 Copied in Letter, William J. Robbins to Trotter, January 30, 1934, series 2, box 2, folder 33, Mildred Trotter Papers, Becker Medical Library, Washington University School of Medicine.

45 Mildred Trotter, interview by Estelle Brodman, May 19, 1972 and May 23, 1972, transcript, Becker Medical Library, Washington University School of Medicine.

46 Patricia Case, "Ruth Sawtell Wallis (1895–1978)," in *Women Anthropologists: Selected Biographies*, ed. Ute Gacs, Aisha Khan, Jerri McIntyre, Ruth Weinberg (Urbana Champaign: University of Illinois Press, 1988), pp. 3631–3636.

47 Earnest A. Hooton, "Radcliffe Investigates Race Mixture," *Harvard Bulletin* 3 (1930): 768–776.

48 Jason M. Sheltzer and Joan C. Smith, "Elite Male Faculty in the Life Sciences Employ Fewer Women," *Proceedings of the National Academy of Sciences* 111, no. 28 (2014): 10107–10112.

49 Margaret W. Rossiter, *Women Scientists in America: Struggles and Strategies to 1940* (Baltimore, MD: Johns Hopkins University Press, 1982), p. 212.

50 Martin J. Finkelstein, Valerie Martin Conley, and Jack H. Schuster, "Taking the Measure of Faculty Diversity," *Advancing Higher Education* (April 2016).

51 Earnest A. Hooton, "Radcliffe Investigates Race Mixture," *Harvard Bulletin* 3 (1930): 768–776.

52 Margaret W. Rossiter, "The Matilda Effect in Science," *Social Studies of Science* 23 (1993): 325–341.

53 Lynne A. Isbell, Truman P. Young, and Alexander H. Harcourt, "Stag Parties Linger: Continued Gender Bias in a Female-Rich Scientific Discipline," *PLoS One* 7, no. 11 (2012): e49682; Trudy

R. Turner, et al., "Participation, Representation, and Shared Experiences of Women Scholars in Biological Anthropology," *American Journal of Physical Anthropology* 165 (2018): 126–157.

54 Stuart W. Smith, "Edith Boyd (1895–1977)," *The Anatomical Record* 198, no. 2 (1980): 302; Edith Boyd and Richard Scammon, *Origins of the Study of Human Growth* (Portland: Oregon Health Sciences University, 1981).

55 Robert F. Spencer and Elizabeth Colson, "Wilson D. Wallis 1886–1970," *American Anthropologist* 73, no. 1 (1971): 257–266, p. 258.

56 *Recollections of the History of Neuropsychopharmacology through Interviews Conducted by William E. Bunney, Jr.*, ed. Peter R. Martin (International Network for the History of Neuropsychopharmacology, 1996), p. 81.

57 No author, "Goldine Gleser, PhD '50 (1915–2004)," *Psychronicle, Washington University Newsletter* (Spring 2007), 11.

58 Goldine C. Gleser, *Getting It All* (Seattle, WA: Keepsake Editions, 2000), p. 92.

59 Letter, Hoyt D. Lemons to Trotter, August 31, 1951, series 2, box 4, folder 16, Mildred Trotter Papers, Becker Medical Library, Washington University School of Medicine. The error is presumably a combination with "Robert J. Terry."

60 Letter, *Goldine Gleser to Trotter, July 14, 1956*, series 2, box 5, folder 1, Mildred Trotter Papers, Becker Medical Library, Washington University School of Medicine.

61 Letter, *Goldine Gleser to Trotter, December 3, 1956*, series 2, box 5, folder 2, Mildred Trotter Papers, Becker Medical Library, Washington University School of Medicine.

62 Letter, *Goldine Gleser to Trotter, July 8, 1956*, series 2, box 5, folder 2, Mildred Trotter Papers, Becker Medical Library, Washington University School of Medicine.

63 William M. Landau, interviewed by Victor W. Henderson and Barbara W. Sommer, American Academy of Neurology Oral History Project. August 10, 2012, St. Louis, MO, American Academy of Neurology.

64 Mildred Trotter, interview by Estelle Brodman, May 19, 1972 and May 23, 1972, transcript, Becker Medical Library, Washington University School of Medicine.

65 Tim Parker, "Texans Attack Shortage of Scientists," *The Victoria Advocate* (Associated Press), January 13, 1956.

66 Mildred Trotter, interview by Estelle Brodman, May 19, 1972 and May 23, 1972, transcript, Becker Medical Library, Washington University School of Medicine.

67 Marion Hunt, "Mildred Trotter: 'With Honor in Her Own Country'," *Outlook Magazine, Washington University School of Medicine* 17, no. 1 (Spring 1980): 8–13, p. 10.
68 Draft, Trotter, "The Department of Anatomy in My Time," pp. 44–45, no date, series 1, box 1, Mildred Trotter Papers, Becker Medical Library, Washington University School of Medicine.
69 Mildred Trotter, interview by Estelle Brodman, May 19, 1972 and May 23, 1972, transcript, Becker Medical Library, Washington University School of Medicine.
70 Stephen Kulis, Diane Sicotte, and Shawn Collins, "More than a Pipeline Problem: Labor Supply Constraints and Gender Stratification across Academic Science Disciplines," *Research in Higher Education* 43, no. 6 (2002): 657–691.
71 Margaret W. Rossiter, *Women Scientists in America: Struggles and Strategies to 1940* (Baltimore, MD: Johns Hopkins University Press, 1982), pp. 197–199, 235.
72 Mildred Trotter, interview by Estelle Brodman, May 19, 1972 and May 23, 1972, transcript, Becker Medical Library, Washington University School of Medicine.
73 Marion Hunt, "Mildred Trotter: 'With Honor in Her Own Country'," *Outlook Magazine, Washington University School of Medicine* 17, no. 1 (Spring 1980): 8–13, p. 10.
74 Mildred Trotter, interview by Estelle Brodman, May 19, 1972 and May 23, 1972, transcript, Becker Medical Library, Washington University School of Medicine.
75 Barbara Vancheri, "At 81, a County Native Goes Strong in the Lab," *Beaver County Times*, Wednesday, August 20, 1980, B-1.
76 "Bulletin of the Washington University School of Medicine," *Publications of Washington University* 39, no. 1 (December 31, 1940), 1–121, p. 10, 59; US Census Bureau 1940, Population schedule. Retrieved from http://www.archives.com/GA.aspx?_act=ImageViewCensus1940&FirstName=gordon&ExactFirstName=1&LastName=scott&ExactLastName=1&MiddleName=h&Location=MO&ExactLocation=1&BirthYear=1901&BirthYearSpan=5&UniqueId=49557077&type=census&folderImageSeq=846; US Census Bureau 1940, Population schedule. Retrieved from http://www.archives.com/1940-census/mildred-trotter-mo-51119212.
77 Draft, Trotter, "The Department of Anatomy in My Time," p. 106, no date, series 1, box 1, Mildred Trotter Papers, Becker Medical Library, Washington University School of Medicine.
78 Margaret W. Rossiter, *Women Scientists in America: Struggles and Strategies to 1940* (Baltimore, MD: Johns Hopkins University Press, 1982), p. 249.

79 Darna L. Dufour, "Alice Mossie Brues (1913–)," in *Women Anthropologists: Selected Biographies*, ed. Ute Gacs, Aisha Khan, Jerri McIntyre, Ruth Weinberg (Urbana Champaign: University of Illinois Press, 1988), 23.
80 Maria Lepowsky, "Charlotte Gower and the Subterranean History of Anthropology," in *Excluded Ancestors, Inventible Traditions: Essays toward a More Inclusive History of Anthropology*, ed. Richard Handler (Madison: University of Wisconsin Press, 2000), p. 131.
81 Frances H. Stewart, interviewed by William R. Massa, May 17, 1977, transcript, Becker Medical Library, Washington University School of Medicine.
82 National Academies of Sciences, Engineering, and Medicine, *Sexual Harassment of Women: Climate, Culture, and Consequences in Academic Sciences, Engineering, and Medicine.* (National Academies Press, 2018).
83 Margaret W. Rossiter, *Women Scientists in America: Struggles and Strategies to 1940* (Baltimore, MD: Johns Hopkins University Press, 1982), pp. 129, 251.
84 Richard Hudgens, quoted in "Lasting Lessons," no author, *Washington University Magazine and Alumni News* 69, no. 2 (Summer 1999), p. 8.
85 Ann Randolph Flipse Gerber, "Remarks Prepared for the Memorial Service for Mildred Trotter, Ph.D. 1899–1991," October 9, 1991, http://beckerexhibits.wustl.edu/mowihsp/bios/FlipseMemTrotter.htm.
86 No author, "A tribute to Mildred Trotter, Ph.D.," *Outlook Magazine, Washington University School of Medicine* 12, no. 3 (Summer 1975), 15; and Ann Randolph Flipse Gerber, "Remarks Prepared for the Memorial Service for Mildred Trotter, Ph.D. 1899–1991," October 9, 1991, http://beckerexhibits.wustl.edu/mowihsp/bios/FlipseMemTrotter.htm.
87 Harriet Smith Kaplan, interview by Paul Anderson, May 6, 1981, transcript, Becker Medical Library, Washington University School of Medicine.
88 Trotter, James. Interview by author. Phone conversation. December 18, 2020.
89 Barbara Vancheri, "At 81, a County Native Goes Strong in the Lab," *Beaver County Times*, Wednesday, August 20, 1980, B-1.
90 Henry Etzkowitz, Carol Kemelgor, Michael Neuschatz, Brian Uzzi, and Joseph Alonzo, "The Paradox of Critical Mass for Women in Science," *Science* 266, no. 5182 (1994): 51–54.
91 Goldine C. Gleser, *Getting It All* (Seattle, WA: Keepsake Editions, 2000), p. 167.

92 Wallis's other titles include *No Bones About It* (New York: Dodd, Mead, and Co., 1944), *Blood from a Stone* (New York: Dodd, Mead, and Co., 1945), *Cold Bed in the Clay* (New York: Dodd, Mead, and Co., 1947), and *Forget My Fate* (New York: Dodd, Mead, and Co., 1950), which is also the title of a musical composition she copyrighted.
93 Ruth Sawtell Wallis. 1943. *Too Many Bones* (New York: Dodd, Mead, and Co.).
94 Ruth Sawtell Wallis. 1943. *Too Many Bones* (New York: Dodd, Mead, and Co.), p. 14.
95 Ruth Sawtell Wallis. 1943. *Too Many Bones* (New York: Dodd, Mead, and Co.), p. 59.
96 June M. Collins, "Ruth Sawtell Wallis 1895–1978," *American Anthropologist* 81, no. 1 (1979): 85–87, pp. 86–87.
97 Ruth Sawtell Wallis. 1943. *Too Many Bones* (New York: Dodd, Mead, and Co.), p. 185
98 Stanley M. Garn and Eugene Giles, "Earnest Albert Hooton, November 20, 1887–May 3, 1954," *Biographical Memoirs* 68 (1995): 167–179, p. 172.
99 Earnest Hooton, *Subverse* (Paris: Finisterre Press, 1961).
Note: Many thanks to Joseph T. Hefner for bringing this collection to my attention.
100 Robert Playfair, "He'd Send Older Men to War," *St. Louis Post-Dispatch*, December 31, 1944, 3D.
101 Draft, Trotter, "The Department of Anatomy in My Time," p. 21, no date, series 1, box 1, Mildred Trotter Papers, Becker Medical Library, Washington University School of Medicine.
102 Margaret W. Rossiter, *Women Scientists in America: Struggles and Strategies to 1940* (Baltimore, MD: Johns Hopkins University Press, 1982), p. 142.
103 Doris Stone, "A Fair Period for a Field Study," *The Radcliffe Quarterly* 66, no. 3 (1980): 20–22. p. 21.
104 Mary Ann Mason, Nicholas H. Wolfinger, and Marc Goulden, *Do Babies Matter?: Gender and Family in the Ivory Tower* (New Jersey: Rutgers University Press, 2013).
105 Christopher D. Lynn, Michaela E. Howells, and Max J. Stein, "Family and the Field: Expectations of a Field-Based Research Career Affect Researcher Family Planning Decisions," *PLoS One* 13, no. 9 (2018): e0203500.
106 Patricia Case, "Ruth Sawtell Wallis (1895–1978)," in *Women Anthropologists: Selected Biographies*, ed. Ute Gacs, Aisha Khan, Jerri McIntyre, Ruth Weinberg (Urbana Champaign: University of Illinois Press, 1988), 363.

107 Maria Lepowsky, "Charlotte Gower and the Subterranean History of Anthropology," in *Excluded Ancestors, Inventible Traditions: Essays toward a More Inclusive History of Anthropology*, ed. Richard Handler (Madison: University of Wisconsin Press, 2000), p. 145.
108 Draft, Trotter, "The Department of Anatomy in My Time," pp. 24–25, no date, series 1, box 1, Mildred Trotter Papers, Becker Medical Library, Washington University School of Medicine.
109 Letter, Trotter to "Donna," September 19, 1951, series 7, box 25, folder 11, Mildred Trotter Papers, Becker Medical Library, Washington University School of Medicine.
110 Letter, William Strauss Jr. to Trotter, March 28, 1957, series 13, box 6, folder 6, Mildred Trotter Papers, Becker Medical Library, Washington University School of Medicine.
111 Carl F. Cori, interview by Paul GW. Anderson, October 18, 1982, transcript, Becker Medical Library, Washington University School of Medicine.
112 Carl F. Cori, interview by Paul GW. Anderson, October 18, 1982, transcript, Becker Medical Library, Washington University School of Medicine.
113 Joseph Larner, "Gerty Theresa Cori: August 8, 1896–October 26, 1957," *Biographical Memoirs, National Academy of Sciences* 61 (1992): 125.
114 Gabriel W. Lasker, *Happenings and Hearsay: Experiences of a Biological Anthropologist* (Detroit, MI: Wayne State University Press, 1999), p. 112.
115 Goldine C. Gleser, *Getting It All* (Seattle, WA: Keepsake Editions, 2000), p. 66.
116 Goldine C. Gleser, *Getting It All* (Seattle, WA: Keepsake Editions, 2000), p. 74.
117 Goldine C. Gleser, *Getting It All* (Seattle, WA: Keepsake Editions, 2000), p. 117.
118 Goldine C. Gleser, *Getting It All* (Seattle, WA: Keepsake Editions, 2000), p. 58.
119 Goldine C. Gleser, *Getting It All* (Seattle, WA: Keepsake Editions, 2000), p. 102.
120 Goldine C. Gleser, *Getting It All* (Seattle, WA: Keepsake Editions, 2000), pp. 121–122.
121 Goldine C. Gleser, *Getting It All* (Seattle, WA: Keepsake Editions, 2000), p. 163.
122 Goldine C. Gleser, *Getting It All* (Seattle, WA: Keepsake Editions, 2000), p. 76.
123 Bernardo A. Houssay, "Memorial to Gerty Theresa Cori," December 15th, 1957 Becker http://beckerexhibits.wustl.edu/mow-ihsp/bios/HoussayMemCori.htm.

124 Stuart W. Smith, "Edith Boyd (1895–1977)," *The Anatomical Record* 198, no. 2 (1980): 302.
125 "Viking Fund Medalist for 1956," *American Journal of Physical Anthropology* 15, no. 2 (1956): 287–291.
126 Letter, Trotter to T. D. Stewart, April 2, 1957, series 13, box 8, folder 11, Mildred Trotter Papers, Becker Medical Library, Washington University School of Medicine.
127 T. Dale Stewart, ed., *Personal Identification in Mass Disasters: Report of a Seminar Held in Washington, DC, 9–11 Dec. 1968, by Arrangement between the Support Services of the Dept. of the Army and the Smithsonian Institution* (National Museum of Natural History, Smithsonian Institution, 1970).
128 Letter, T.D. Stewart to Trotter, October 16, 1968, series 13, box 6, folder 12, Mildred Trotter Papers, Becker Medical Library, Washington University School of Medicine.
129 Barbara Vancheri, "At 81, a County Native Goes Strong in the Lab," *Beaver County Times*, Wednesday, August 20, 1980, B-1.
130 Niki Scott, "Beneath the Anger are Their Unfulfilled Needs," Beaver County Times, Wed August 20, 1980, B-1.
131 "Washington University Portrait: Mildred Trotter - Feminine Bone Detective. MS 21; PhD 24," *Washington University Magazine* (June 1957), 12.
132 Mary Kimbrough, "Bone Detective," *The Everyday Magazine in the St. Louis Post-Dispatch*, May 8 1955, 1G.
133 Mary Kimbrough, "Bone Detective," *The Everyday Magazine in the St. Louis Post-Dispatch*, May 8 1955, 1G.
134 Helen Dudman, "He's Bone Detective for the FBI," *St. Louis Post-Dispatch*, April 17, 1958, 3E.
135 Quote from Virgil Loeb in Candace O'Connor, "First Class Teachers; Endowing Students with a love of Science: Mildred Trotter," *Outlook Magazine, Washington University School of Medicine* 40, no. 2 (Summer 2003), 13.
136 Ann Randolph Flipse Gerber, "Remarks Prepared for the Memorial Service for Mildred Trotter, Ph.D. 1899–1991," October 9, 1991, http://beckerexhibits.wustl.edu/mowihsp/bios/FlipseMemTrotter.htm.
137 Margaret W. Rossiter, *Women Scientists in America: Struggles and Strategies to 1940* (Baltimore, MD: Johns Hopkins University Press, 1982), pp. 249, 258.
138 Mildred Trotter, interview by Estelle Brodman, May 19, 1972 and May 23, 1972, transcript, Becker Medical Library, Washington University School of Medicine; and Jenelle Pifer, "The Great Equalizer, How to Teach Anatomy." *Pittmed* (Summer 2012): 27–31, p. 28.

139 Letter, Grant Izmirlian to Trotter, March 22, 1957, series 13, box 4, folder 5, Mildred Trotter Papers, Becker Medical Library, Washington University School of Medicine.
140 "Miss Erganian Plans Wedding," *St. Louis Post-Dispatch*, May 13, 1953, 4D.
141 "State to Have New 'Miss Missouri'," *The Chillicothe Constitution-Tribune* (June 27, 1957), 23.
142 Mary Anne Schofield, "Miss America, Rosie the Riveter, and World War II," in *"There She Is, Miss America": The Politics of Sex, Beauty, and Race in America's Most Famous Pageant*, eds. Elwood Watson and Darcy Martin, eds. (Macmillan, 2004), pp. 53–66, 60.
143 "Don Blasingame to Wed Missouri Girl in the Fall," *Lawrence Daily Journal-World*, April 26, 1960, 5.
144 Adele Starbird, "The Dean Speaks Up: Sitting in Judgment on Beauty," *St. Louis Post-Dispatch*, June 27 1957, 3F.
145 Adele Starbird, "The Dean Speaks Up: Sitting in Judgment on Beauty," *St. Louis Post-Dispatch*, June 27 1957, 3F.
146 Margaret W. Rossiter, *Women Scientists in America: Struggles and Strategies to 1940* (Baltimore: Johns Hopkins University Press, 1982), p. 78.
147 Letter, Trotter to Hertha De Villiers, November 25, 1964, series 13, box 3, folder 1, Mildred Trotter Papers, Becker Medical Library, Washington University School of Medicine.
148 Isis H. Settles and Rachel C. O'Connor, "Incivility at Academic Conferences: Gender Differences and the Mediating Role of Climate," *Sex Roles* 71, nos. 1–2 (2014): 71–82.
149 National Academies of Sciences, Engineering, and Medicine, *Sexual Harassment of Women: Climate, Culture, and Consequences in Academic Sciences, Engineering, and Medicine* (National Academies Press, 2018), p. 244.
150 Mildred Trotter, "Notes on the History of the American Association of Physical Anthropologists," *American Journal of Physical Anthropology* 14, no. 2 (1956): 350–364; Letter, T.D. Stewart to Trotter, April 19, 1955, series 3, box 7, folder 9, Mildred Trotter Papers, Becker Medical Library, Washington University School of Medicine.
151 Letter, T.D. Stewart to Trotter, April 26, 1956, series 3, box 7, folder 19, Mildred Trotter Papers, Becker Medical Library, Washington University School of Medicine.
152 Mildred Trotter, "Notes on the History of the American Association of Physical Anthropologists," *American Journal of Physical Anthropology* 14, no. 2 (1956): 350–364.

153 Letter, Hrdlička to Trotter, March 12, 1934, series 3, box 3, folder 13, Mildred Trotter Papers, Becker Medical Library, Washington University School of Medicine.
154 Mildred Trotter, "Notes on the History of the American Association of Physical Anthropologists," *American Journal of Physical Anthropology* 14, no. 2 (1956): 360–361. Stewart also recalled this event, see Douglas Ubelaker, "T. Dale Stewart's Perspective on His Career as a Forensic Anthropologist at the Smithsonian," *Journal of Forensic Sciences* 45, no. 2 (2000): 269–278, p. 276.
155 Mildred Trotter, "Notes on the History of the American Association of Physical Anthropologists," *American Journal of Physical Anthropology* 14, no. 2 (1956): 355.
156 Letter, Trotter to T.D. Stewart, September 28, 1979, series 13, box 6, folder 12, Mildred Trotter Papers, Becker Medical Library, Washington University School of Medicine.
157 Letter, Trotter to Henrietta Washburn, April 10, 1956, series 3, box 8, folder 20, Mildred Trotter Papers, Becker Medical Library, Washington University School of Medicine.
158 Letter, Trotter to Suzanne Hyman, October 26, 1983, series 13, box 7, folder 3, Mildred Trotter Papers, Becker Medical Library, Washington University School of Medicine.
159 Letter, Trotter to Sharon S. McKern, November 13, 1974, series 3, box 6, folder 41, Mildred Trotter Papers, Becker Medical Library, Washington University School of Medicine.
160 *The National Elementary Principal* 34, no. 2–7 (1954), p. 79; Yearbook, *National Education Association of the United States. Dept. of Elementary School Principals* (1946), p. 359.
161 Draft, Trotter, "The Department of Anatomy in My Time," p. 99, no date, series 1, box 1, Mildred Trotter Papers, Becker Medical Library, Washington University School of Medicine.
162 "Funeral Notices," *St. Louis Post-Dispatch*, July 10, 1991, 4C.
163 Letter, Trotter to Robert J. Terry, October 31, 1963, series 13, box 7, folder 6, Mildred Trotter Papers, Becker Medical Library, Washington University School of Medicine.
164 Draft, Trotter, "The Department of Anatomy in My Time," p. 20, no date, series 1, box 1, Mildred Trotter Papers, Becker Medical Library, Washington University School of Medicine.
165 Adele Chomeau Starbird, *Many Strings to My Lute* (Chicago, IL: The Lakeside Press, 1977).
166 Emma Jane Wilder and Keats Browning, "Many New Teachers Will Greet Students this Year," *Belton Journal and Bell Bounty Democrat* (August 28, 1941), 1.

167 Letter, Trotter to Chrissie (Christianna Smith), June 17, 1969, series 13, box 6, folder 9, Mildred Trotter Papers, Becker Medical Library, Washington University School of Medicine.
168 Letter, Trotter to Dorothy (Mrs. Roy R McCormack), December 5, 1969, series 13, box 7, folder 5; and letter, Trotter to T.D. Stewart, June 17, 1970, series 13, box 6, folder 12, Mildred Trotter Papers, Becker Medical Library, Washington University School of Medicine.
169 Letter, Trotter to Dempsey, January 5, 1973, series 13, box 3, folder 1, Mildred Trotter Papers, Becker Medical Library, Washington University School of Medicine.
170 Letter, Robert J. Terry to Marjorie [Mullins], February 3, 1961, series 13, box 7, folder 6, Mildred Trotter Papers, Becker Medical Library, Washington University School of Medicine.
171 "Mary Institute Teacher Gets Sabbatical in France," *St. Louis Post-Dispatch*, April 26, 1962, 3A.
172 Letter, Marc Goldstein to Trotter, September 15, 1977, series 13, box 1, folder 5, Mildred Trotter Papers, Becker Medical Library, Washington University School of Medicine.
173 *Missouri Botanical Garden Bulletin* 70, no. 1 (January/February 1982), 11.
174 Trotter, James. Interview by author. Phone conversation. December 18, 2020.
175 "Marjorie D. Mullins," *St. Louis Post-Dispatch*, March 1, 1989, 5A.
176 Ann Karus Meeropol, *A Male President for Mount Holyoke College: The Failed Fight to Maintain Female Leadership, 1934–1937* (North Carolina: McFarland, 2014).
177 Ann Karus Meeropol, *A Male President for Mount Holyoke College: The Failed Fight to Maintain Female Leadership, 1934–1937* (North Carolina: McFarland, 2014), p. 66.
178 Ann Karus Meeropol, *A Male President for Mount Holyoke College: The Failed Fight to Maintain Female Leadership, 1934–1937* (North Carolina: McFarland, 2014), p. 128.
179 Marion Hunt, "Mildred Trotter: 'With Honor in Her Own Country'," *Outlook Magazine, Washington University School of Medicine* 17, no. 1 (Spring 1980): 8–13.
180 Letter, Trotter to Alva Morrison, May 8, 1935, rg03-s03-ss04-b01-f03-i015, Board of Trustees Records, Mount Holyoke College Archives and Special Collections.
181 Photograph, "President Roswell Gray Ham (back row, center) with other presidents and deans from the Seven Sisters colleges," Office of the President records, Mount Holyoke College Archives and Special Collections.

182 Letter, Trotter to Lynn Bloom, August 7, 1978, series 3, box 5, folder 11, Mildred Trotter Papers, Becker Medical Library, Washington University School of Medicine.
183 Letter, Trotter to Lynn Bloom, August 7, 1978, series 3, box 5, folder 11, Mildred Trotter Papers, Becker Medical Library, Washington University School of Medicine.
184 Letter, Trotter to Julep [Minton], May 28, 1971, series 13, box 7, folder 5, Mildred Trotter Papers, Becker Medical Library, Washington University School of Medicine.
185 Draft, Trotter, "The Department of Anatomy in My Time," pp. 58–59, no date, series 1, box 1, Mildred Trotter Papers, Becker Medical Library, Washington University School of Medicine.
186 Document, "Travel and Final Salary Payment Authority for Civilian Employees Returning from Overseas Employment," August 19, 1949, series 3, box 4, folder 16, Mildred Trotter Papers, Becker Medical Library, Washington University School of Medicine.
187 Letter, Trotter to Oliver Duggins, August 1, 1947, series 3, box 5, folder 41; and letter, Trotter to Robert J. Terry, September 1, 1964, series 13, box 7, folder 6, Mildred Trotter Papers, Becker Medical Library, Washington University School of Medicine.
188 "Four are Killed in St. Louis Area Auto Accidents," *St. Louis Post-Dispatch*, April 11, 1955, 9A.
189 1930 US Census, ED 95-77 Washington University, sheet 1A, by Harold Hanke enumerator (May 3, 1930).
190 "I do not have either a middle name or initial." Letter, Trotter to A.H. Onthank, July 13, 1951, series 3, box 4, folder 16, Mildred Trotter Papers, Becker Medical Library, Washington University School of Medicine.
191 Draft, Trotter, "The Department of Anatomy in My Time," 85, no date, series 1, box 1, Mildred Trotter Papers, Becker Medical Library, Washington University School of Medicine.
192 1940 US federal census, Retrieved from http://www.archives.com/1940-census/mildred-trotter-mo-51119212
193 "Schools Give Diplomas This Week to 1257," *St. Louis Post-Dispatch*, January 19, 1908, 12B.
194 Robert Jenkins, "Procedural History of the 1940 Census of Population and Housing," Prepared at the Center for Demography and Ecology (Madison: University of Wisconsin, 1983), p. 3.
195 "Sixteenth Decennial Census of the United States, Instructions to Enumerators, Population and Agriculture 1940" (Department of Commerce, Bureau of the Census, January 2, 1940), p. 43.
196 Oxford English Dictionary, OED Online, Oxford University Press, June 2019.

197 Letter, Trotter to Goldine Gleser, October 6, 1958, series 13, box 6, folder 11, Mildred Trotter Papers, Becker Medical Library, Washington University School of Medicine.
198 No author, "Charles E. Minton dies," *The Santa Fe New Mexican* (May 7, 1976), 42.
199 Draft, Trotter, "The Department of Anatomy in My Time," p. 67, no date, series 1, box 1, Mildred Trotter Papers, Becker Medical Library, Washington University School of Medicine.
200 Letter, Trotter to Danforth, September 5, 1961, series 13, box 3, folder 1, Mildred Trotter Papers, Becker Medical Library, Washington University School of Medicine.
201 Letter, Trotter to Hertha De Villiers, November 25, 1964, series 13, box 3, folder 1, Mildred Trotter Papers, Becker Medical Library, Washington University School of Medicine.
202 Letter, Trotter to Carol Samet, January 24, 1969, series 13, box 6, folder 9, Mildred Trotter Papers, Becker Medical Library, Washington University School of Medicine.
203 Letter, Trotter to Julep [Minton], May 28, 1971, series 13, box 7, folder 5, Mildred Trotter Papers, Becker Medical Library, Washington University School of Medicine.
204 No author, "Notice of Hearing and Final Report of Account," *The Santa Fe New Mexican* (March 12 1974), 52.
205 Ann Randolph Flipse Gerber, "Remarks Prepared for the Memorial Service for Mildred Trotter, Ph.D. 1899–1991," October 9, 1991, http://beckerexhibits.wustl.edu/mowihsp/bios/FlipseMemTrotter.htm.
206 "Washington U. Professor to Teach in East Africa," *St. Louis Post-Dispatch*, June 18, 1963, 3A.
207 Mary Kimbrough, "Bone Detective," *The Everyday Magazine in the St. Louis Post-Dispatch*, May 8 1955, 1G.
208 See David K. Johnson, *The Lavender Scare: The Cold War Persecution of Gays and Lesbians in the Federal Government* (Chicago: University of Chicago Press, 2009).
209 George Gatewood, William F. Micarelli, David M. Pemberton, Michael A. Hovland, and Marilyn Huss Moore, "A Monograph on Confidentiality and Privacy in the US Census," Policy Office of the US Census, July 2001, 11–12. https://www.census.gov/history/pdf/ConfidentialityMonograph.pdf.

CHAPTER 7

Marginalized Contemporaries

Another woman was active in physical anthropology during this time, though she never appeared in the American Association of Physical Anthropologists (AAPA) membership lists. Caroline Bond Day (1889–1948) was the first Black woman to earn a graduate degree in anthropology in the US. Similar to the pattern of White women in anthropology who matriculated at women's colleges, Day attended a historically Black university. She completed her BA at Atlanta University (now Clark Atlanta University) in 1912 where she studied under W.E.B. Du Bois and worked as a research assistant on one of his books, *The Negro American Family*.[1] She then attended Radcliffe starting in 1916 where she was required to complete another bachelor's degree in 1919 (the same year as Ruth Sawtell Wallis) before being allowed to begin graduate work. In the meantime, she held a variety of jobs, including as a World War I relief worker, YWCA secretary, dean of women at Paul Quinn College, head of the English Department at Prairie View College, and returning to Atlanta University as director of dramatics and instructor of English.[2] She married in 1920.

Throughout this time, Day had been collecting the data necessary for her master's thesis under Hooton. It was Day to whom Hooton was referring when he wrote, in an entreaty to secure more funding for her thesis project, that "a perspicacious professor… can often manage to get these brainy Radcliffe graduates to do almost all of the harder work… I found such a rare individual in the class of '19."[3] Because he gave speeches at universities encouraging Black students to study anthropology, Day and others may have found him to be a Black ally, at least when compared to other anthropologists.[4] Hooton had a large interest in race studies, and studies of "mixed" people, in particular, when the emphasis of the discipline as a whole was on studying only White populations. But at the same time that he stated that no "pure" race exists and that all features are arbitrary, he also ardently attempted to categorize and

DOI: 10.4324/9781003252818-7

define "the American Negro." To accomplish this work, he would need a Black person to use as entrée into the population he wanted to study. This parallels the pattern of only including women in research positions specifically for their unique physical access to women's bodies. He described the person he was looking for: "the colored investigator had to be a person not only of scientific gifts and understanding, but also of such unquestioned honesty and impartiality as to guarantee the validity of his findings. And these, to be acceptable, should be checked rigorously by a disinterested white scientist."[5] He was, of course, not a disinterested party and his Whiteness certainly did not confer on him objectivity, but the researcher he described was Day.

Her master's thesis, "A Study of Some Negro-White Families in the United States," appeared in a 1932 publication within the Harvard African Studies.[6] Day assembled genealogies, hair samples, and anthropometric data from 346 families, comprising 2,537 individuals, with mixed "Negro," "White," and American "Indian" "blood." All of these individuals were socially regarded as "colored." Out of these 346 families, Day notes that 35 report individual family members who are "passing for white," most of whom are not included in the study due to concerns that they would be exposed.[7] She estimated that another 50 or so entire families that she had contacted were, for a similar reason, not studied at all. Day rightly suggested that the White population must also then contain "mixed" individuals, though she does not include them in this study.[8] Specific families were featured, with corresponding photographs and details of physical traits. Following this section, Day also presents descriptions and measurement procedures for physical features, such as hair type, nose breadth, and lip thickness. Day included Du Bois's family as well as her own and her husband's in the study. Each featured individual also has a self-reported, quantified admixture listed, Day's own being "7/16 N[egro] 1/16 I[ndian] 8/16 W[hite]."[9]

While Day makes brief sociological and anecdotal notes relevant to her data, the overall content of this paper is a presentation of information that implicitly supports her goal to demonstrate the similarities between the Black/mixed middle class and White middle class in America.[10] This was, of course, not in line with Hooton's main goal. The foreword and anthropometric chapters focus on Hooton's own primary intention, which he, of course, was not able to achieve, of categorizing a distinct American mixed-race "type" by quantifying biological differences resulting from "race crossings."[11] In another chapter, Hooton provided the enumerated anthropometrics that Day had collected on features such as nose width and hair type, along with relevant statistics. He was so eager to get this work finished that he used other graduate students (two men and one woman, whom he acknowledges in the foreword) to write up the data.[12] In this chapter and his foreword, Hooton laments the small sample size due to the difficulty in finding appropriate individuals and obtaining their permission for study. He clearly did not, at least prior to the study, recognize that "mixed" people would not be discoverable as some discrete group that he could just send someone out to measure. He details deficiencies of the study, takes responsibility for them, and recognizes that Day performed an amount of work that should not all have been shouldered by just one person.[13] Day's fastidious attention to data collection, and the full publication of her actual data, has allowed for modern re-analysis and re-purposing of her work by Joseph T. Hefner and Amber M. Plemons, undertaking geometric morphometric analyses from the data included in Day's thesis.[14]

Day's research did not garner much scientific or popular attention when it first appeared. Mixed race studies and blood quantification had fallen out of favor in the time between when Day started this work and when it was published, over a decade later.[15] Reactions of the families included in the study were not all positive, and some even regretted that they had participated.[16] Day's research had made visible some sensitive details of family histories that were not often shared, such as rape, out-of-wedlock births, and the identities of some individuals who had agreed to their inclusion but normally preferred to pass as White.[17] Some family trees unavoidably demonstrated cases of White men's abuses of Black women.

More recently, Day's research has been used as an example by anthropologist Rachel J. Watkins of how scientific researchers have at once dispelled and perpetuated racial concepts.[18] While attempting to deconstruct theories of racial differences, Day herself used those same racial ideas as the supposed fixed physical "Negro traits" as opposed to "white traits," and noted that mixed individuals could be "mistaken" for White. At the time, Day must have seen this as an opportunity to critique racial concepts through scientific bases, but she also had to work within Hooton's desired framework, and the scientific language available to her at the time. She struggled to provide a type of information in the then recent vein of Melville Herskovits' 1929 book *The American Negro*, which demonstrated that the majority of Black Americans are in fact "mixed" and do not constitute a discernibly different group or race. Herskovits indeed did not support any categorization of races.

Day's research had also previously appeared in a briefer, more explicitly anti-racist form in a 1930 issue of *Crisis* magazine (the official publication of the NAACP).[19] Many of the views left unspoken in her thesis are more plainly stated in the *Crisis* version, such as the extreme variability of physical appearance relative to blood quantification and the indistinguishability between "White," "Negro," and "mixed" individuals as disparate groups. She further dispels unfortunately popular myths from the time, such as the infertility of mixed-race individuals or their children. It seems this magazine provided the outlet that she could not get from the Harvard thesis under Hooton. Writing in more accessible, popular magazines with national reach was a common method for some Black academics at the time who were underrepresented or found their content limited in scholarly literature.[20]

Like Ruth Sawtell Wallis with *Too Many Bones*, Day also used fictional spaces to address very factual discriminatory experiences. One of Day's short stories, "The Pink Hat," first appeared in 1926 in a Black literary magazine, *Opportunity*, which was "dedicated to depicting Negro life as it is with no exaggerations" and featured writing by women.[21] This story helps clarify the perspective she brought to her thesis research. Day's protagonist is a teacher in a southern town who is "a mulatto—anthropologically speaking, I am a dominant of the white type of the F3 generation of secondary crossings."[22] This language mimics the phenotypic descriptions in her 1932 thesis. She wears a new pink hat that reflects its color on her skin, and is surprised when she walks around town and is, for the first time, addressed and treated with respect. She is perceived as a White woman. She then takes advantage of all the opportunities this provides, like access to cultural events, drinking at a soda fountain, and seeing a movie. At this point, she falls and breaks her ankle, and is returned to her home where she is with her "family—a colored family—and in the colored section of the town." When she seeks treatment, a friend reminds her that "it is against the rules of the osteopathic association to serve Negroes." She can no longer pass, and is again denied the basic privileges that a White woman can take for granted. In the last paragraph, the protagonist comes to a new perspective on her situation, and decides that she prefers her family, her neighborhood, and her own students. She doesn't want the pink hat. This pink hat unambiguously stands for "passing" as White, and this story relates a fictionalized version of what she may have hoped to communicate through a different avenue with her thesis data. Supposed races are anatomically indistinguishable; race is culturally construed and this construction is harmful.

Carline Bond Day was never a member of the AAPA, and there were no founding members of the AAPA who were *not* White. But by at least 1935, one Black man did appear in the membership listing, prodigious anthropologist William Montague Cobb (1904–1990). Cobb graduated from Amherst College in 1925, where he ran cross-country, boxed, and played violin.[23] That year he was awarded the Blodgett Scholarship to work at Woods Hole Marine Biological Laboratory studying embryo development. He went on to complete an MD at Howard in 1929, the same year he married. The University had decided to foster an all-Black faculty, and as part of that initiative, they supported Cobb in earning a PhD in a field not represented by Black Americans at the time – physical anthropology – at Western Reserve under T. W. Todd in 1932. He was the first Black person in the US to do so, the same year that Caroline Bond Day completed her AM. He would continue to teach at Howard for his entire career. Cobb would serve as President of the AAPA directly following Trotter from 1957 to 1959, and as President of the NAACP from 1976 to 1982. He was the first and, to this day, only Black person to be President of the AAPA.

If anthropology as a field can be described as unwelcoming to women in the early 20th century, then it was hostile to people who were not White. As a discipline, it has historically produced interpretations that reinforce racist and sexist concepts, under the guise of scientific scholarship. The AAPA was founded with the primary purpose to investigate and explain what were then seen as discrete races. In Hrdlička's 1918 foundational document of the *AJPA* and call for what would become the AAPA, he stated that "the paramount scientific object of Physical Anthropology is the gradual completion ... of the study of the normal white man....The choice of the white man for the standard is only a matter of most direct concern and convenience; the yellow-brown or the black man would serve equally well, if not better, were we of his blood and were he as readily available."[24] Secondary to that aim is the study of living and fossil primate anatomy; third is human evolution, and fourth is "primitive human races;" fifth is the "physical, physiological, and intellectual effects of racial mixing on progeny;" the sixth is human development; and he continues on to note that "the growing science of eugenics will essentially become applied anthropology."[25] Hrdlička further stated that "in the United States we are confronted with the grave problem of mixture of white and negro."[26] Though there were many dissenting views from Hrdlička, this was a field explicitly of White men, for White men.

Cobb was present at early AAPA meetings, and despite the heavy interest in race studies, he felt that the anthropologists were "not taking any crusading attitudes on race or anything like that," compared to the rest of society at the time.[27] Hrdlička had held that Black people were mentally and physically inferior to White. Yet he also chose to publish Cobb's papers in the *AJPA* and maintained a longtime professional relationship. When Cobb asked him how, with his extremely disparaging view of Black people, Hrdlička could work with Cobb, Hrdlička replied that "well the Negro is alright when he's had the hardships the white man has had. You have the vigor of the hybrid."[28] As Cobb later explained the man's racist and contrived response, "anytime you see anything you cannot explain, you invent an explanation."[29]

It is not surprising that of all the anthropologists, Cobb chose to and was chosen to work under Todd for his PhD at Western Reserve. Todd was reticent to support the split of physical anthropology from anatomy in 1930, partially for the reason that anthropology was so preoccupied with race, and possibly due to its inherent connection to Hrdlička. Unlike Hrdlička, Todd was a critic of the strict race concept, particularly of racial determinism, and found research which claimed to identify racial differences to result from misinterpreted data which ignored the social injustices that cause detrimental effects in Black populations to a greater extent than in White populations.[30] In an oral history interview, Cobb recalled a set of skulls that Todd kept as his "Humiliators."[31] Their appearance would fool anthropologists by exhibiting supposedly "typical" traits of one race, but Todd had documentation and photographs to show that they would in life have been considered another. Todd had begun to amass a large human skeletal collection for study, in the manner Robert J. Terry had at Washington University. Their work would encourage Cobb to create the Howard Laboratory of Anatomy and Physical Anthropology as well as the collection of the skeletal remains of Black individuals from medical school cadavers. When preparing the 1955 summer seminar in human identification, Stewart and Trotter planned to imitate the 'Humiliators' test, borrowing specimens from Cobb's collection.[32]

Cobb intentionally focused his career on disproving racist science. He stated that "nearly every distinguished living American anthropologist, and I know them all now, has private reservations about the intellectual possibilities of the Negro. We cannot expect them to be willing to go very far."[33] Cobb decided he would have to be the one to go the distance. Cobb found himself and Howard University uniquely situated to correct the pervasive racism within the scientific community. To do this, Cobb understood that anthropologists required large samples of Black cadavers and skeletons for anatomical studies.

Cobb directly involved himself in countering unsupported scientific claims of Negro inferiority and other racist myths. He was prolific and published this information in a variety of scholarly, "Negro," and popular venues, just as Caroline Bond Day had. He once wrote in *Crisis* in 1938, citing Day, to refute a potentially distressing claim in a *Collier's* article written by a physician that nasal cartilage exposes people who are passing for White as being Black.[34] One of the most well-known of his publications was his 1936 "Race and Runners" in the *Journal of Health and Physical Education*.[35] After the 1936 Berlin Olympics where American Jesse Owens won four gold medals, Cobb took this globally popular moment to dispel racist myths which were perceived as scientific fact. Many simultaneously believed in White superiority and that Black people were physically more adept than White people, making Owens' victory a result not of training and unique individual ability, but a replayed myth of the physical brutishness of Black men. But Cobb showed that there are no demonstrable anatomical differences between the legs and feet of White and Black runners, or therefore with innate physical ability. He even took physical measurements and radiographs of Owens' body for comparison to a documented skeletal collection to accomplish this. It was not Owens' race which conferred on him the gold, but, as with anyone, a combination "dependent on physical constitution, technique, and the will to achieve," which are not linked to physiological race. As he further explained in "The Negro as a Biological Element in America" in 1939, despite claims of Black peoples' physical superiority, he found it to be non-genetic features and social constructs and constraints that have had the most effect, and that no discernible and categorical physical differences are evident between White and Black groups.

While his anatomical studies were objective, he also used this data to, as Rankin-Hill and Blakey put it, "realize his agenda," particularly viewing education as a means of social change.[36] He knew that when the scientific community continues racist ideas, that science informs and bolsters public opinion and, even more importantly, affects medical care, social programs, and education. Not only did Cobb undertake the relevant scientific research, but he directly linked it back to health and the improvement of lives. He demonstrated the effects that racism itself has had on Black populations, and how that harms all of society. He would continue to caution that racism is subtle and insidious and has an effect on public health.

At the Central Identification Unit (CIU) in Manila, Philippines in the early 1950s, Trotter crossed paths with another Black anthropologist who would much later join the AAPA. Charles P. Warren (1921–1987) served as a staff sergeant in the Army Air Corps during World War II, in the Pacific Theater. He then completed a BS in zoology at Northwestern University in 1947, where he was the first Black quarterback on a Big Ten football team, and was a member of the first African American intercollegiate fraternity, Alpha Phi Alpha.[37] In 1945, he married music teacher and New Orleans native Lastinia Martinez, and they would have two children. Warren credited Melville Herskovits, a vocal critic of the concept of distinct and "pure" races, at Northwestern for encouraging him to study anthropology, and went on to complete an MA at Indiana University in 1950.[38] That year he received a Fulbright Scholarship to conduct ethnological research in the Philippines. In Manila and in Indiana, he had undertaken some work with human remains from archaeological sites. He then worked with the US military in Manila on identifying World War II war unknown cases. He would work until 1955 at the laboratory in Kokura, Japan on Korean War cases with many physical anthropologists including T. Dale Stewart. When he returned to the US, he was an instructor at the University of Illinois at Chicago and a research associate in Philippine Studies at the University of Chicago.[39] His research focused on cultural studies of the Batak of Palawan in the Philippines. In 1961, he earned an MA in anthropology at the University of Chicago. During the Vietnam Conflict, he took leave from his teaching position to work with CIL-Thai from 1973 to 1975 identifying remains. In 1978, he and Clyde Snow were called on to identify victims from the John Wayne Gacy case.[40]

Trotter expressed her negative impressions of Warren during his time with the American Graves and Registration Service (AGRS). In 1953, prior to Stewart meeting Warren in Japan, Trotter described him as "a Negro with a little formal training in Social Anthropology. He went to Manila under a Fulbright and has been anthropologist for the Army almost ever since."[41] Stewart once mistakenly referred to him as "Dr. Warren." Trotter then ungenerously asked Stewart in 1954,

> How do you like Warren (surely he is not Dr.) by now? Or rather, what I want to know is how much do you think he knows? We came to odds when he wanted to make identifications to please the two women clerks who had been sent to Manila to shuffle and sort earlier records and who had made identifications from these earlier records. Oh well—perhaps Warren has learned from [Furue]. (I saw Warren for only 17 days.)[42]

Stewart responded that, "'Dr' Warren is generally regarded as not being top in identification work. Mrs Madine shares your opinion of him. Yet Warren is a good mixer. I feel it is unfortunate that he has stayed so long in these foreign parts; I doubt that he will ever complete his education."[43] Stewart had also commented that "Warren, of course, is trying to make a good impression of me and Newman. Under the circumstances, I'm trying to be nice too; but I'm observing and sizing up capabilities of the Japanese anthropologist."[44] In 1953, Sherwood Washburn and Charles Shade had recommended Warren for AAPA membership.[45] In 1956, Stewart wrote to Trotter that they would have to deal with "the problem of membership" for Warren at the upcoming AAPA meeting.[46] Despite trying for years, he would only be granted membership by 1972.

At the time Trotter worked with Warren in Manila in 1951, he had only recently finished his master's degree in cultural anthropology. Though he was working on ethnological research during his Fulbright Scholarship, he was called on to assist the AGRS in identifying the remains from an aircraft crash in 1950 while the curator of anthropology at the Philippine National Museum, Robert B. Fox, was away.

By virtue only of being an American anthropologist physically present in the Philippines at that moment, and being known to the AGRS, in 1951 he was put in charge of a large, commingled skeletal project (from the Cabanatuan prison camp) which existed for the very fact that there were so many problems with identifying these remains.[47] It appears that he, unsurprisingly, struggled in this role. Warren himself noted the difficulties of the task at hand for such a young anthropologist.[48] In the end, Trotter was brought in as the expert to sort the project out and determined that it, in fact, could not be sorted out at the time.[49] These remains have since been exhumed in the effort to identify them today at DPAA.

Trotter had decided that Warren could not defend his professional opinions against those of two "women clerks," that he was not capable of doing the job, and she seems to have believed he should already have been – but never would be – competent. We cannot know today if this was simply true about Warren (particularly since he was formally trained only in cultural anthropology at that point), but perhaps Trotter was not cognizant of her own prejudiced ideas about a young Black anthropologist and the double standard to which she was holding him, like so many had done to her.[50] Warren agreed with Trotter that the overall AGRS work in the Philippines was problematic, later openly stating that it was "a small and relatively unproductive operation, so it is quite understandable that when Mildred Trotter of Washington University in St. Louis visited...she... recommended that it be terminated."[51] And he shared some of the same complaints that Trotter would also express about having no input in the work and receiving no feedback: that he was asked to reprocess partial sets of remains that were selected by a board, and was never permitted access to records or to the final results of any of his analyses. Unlike Trotter though, he did not have the professional experience or standing at the time to make a formal critique.

Trotter was particularly vexed by Warren's continued employment with the Army identification efforts, and used him, indirectly but repeatedly, as her example for the risk of using inexperienced anthropologists. This was related to her and Stewart's campaign to improve education and training in human identification. She felt that Warren was "working conscientiously but had had too little experience with skeletons to cope with the problem" in Manila.[52] He apparently had, prior to her arrival, arbitrarily removed the right radius or ulna when their lengths varied considerably from the left side. Trotter was struck by the mistake for years, and used this particular example when corresponding with Washburn on how to address what they considered a dearth of basic anatomical training in physical anthropologists, claiming that even tailors and dressmakers know how much an individual's left and right arm lengths can differ.[53] In Trotter and Gleser's 1952 publication though, they noted that "the differences in length between the bones of the two sides are small."[54] Of course, Warren's decision to remove one side had absolutely no logical basis, and was likely evidence his inexperience.

Despite Trotter's recommendation against him, the Army soon sent Warren to the CIU in Kokura, Japan in 1952. He joined Charles Shade and Tadao Furue in processing Korean War remains, replacing Alexander Tardy. More anthropologists would later join, including Ellis Kerley, Rex Gerald, and David L. Cole. Also joining were Thomas McKern and T. Dale Stewart, who served as senior anthropologists, during which time they undertook a large-scale research project which resulted in the 1957 manuscript *Skeletal Age Changes in Young American Males.*[55] Warren claimed that he received 1 week of on-the-job training, and then worked a separate shift from the others, 6–7 days a week.[56] He and the other relatively novice anthropologists were surprised by the conditions of the remains, which were in variable states of soft tissue decomposition. He noted positively that he had more responsibilities and access to the remains and records than he had in the Philippines, which, whether he knew it at the time or not, was likely due to Trotter's efforts. Still, this low level of training and competency verification, and working in professional isolation, is not an ideal milieu for producing high caliber anthropologists or work.

Trotter and Stewart corresponded regarding the other anthropology technicians in Kokura too. After one letter, Trotter wondered to Stewart "who is Kerley?"[57] To describe the now well-known White anthropologist who was "getting a Ph.D. and a divorce," Stewart wrote to Trotter in 1954 that "like most anthropologists he has a minimum of preparation for this sort of work... It must be a subject for discussion at the seminar."[58] So, Warren was typical of the anthropologists employed by the AGRS in being undertrained and underprepared, and Stewart and Trotter hoped to rectify this overall situation. But Kerley received a much kinder introduction than Warren had, and perhaps greater encouragement as well. Kerley would certainly come to have an impressive career as an anthropologist over the following decades, but Stewart had somewhat overstated Kerley's qualifications in 1954. Kerley had in fact barely started his graduate work months before and only held a BA; he would finish his MA in 1956 and PhD in 1962.

While the more senior anthropologists at the AGRS may not have held Warren in high esteem, Warren later expressed some possible reasons to return the sentiment. He believed that a military research paper he coauthored in 1955 with Tadao Furue on using ultraviolet light to help with segregating commingled remains was partially plagiarized by Thomas McKern in his 1958 paper on the same topic, in which he did not even provide reference to the earlier paper.[59] He also asserted that a staff paper written by Cole, Furue, Kerley, and himself was coopted without acknowledging the authors for a panel discussion Russell Newman led at the 1956 AAPA annual meeting.[60] While papers authored for the military would have been open for any official uses such as these, the earlier work should likely have been properly referenced.

Warren also noted the inconsistencies and inaccuracies of anthropological race determination at Kokura. The anthropologists were instructed to make a determination of "*White*, Negroid, or Mongoloid" [my emphasis], with the allowed addition of "probably" or a determination of which race was "predominant." Warren stated that "underlying this directive was the belief that there are three major races in the world, and that all other human types are the result of the mixing of two (or three) of the major groups. This kind of logic is not foreign to some anthropologists."[61] The inconsistent terminology also indicated to Warren that "White" was considered the standard. By his comments, Warren clearly rejected the race concept and found its application for the AGRS to be problematic, though he did not go into further detail. An indirect colleague of Warren's who worked with the AGRS earlier, Japanese anthropologist Hanihara Kazuro, took a different stance. He considered himself an expert on determining race from the skeleton, and in 1965 wrote a book on his experiences at the AGRS. He cataloged what he considered the physical differences between races, and organized an evolutionary tree with the "black race" closest to the animal kingdom. As historian Tessa Morris-Suzuki describes this treatment of the remains of US war dead, "even in death – even in the effort to return their bodies to their families – their mortal remains were viewed through the prism of the race that had overshadowed their lives."[62]

I have not found documentation of Warren's own perceptions of his personal and professional treatment due to race during his military work. However, he was certainly aware of the differential experiences based on skin color and addressed this in an article he published on student responses to anthropological films. He noted that for over a decade he "carried the burden" of introductory courses at the University of Illinois at Chicago.[63] He used visual media in the classroom, and his research interests often centered on Negrito groups in Southeast Asia. Nearly half of his students were described as "minorities," and he noted that many of these students reacted negatively to seeing films of "black and brown populations," often nude or semi-nude. Their concern, and clearly Warren's as well, was not the nudity itself, but the exclusive portrayal of people of color living in relative poverty and having poor hygiene. The students were perceptive, and saw the racist categorizations and portrayals of these people in films, which he noted ethnographers have lumped as Negrito or pygmy groups worldwide, despite their greater genetic connection to respective local populations than to each other.

Warren encouraged researchers and educators not to misrepresent ancestry, and to be cautious to not present certain populations as savages.

Later in his career, Warren was actually quite active in improving the training of anthropologists at the AGRS labs, perhaps because of his own acknowledged early inexperience and continued lack of support. He developed training manuals for incoming workers and provided instruction equivalent to coursework. In 1975, he received a Meritorious Civilian Service Award from the Army for his work in "upgrading the skills and the performance levels of the laboratory personnel by providing university-level classroom experiences and on-the-job training."[64]

Warren's colleague, Tadao Furue, also started working for the AGRS in 1951. He was a Japanese citizen who, according to some accounts, had been chosen as a kamikaze pilot during World War II, but fortunately for him the War soon ended.[65] After finishing an undergraduate degree at Tokyo University, he and classmate Hanihara Kazuro started working for the AGRS in Kokura. Eventually Furue was the only non-US citizen anthropologist there, and the US government at one earlier point had actually touted its multi-national team performing identification work.[66] Stewart described Furue's work as "good," even remarked on an osteometric board Furue had designed, and that he would like Furue to come to the US.[67] His only reservation was that Furue was not interested in research, which Stewart stated he believed to be common among Japanese anthropologists.[68] Furue fit the pattern of AGRS anthropologists being undereducated and underprepared at that time. And, despite Trotter's claim that maybe Warren might be learning from him, Furue actually seems to have been the least educated and trained of the anthropological team. But at the time, he was well-received by Trotter and Stewart.

Furue continued to work with the US identification effort as it changed names and moved around the globe. By the 1980s, he was the sole anthropologist working in Hawaii at what was called CILHI and had become a controversial figure in the accounting community. Furue developed a technique he called "morphological approximation," in which he estimated the measurements of fragmentary bones by sizing them up against other, intact bones, which he would then measure as a proxy.[69] This is not a tenable method. In 1985, University of Florida anthropologist William Maples, along with Ellis Kerley (in whose second wedding Furue had served as best man while in Japan) and forensic dentist Lowell Levine, were called in to assess the quality of Furue's work on a commingled case from the Vietnam War. Maples described Furue's identifications as being "made on distressingly little evidence."[70] Still, colleagues politely described his choices less as fraudulence or professional dishonesty, and more as "a lack of support," the result of being "literally and intellectually cut off," or as the over-eagerness of a "man of intense pride" to provide identifications.[71] Regardless of the description, Furue was under- and misperforming for decades. But for whatever personal or other reasons, Furue was perceived generally positively, and at a minimum benignly, while Warren certainly was not. Only after this incident, in 1986 and just a few years before his death, was Furue added as a member of the AAPA, perhaps in an attempt to provide him with opportunities for professional education, interaction, or credibility.

One of Trotter's PhD students also appeared only briefly as a member of the AAPA, despite her and Stewart's glowing impressions of him. Chinese student Ju-Kang Woo, later written as Wu Rukang, studied at Washington University from 1946 to 1949. He was recommended by Washington University anatomy department head E. V. Cowdry, who had earlier established the anatomy department at Peking Union Medical College in Beijing. Trotter even corresponded with Wu while she was in Hawaii on topics related to her stature estimation project. While she was on leave, Wu went to Washington, DC to study with Stewart and Russell Newman at the Smithsonian. During this time, he undertook independent reading and research on fossil specimens, data collection for his dissertation on palatine tori, and attended the Summer Seminar in Physical Anthropology. Though a student at Washington University and not an employee of the AGRS, Stewart used the same method with Wu of judging a junior anthropologist's competency and potential based primarily on conversations and impressions, and not on objective examinations or publications. In a letter to Washington University in regard to giving Wu academic credit for his work, Stewart wrote that

> Mr. Woo was not given a formal examination covering his work in Washington but either Dr. Stewart or Dr. Newman talked to him almost daily and feel satisfied that he pursued his studies intelligently and acquired an extensive knowledge of Early Man. They recommend that he receive full university credit for this work.[72]

Following completion of his PhD, Wu returned to China and became best known for his studies in paleoanthropology and started the country's first biological anthropology journal, *Acta Anthropologica Sinica*. Political conditions kept Wu from returning to the US or working with former colleagues for decades after.[73] Trotter and Wu remained in infrequent mail contact. She received a warm welcome and tour with him on a trip to Beijing in 1979 ("Surprise! I'm coming to China as a tourist"),[74] where she was also delighted to see pandas. She later helped his daughter acclimatize when she started graduate school at Washington University in 1982.[75]

In "The Department of Anatomy in My Time," Trotter also details her memories of Kehar Singh Chouké. Chouké had completed medical school in India in 1906, then had to repeat a portion of medical school at Washington University, graduating with an MD in 1922. Trotter described him as Sikh, always wearing a turban, untrimmed beard, long hair, a metal bracelet, and American clothing. There was, evidently, some widespread interest in his presence at the medical school. His smiling photograph was featured in the local paper, noting that he had worn a turban instead of a mortarboard at graduation, due to his "religious scruples."[76] For the 2 years he taught at the school though, Trotter noted that he was generally not liked by students. Although Chouké believed this was due to his dark skin, she claimed that it was instead due to what she alleged was his "haughty manner."[77] Trotter went on to explain that he left St. Louis for the University of Colorado, where 6 years later, the Board of Regents demanded that he either remove his beard and turban or be fired. At this point he made one final trip to India to see his wife and three sons, obtained a divorce, and severed all ties to India. He then complied with the University's ultimatum. This coerced erasure of his identity is observable in his photographs archived at Washington University, depicting him before and after. He later joined the University of Pennsylvania and married a faculty member from Bryn Mawr.

In her oral history, Trotter recounted some experiences in 1963 teaching anatomy at Makerere University in Uganda.[78] The head of the anatomy department was a White English man (David Allbrook) whose aim was to properly train Ugandans in medicine who would hopefully stay on as faculty at the medical school. All 12 students were men, and they were surprised the first day to see an American woman as their teacher. All of the students had been born in Africa. Of the group, five were ethnic East Indian and trained in India, and two were White British and trained in Britain, one being Louis Leakey's nephew, and the rest were not further described but were likely local Ugandans.

Trotter claims to have had only one real difficulty in teaching these men, which was that she initially called them "boys," a term she states she also called her students in St. Louis. She recognized the shared problem with this term, stating that "I later learned the term "boys" is very much resented by Africans – as it is by *our own* American blacks" [my emphasis].[79] The students laughingly recognized her genuine ignorance in using the word, even signing a going away present "To 'Mamma' Trotter," from the "Boys."[80] From this story, it sounds as if she had not, at least by 1963, taught any Black students, since she apparently was able to call her American male students "boys" without incident. At this point, only one Black student had graduated from the Washington University School of Medicine, James L. Sweatt III, in 1962.[81] I have no record to show whether she ever had Sweatt in her classes. The next Black student did not graduate until one full decade later (Julian Mosley in 1972).

Trotter noted that in Uganda "there was a great feeling of color."[82] She had earlier recalled how one student was "surprised and delighted" when Trotter shook his hand. Less than a year before she arrived, Uganda had gained its independence from Britain. In 1972, she noted that her time in Africa gave her some "appreciation of the problems involved when a government [South Africa] ranks a population in five classes with privileges decreasing as the color increases from White to Black."[83] Trotter remembered in her oral history that the second Black US Congressman, Adam Clayton Powell, Jr., visited Kampala while she was there. Powell, by his own and others' accounts, easily passed as White.[84] She explained that "he was well received. But I thought he wasn't particularly good for the job and I couldn't understand why we couldn't have more American Negroes there... The answer to that was that they never came as a member of their race. They came in a very superior way which just upset the native Africans."[85] Trotter's sentiment mirrors her comments on Chouké, alleging that these men were arrogant and superior, acting above what she seems to have considered their rightful station designated by society. Of course, Trotter also felt a similar way about at least one woman, having stated that "the reason people tend not to like" joint 1977 Nobel Prize-winning medical physicist Rosalyn Yalow "is because she is conceited."[86]

Somehow, despite these experiences and her own explicit recognition of race discrimination in Uganda, Trotter did not seem as reflective about the same discrimination in the United States, even though she was living in St. Louis and must have been aware of the growing civil rights movement. And prior to the body donation law that Trotter helped to pass in 1956, she specifically noticed the disproportionate number of Black male cadavers of indigent men who arrived at the university because no one claimed them or the responsibility for their burial. But it is quite possible to identify someone else's faults in sharp relief, even while maintaining obliviousness to similar faults of your own, especially when those thoughts are socially, structurally, and pseudo-scientifically ingrained.

NOTES

1 Anastasia C. Curwood, "Caroline Bond Day (1889–1948): A Black Woman Outsider Within Physical Anthropology" *Transforming Anthropology* 20, no. 1 (2012): 79–89, p. 81.

2 Hubert B. Ross, Amelia Marie Adams, and Mallory Williams, "Caroline Bond Day: Pioneer Black Physical Anthropologist," in *African American Pioneers in Anthropology*, ed. Faye V. Harrison and Ira E. Harrison (Urbana Champaign: University of Illinois Press, 1999), 37–50, p. 41.

3 Earnest A. Hooton, "Radcliffe Investigates Race Mixture," *Harvard Bulletin* 3 (1930): 768–776.

4 Anastasia C. Curwood, "Caroline Bond Day (1889–1948): A Black Woman Outsider within Physical Anthropology," *Transforming Anthropology* 20, no. 1 (2012): 79–89, p. 82; Eugene Giles, "The Two Faces of Earnest A. Hooton." *American Journal of Physical Anthropology* 149, S55 (2012): 105–113.

5 Hubert B. Ross, Amelia Marie Adams, and Mallory Williams, "Caroline Bond Day: Pioneer Black Physical Anthropologist," in *African American Pioneers in Anthropology*, ed. Faye V. Harrison and Ira E. Harrison (Urbana Champaign: University of Illinois Press, 1999), 37–50, p. 43.

6 Caroline Bond Day, "A Study of Some Negro-White Families in the United States," *Harvard Africa Studies Volume X: Varia Africana* V, ed. Earnest A. Hooton and Natica I. Bates (Cambridge, MA: Harvard University Press, 1932).

7 Caroline Bond Day, "A Study of Some Negro-White Families in the United States," *Harvard Africa Studies Volume X: Varia Africana* V, ed. Earnest A. Hooton and Natica I. Bates (Cambridge, MA: Harvard University Press, 1932), p. 5.

8 Caroline Bond Day, "A Study of Some Negro-White Families in the United States," *Harvard Africa Studies Volume X: Varia Africana* V, ed. Earnest A. Hooton and Natica I. Bates (Cambridge, MA: Harvard University Press, 1932), p. 11.

9 Caroline Bond Day, "A Study of Some Negro-White Families in the United States," *Harvard Africa Studies Volume X: Varia Africana* V, ed. Earnest A. Hooton and Natica I. Bates (Cambridge, MA: Harvard University Press, 1932), plate 34.

10 Hubert B. Ross, Amelia Marie Adams, and Mallory Williams, "Caroline Bond Day: Pioneer Black Physical Anthropologist," in *African American Pioneers in Anthropology*, ed. Faye V. Harrison and Ira E. Harrison (Urbana Champaign: University of Illinois Press, 1999), 37–50, p. 45.

11 Hubert B. Ross, Amelia Marie Adams, and Mallory Williams, "Caroline Bond Day: Pioneer Black Physical Anthropologist," in *African American Pioneers in Anthropology*, ed. Faye V. Harrison and Ira E. Harrison (Urbana Champaign: University of Illinois Press, 1999), pp. 37–50.

12 Hubert B. Ross, Amelia Marie Adams, and Mallory Williams, "Caroline Bond Day: Pioneer Black Physical Anthropologist," in *African American Pioneers in Anthropology*, ed. Faye V. Harrison and Ira E. Harrison (Urbana Champaign: University of Illinois Press, 1999), 37–50, pp. 41–42.
13 Hooton, Foreword to Caroline Bond Day, "A Study of Some Negro-White Families in the United States," *Harvard Africa Studies Volume X: Varia Africana* V, ed. Earnest A. Hooton and Natica I. Bates (Cambridge, MA: Harvard University Press, 1932), p. iv.
14 Joseph T. Hefner and Amber M. Plemons, "A Geometric Morphometric Approach to Quantify the Impact of Admixture on Craniofacial Form," American Academy of Forensic Sciences, Proceedings 2020.
15 Hubert B. Ross, Amelia Marie Adams, and Mallory Williams, "Caroline Bond Day: Pioneer Black Physical Anthropologist," in *African American Pioneers in Anthropology*, ed. Faye V. Harrison and Ira E. Harrison (Urbana Champaign: University of Illinois Press, 1999), 37–50, p. 42
16 Hubert B. Ross, Amelia Marie Adams, and Mallory Williams, "Caroline Bond Day: Pioneer Black Physical Anthropologist," in *African American Pioneers in Anthropology*, ed. Faye V. Harrison and Ira E. Harrison (Urbana Champaign: University of Illinois Press, 1999), 37–50, p. 47.
17 Anastasia C. Curwood, "Caroline Bond Day (1889–1948): A Black Woman Outsider within Physical Anthropology" *Transforming Anthropology* 20, no. 1 (2012): 79–89, p. 82.
18 Rachel J. Watkins, "Biohistorical Narratives of Racial Difference in the American Negro: Notes toward a Nuanced History of American Physical Anthropology," *Current Anthropology* 53, no. S5 (2012): S196-S209, S205.
19 Caroline Bond Day, "Race Crossings in the United States," *Crisis* 37, no. 3 (Mar 1930): 81–82, 103, p. 45.
20 Faye V. Harrison and Ira E. Harrison, "Anthropology, African Americans, and the Emancipation of a Subjugated Knowledge," in *African American Pioneers in Anthropology*, ed. Faye V. Harrison and Ira E. Harrison (Urbana Champaign: University of Illinois Press, 1999), pp. 1–36.
21 Caroline Bond Day "The Pink Hat" *Opportunity* 4, no. 48 (December 1926): 379–280, reprinted in Judith Musser (ed.), *'Tell It to Us Easy' and Other Stories: A Complete Short Story Fiction Anthology of African American Women Writers in Opportunity Magazine (1923-1948)* (Jefferson, North Carolina: McFarland, 2011).

22 Caroline Bond Day "The Pink Hat" *Opportunity* 4, no. 48 (December 1926): 379-280, reprinted in Judith Musser (ed.), *'Tell It to Us Easy' and Other Stories: A Complete Short Story Fiction Anthology of African American Women Writers in Opportunity Magazine (1923–1948)* (Jefferson, NC: McFarland, 2011), p. 77.
23 Lesley Rankin-Hill and Michael L. Blakey, "W. Montague Cobb: Physical Anthropologist, Anatomist, and Activist," in *African American Pioneers in Anthropology*, ed. Faye V. Harrison and Ira E. Harrison (Urbana Champaign: University of Illinois Press, 1999), pp. 101–136.
24 Aleš Hrdlička, "Physical Anthropology: Its Scope and Aims; Its History and Present Status in America," *American Journal of Physical Anthropology* 1 (1918): 3–23, p. 18.
25 Aleš Hrdlička, "Physical Anthropology: Its Scope and Aims; Its History and Present Status in America," *American Journal of Physical Anthropology* 1 (1918): 3–23, pp. 18–21.
26 Aleš Hrdlička, "Physical Anthropology: Its Scope and Aims; Its History and Present Status in America," *American Journal of Physical Anthropology* 1 (1918): 3–23, p. 20.
27 Lesley M. Rankin-Hill and Michael L. Blakey, "W. Montague Cobb (1904-1990): Physical Anthropologist, Anatomist, and Activist," *American Anthropologist* 96 (1994): 74–96, p. 81.
28 Lesley M. Rankin-Hill and Michael L. Blakey, "W. Montague Cobb (1904–1990): Physical Anthropologist, Anatomist, and Activist," *American Anthropologist* 96 (1994): 74–96, p. 80.
29 Lesley M. Rankin-Hill and Michael L. Blakey, "W. Montague Cobb (1904–1990): Physical Anthropologist, Anatomist, and Activist," *American Anthropologist* 96 (1994): 74–96, p. 80.
30 Lesley M. Rankin-Hill and Michael L. Blakey, "W. Montague Cobb (1904–1990): Physical Anthropologist, Anatomist, and Activist," *American Anthropologist* 96 (1994): 74–96, p. 78.
31 Lesley Rankin-Hill and Michael L. Blakey, "W. Montague Cobb: Physical Anthropologist, Anatomist, and Activist," in *African American Pioneers in Anthropology*, ed. Faye V. Harrison and Ira E. Harrison (Urbana Champaign: University of Illinois Press, 1999), cited on p. 115.
32 Letter, T.D. Stewart to Trotter, April 18, 1955, series 3, box 7, folder 19, Mildred Trotter Papers, Becker Medical Library, Washington University School of Medicine.
33 Rachel J. Watkins, 2007 "Knowledge from the Margins: W. Montague Cobb's Pioneering Research in Biocultural Anthropology" *American Anthropologist* 109, no. 1 (2007): 186–196, cited on p. 188.
34 W. Montague Cobb, "Your Nose Won't Tell," *The Crisis* (October 1938), 332.

35 W. Montague Cobb, "Race and Runners," *The Journal of Health and Physical Education* 7, no. 1 (1936): 3–7, 52–56.
36 Lesley M. Rankin-Hill and Michael L. Blakey, "W. Montague Cobb (1904–1990): Physical Anthropologist, Anatomist, and Activist," *American Anthropologist* 96 (1994): 74–96, p. 88.
37 "Charles P. Warren, 66, Anthropology Professor," *Chicago Tribune*, (December 28, 1987); "Voice of the Sphinx," *The Sphinx (Official Publication of Alpha Phi Alpha)* 26, no. 4 (December 1940).
38 Robert B. Pickering and David Bachman, *The Use of Forensic Anthropology* (New York: CRC Press, 1996), 4.
39 Wilhelm G. Solheim II, "Charles Preston Warren, 1921–1987," Asian Perspectives 27, no. 2 (1986-1987): 183–184.
40 "Charles P. Warren, 66, Anthropology Professor," *Chicago Tribune*, December 28, 1987.
41 Letter, Trotter to T.D. Stewart, November 17, 1953, series 13, box 6, folder 11, Mildred Trotter Papers, Becker Medical Library, Washington University School of Medicine.
42 Letter, Trotter to T.D. Stewart, November 10, 1954, series 3, box 7, folder 18, Mildred Trotter Papers, Becker Medical Library, Washington University School of Medicine.
43 Letter, T.D. Stewart to Trotter, November 18, 1954, series 3, box 7, folder 18, Mildred Trotter Papers, Becker Medical Library, Washington University School of Medicine.
44 Letter, T.D. Stewart to Trotter, October 25, 1954, series 3, box 7, folder 18, Mildred Trotter Papers, Becker Medical Library, Washington University School of Medicine. The anthropologist he references appears to read 'Kanasaki'.
45 Letter, Trotter to T.D. Stewart, November 17, 1953, series 13, box 6, folder 11, Mildred Trotter Papers, Becker Medical Library, Washington University School of Medicine.
46 Letter, T.D. Stewart to Trotter, March 22, 1956, series 3, box 7, folder 19, Mildred Trotter Papers, Becker Medical Library, Washington University School of Medicine.
47 The Defense Prisoner of War/Missing Personnel Office, World War II Division Memo, To: Philippines Geographic File, From: Heather Harris and Lisa Breckinbaugh, dtd 13 Oct 2005, Revised 20 Feb 2014. Re: Casualties of Cabanatuan Prisoner of War Camp #1 and the history of their burials.
48 Charles Warren, "Forensic Anthropology in a Military Setting," *Human Organization* 40, no. 2 (1981): 172–180, p. 173.
49 Document, Trotter and Charles Warren, "Statements re Cabanatuan graves, 1951," series 3, box 4, folder 24, Mildred Trotter Papers, Becker Medical Library, Washington University School of Medicine.

50 Anecdotally, Alec Christensen's cursory comparison for a modern study of Korean War stature data found Warren's measurements to be nearly identical to those of a current DPAA anthropologist; at the very least Warren's measurement skills were on par with his peers (Alec Christensen, personal communication, April 2018).
51 Charles Warren, "Forensic Anthropology in a Military Setting," *Human Organization* 40, no. 2 (1981): 172–180, p. 173.
52 Draft, Trotter, "The Department of Anatomy in My Time," p. 82, no date, series 1, box 1, Mildred Trotter Papers, Becker Medical Library, Washington University School of Medicine.
53 Trotter to Sherwood Washburn, October 15, 1954, series 3, box 8, folder 18, Mildred Trotter Papers, Becker Medical Library, Washington University School of Medicine.
54 Mildred Trotter and Goldine C. Gleser, "Estimation of Stature from Long Bones of American Whites and Negroes," *American Journal of Physical Anthropology* 10, no. 4 (1952): 463–514, p. 512.
55 Thomas W. McKern and T. Dale Stewart, *Skeletal Age Changes in Young American Males* (Natick, MA: Quartermaster Research and Development Command Technical Report EP-45, 1957).
56 Charles Warren, "Forensic Anthropology in a Military Setting," *Human Organization* 40, no. 2 (1981): 172–180, p. 173.
57 Letter, *Trotter to T.D. Stewart, November 10, 1954*, series 3, box 7, folder 18, Mildred Trotter Papers, Becker Medical Library, Washington University School of Medicine.
58 Letter, *Stewart to Trotter, October 25, 1954*, series 3, box 7, folder 18, Mildred Trotter Papers, Becker Medical Library, Washington University School of Medicine.
59 Charles Warren, "Forensic Anthropology in a Military Setting," *Human Organization* 40, no. 2 (1981): 172–180, p. 175. The papers are Tadao Furue and Charles P. Warren, *1955 Final Report on Ultraviolet Ray Research* (CIU, AGRS Group, 8204th Army Unit, US Army, 1955); David L. Cole, Tadao Furue, Ellis R. Kerley, and Charles P. Warren, *The Physical Anthropologist in Military Identification* (CIU, AGRS, 8204th Army Unit, US Army, 1955); and Thomas W. *McKern, The Use of Short Wave Ultra-violet Rays for the Segregation of Commingled Skeletal Remains. Technical Report EP-98* (Natick, MA: Headquarters Quartermaster Research and Engineering Command, US Army Quartermaster Research and Engineering Center, 1958).
60 Charles Warren, "Forensic Anthropology in a Military Setting," *Human Organization* 40, no. 2 (1981): 172–180, p. 175.
61 Charles Warren, "Forensic Anthropology in a Military Setting," *Human Organization* 40, no. 2 (1981): 172–180, p. 178.

62 Tessa Morris-Suzuki, "Lavish are the Dead: Re-envisioning Japan's Korean War," *The Asia-Pacific Journal* 11(52), no. 3 (2013): 8.
63 Charles P. Warren, "Minority Student Response to the Anthropology of Asian Black Populations," *Philippine Quarterly of Culture & Society* 10 (1982): 211–224.
64 Charles Warren, "Forensic Anthropology in a Military Setting," *Human Organization* 40, no. 2 (1981): 172–180, p. 177.
65 William R. Maples and Michael Browning, *Dead Men Do Tell Tales: The Strange and Fascinating Cases of a Forensic Anthropologist* (New York: Broadway Books, 2010), p. 198.
66 Tessa Morris-Suzuki, "Lavish are the Dead: Re-envisioning Japan's Korean War," *The Asia-Pacific Journal* 11(52), no. 3 (2013): 4.
67 Letter, T.D. Stewart to Trotter, October 25, 1954, series 3, box 7, folder 18, Mildred Trotter Papers, Becker Medical Library, Washington University School of Medicine.
68 Letter, T.D. Stewart to Trotter, November 18, 1954, series 3, box 7, folder 18, Mildred Trotter Papers, Becker Medical Library, Washington University School of Medicine.
69 Michael Sledge, "*Soldier Dead: How We Recover, Identify, Bury, and Honor Our Military Fallen,*" (New York: Columbia University Press, 2005), p. 125.
70 William R. Maples and Michael Browning, *Dead Men Do Tell Tales: The Strange and Fascinating Cases of a Forensic Anthropologist* (New York: Broadway Books, 2010), p. 201.
71 William R. Maples and Michael Browning, *Dead Men Do Tell Tales: The Strange and Fascinating Cases of a Forensic Anthropologist* (New York: Broadway Books, 2010), 201; Michael Sledge, *Soldier Dead: How We Recover, Identify, Bury, and Honor Our Military Fallen* (New York: Columbia University Press, 2005), p. 125.
72 Letter, T.D. Stewart to Trotter, September 23, 1948, series 3, box 4, folder 23, Mildred Trotter Papers, Becker Medical Library, Washington University School of Medicine.
73 Wu Rukang and Wu Xinzibi, "China," in *History of Physical Anthropology*, ed. Frank Spencer (New York: Garland, 1997), 273–282, p. 274.
74 Trotter to Ju-Kang Woo, February 23, 1979, series 3, box 8, folder 40, Mildred Trotter Papers, Becker Medical Library, Washington University School of Medicine.
75 Letter, Trotter to Wu Rukang, November 4, 1982, series 13, box 7, folder 11, Mildred Trotter Papers, Becker Medical Library, Washington University School of Medicine.
76 "Graduate Wore Turban Instead of Mortar Board at Exercises," *St. Louis Post-Dispatch*, June 9, 1922, 3 and 37.

77 Draft, Trotter, "The Department of Anatomy in My Time," p. 28, no date, series 1, box 1, Mildred Trotter Papers, Becker Medical Library, Washington University School of Medicine.
78 Mildred Trotter, interview by Estelle Brodman, May 19, 1972 and May 23, 1972, transcript, Becker Medical Library, Washington University School of Medicine.
79 Mildred Trotter, interview by Estelle Brodman, May 19, 1972 and May 23, 1972, transcript, Becker Medical Library, Washington University School of Medicine.
80 Card, undated, series 9, box 26, folder 1, Mildred Trotter Papers, Becker Medical Library, Washington University School of Medicine.
81 Rosalind Early, "First in Class," *The Source, Washington University* (December 7, 2015).
82 Mildred Trotter, interview by Estelle Brodman, May 19, 1972 and May 23, 1972, audio, Becker Medical Library, Washington University School of Medicine.
83 Draft, Trotter, "The Department of Anatomy in My Time," p. 99, no date, series 1, box 1, Mildred Trotter Papers, Becker Medical Library, Washington University School of Medicine.
84 Lawrence Rushing, "The Racial Identity of Adam Clayton Powell Jr.: A Case Study in Racial Ambivalence and Redefinition," *Afro-Americans in New York Life and History* 34, no. 1 (2010): 7.
85 Mildred Trotter, interview by Estelle Brodman, May 19, 1972 and May 23, 1972, audio, Becker Medical Library, Washington University School of Medicine.
86 Letter, Trotter to Christianna Smith, March 6, 1978, series 13, box 7, folder 5, Mildred Trotter Papers, Becker Medical Library, Washington University School of Medicine.

CHAPTER 8

Race, Sex, and Research

The early union of physical anthropology with support for a biological basis of race has had long repercussions for the field, including the continued underrepresentation of marginalized individuals today.[1] Two incidents that occurred around Trotter's American Association of Physical Anthropologists (AAPA) presidency highlight the conflicted status of the race concept and racism within physical anthropology during the prime of her career.

In 1953, W. Montague Cobb was alerted that the 1955 AAPA meetings would be changed from Chicago to Atlanta, where Jim Crow laws were in effect and the participants at the annual meeting of the AAPA and its parent organization, the American Association for the Advancement of Science (AAAS), would not be excepted from these laws.[2] Cobb was at that time on the council of the AAAS, and poignantly inquired as to whether the Association had any official rule that its meetings could only take place in cities where its members could be treated equally. No such rule existed, and Cobb decided not to attend any meeting which would condone racial segregation and restrict its members from their basic human rights. He even wrote to the President of the United States about the matter.

The AAPA then unanimously adopted a resolution to not hold meetings in places where racial segregation is practiced, even though they normally held their meetings in conjunction with the AAAS. Ahead of the meeting in 1955, J. Lawrence Angel wrote to William Strauss that he and Trotter planned to write a letter of support for Cobb to the AAAS: "at least we can show how strongly we feel against holding scientific meetings in place where our Negro members will be hurt."[3] The AAAS soon followed the AAPA's lead. Cobb's position had not gone unchallenged, however, and he had at least one notable encounter. Anthropologist Margaret Mead, at a dinner in her own honor, told Cobb that his position was not supported by Negro leaders. As Cobb noticed, her mistake arose because she confused one Black man she spoke with for another (Channing Tobias), and in doing so inexplicably misconstrued that the Chairman of the Board of the NAACP somehow did not support

DOI: 10.4324/9781003252818-8

integration.[4] This larger issue began a continuing conversation within the AAPA, the history of which Juan Comas compiled in 1969, about the social responsibility of the AAPA in addressing and delegitimizing purportedly scientific claims supporting racism.[5]

Another incident occurred in 1956. An anatomist, eugenicist, and segregationist, Wesley Critz George, at the University of North Carolina at Chapel Hill (UNC) medical school had been publicly espousing false, pseudo-scientific claims opposing integration following the 1954 *Brown vs. the Board of Education* decision. A UNC anthropologist, John Gillin, wrote a statement in the *Daily Tar Heel* in 1956, directly in response to George, that no scientific evidence supports the superiority or inferiority of any of the races.[6] The articles started a debate in the anthropological community, and many called on the AAPA to take a professional stance in support of Gillin's comments. AAPA members, at that time presided over by Trotter, argued over the role the Association should have in addressing "race propaganda." Two members, one being Carleton S. Coon, an anthropologist at the University of Pennsylvania who had trained under Hooton in the 1920s, argued that no scientific society could "pass judgment" on a "political matter." Of course, these were not just political arguments, at issue was the intentional misuse and fabrication of scientific (specifically anatomical and anthropological) data for political purposes.

Despite Coon's comments, the majority did indeed recognize the need for a statement on the subject of race and the misuse of biological data. Coon would later unofficially (and unsuccessfully) resign from his AAPA Presidency in 1962 due to his conflicting views. In the end, the AAPA then passed a resolution that "despite hundreds of investigations, no conclusive evidence has been offered of superiority or inferiority of any of the races... with respect to their innate psychological or cultural abilities or potentialities," and that "nothing can be gained by basing discussions of segregation and other aspects of race relations upon misapprehension or misrepresentation of the findings of physical anthropology."[7] This issue was somewhat mirrored, under different circumstances and with a different result, by the American Academy of Forensic Sciences Board's dissolution of the Anthropology Section's Diversity and Inclusion Committee in 2020 (having only been officially sanctioned in 2018) after it distributed an anti-racist statement in response to the disproportionate killings of Black individuals by law enforcement.

Gillin wrote to thank Trotter, as President of the AAPA, for the Association's public declaration. He noted his disappointment in the silence of scientists at UNC, who, despite considerable private support, never publicly endorsed him. He stated that he was "not by nature a 'radical or a 'troublemaker' ... However, I will not have the scientific truth flouted."[8] Trotter's personal perspectives in this debate were not made explicit at the time, but in a letter to Stewart in March 1956, she stated that, as the current President, she wanted to appoint a specific individual as chairman for the next year because she "know[s] he is aware of and sympathetic with Cobb's position."[9] She intended to leave a committee that would reject unscientific claims that support racism, and would work well with Cobb, the incoming President. The discipline as a whole was already slowly heading away from racial typologies and descriptive studies, and toward new questions and analytical methods, partially heralded by Sherwood Washburn's 1951 "The New Physical Anthropology."[10]

In the early 20th century, women, though fewer in number, were more likely than their male counterparts in anthropology to reject the race concept and to speak against institutional racism. Leonard Lieberman (1997) details the roles women in anthropology have played in deconstructing the race concept.[11] Women, having been marginalized from the primarily male scientific establishment where they are "both members and outsiders," have been more likely than men to question racial arguments for other marginalized groups.[12] In Goldine Gleser's words, "I guess my being Jewish and a woman helped me identify with the 'underdog'."[13] Ruth Sawtell Wallis published on topics critical of eugenicist concepts of racial purity.[14] Caroline Bond Day attempted to build her master's thesis around discrediting the concept of fixed racial traits. One exception to this pattern from the women discussed earlier was Alice Brues, who rejected racism, but continued to support some aspects of the race concept.[15] Despite this recognition, race has been a core tenet throughout the history of anthropology, and women, including Trotter, also actively contributed to the centrality of race in anthropological studies and perpetuating racist science within the discipline.

Perhaps because Trotter's osteological research included race, but did not often directly pertain to studies of racial variation and determination, her name does not often come up in contemporary or subsequent discussions of the race concept. What remains is her academic work to infer her more underlying scientific views on race/ancestry and sex. Unlike many American physical anthropologists at the time, Trotter did actually include Black populations in her research. However, they were always presented separately from White populations. In multiple publications, she defined the term "American Negro" to imply a mixture of White, American Indian, and Black ancestry.[16] No similar clarification was ever provided for such mixture being present in White populations, though the inference should be obvious. And despite her recognition of variability and "mixture" within these large-scale populations, she still presented racial subsamples as if they were biologically discrete racial groups.[17] In each and every study where she included both White and Black individuals, she divided her samples, prior to any analysis, usually first by race, then by sex. Occasionally, she divided first by sex then by race. Some samples are thirdly grouped by age ranges. She used these race and sex divisions even for fetuses.[18] And when American Black, African Black, American White, and European White populations are provided, she noted the inclusions in sample descriptions and tables, then divides them into Black and White categories before undertaking analyses.

In her most well-known and well-used publications dealing with stature estimation, Trotter and Gleser 1952 and 1958, she applied this same method of grouping separately males by race, and females by race. In a letter written in 1949 in reference to, but prior to, her analysis of the stature data, Trotter had already stated that "'Americans' represent many stocks and mixtures of stocks. For this reason any problem studied on Americans would necessarily involve extensive 'sorting' at the outset in order to reduce to a minimum the deviation and variation."[19] She had decided to divide her samples by sex and race before she even had the data to analyze whether or not it benefited from or even supported this division. She took for granted the advantage of using race-grouped formulas, paraphrasing Pearson (1929) that "better results from regression formulae will be obtained by applying a formula peculiar to a race itself than by applying a formula from a second race."[20] She did acknowledge that racial categories may be problematic: "insofar as racial admixture of Whites and Negroes is concerned ... there is not complete agreement on the question of extent of hybridization of the Negro (Herskovits, '28; Terry, '29, '32; Todd and Lindala, '28)."[21] But she immediately went on to use these categories anyway.

Trotter supported her decision to group by race and sex by referencing the work of Stevenson (1929) who compared data and formulas on a contemporary Chinese male sample with the Rollet sample (and Pearson formulas).[22] He found that each sample did not provide satisfactory estimations for the other. Only after she had already compiled and grouped her 1952 data did Trotter compare her Terry Collection sample across race and sex. Hrdlička (1947) and Dupertuis and Hadden (1951) had already found that for a given length of bone, there is little to no difference by sex to stature.[23] But Trotter found that to be inaccurate for her sample. She determined that "it is evident that the males of each race are taller than the females for a given length of femur, and that the Whites are taller than the Negroes."[24] She only provides a graph to support this assertion and does not indicate if she adjusted data for age-related stature changes as she had done in other sections of this article.

Before even looking at the data though, Trotter declared, a priori, a supposed requirement and benefit of using group-specific formulas. This method was and still commonly is typical of anthropological studies, whether they support the biological race concept or not. Trotter's sample groupings and descriptions followed suit with those of Terry and Todd at the time, who were openly opposed to the race concept. Even so, both anthropologists regularly and systematically grouped their data, without providing any scientific reason to support these divisions, by race and sex. Trotter further asserted that "there is no method that I know of by which you can estimate female stature from male stature, even though both sexes are from the same race… there is always danger connected to such an extrapolation."[25] Indeed, the final sentence of Trotter and Gleser reads: "These comparisons… indicate the necessity of independent equations for estimation of stature for each sex of the White and Negro races."[26] She grouped the samples by race and sex before analyzing any data and then claimed that the results proved the necessity of those divisions.

The actual racial classifications of individuals in her reference samples must, of course, be questioned as well. In their description of the Terry Collection, Hunt and Albanese (2005) explain that "caution should be used," because "it is most likely that the criteria for inclusion in any given racial category also varied over the decades of the collection period as social and academic views regarding the race concept changed in the US."[27] Trotter and colleagues categorized individuals into racial groups as they were socially perceived at one moment in time, then divided groups by these categories, regardless of the final data.

Trotter firmly believed that racial categorization was fundamental to the accuracy and efficacy of anthropological analysis. In the 1970s, Trotter and Gleser expressed skepticism in anthropologist Georges Olivier's research that claimed one could determine stature without regard to race.[28] When Stewart was assembling his data on skeletal aging in Korean War remains for publication in the 1950s, he did not distinguish his sample based on race. Trotter wrote to him, "Why do you shy away from race? You don't consider, do you, that the only difference between racial groups is socio-economic background?"[29] In this comment, she makes it clear that she believes race, even if not solely biological, is a meaningful biological category that is absolutely required for the organization of data.

Through a computer program, *FORDISC*, new equations based on Trotter and Gleser's original equations, along with many others, are still used today. *FORDISC* continues to use these sex- and race-divided groups. That is, to estimate stature, the user should select the race and sex of the unknown individual's stature being estimated. The input measurements are then compared exclusively to the reference data for the group selected. One may also select "Any" (i.e., White and Black) if the racial category is not known or is anthropologically determined. *FORDISC* creators Jantz and Ousley clarify the complications of assessing racial classifications by comparison to reference groups, as well as the limits of the program, even explaining that the ability "to classify individuals does not validate the classic biological races."[30] But because these categorizations are socially relevant, *FORDISC* still directs users in race-grouped formats.

As Trotter described it, "race is very important in physical anthropology."[31] Hrdlička's founding sentiments for the AAPA in 1918 established this, since two main goals of the Association were "the study of the normal white man," and "of the more primitive human races and their subdivisions."[32] The precedent has continued, in different forms, into even more recent scholarship, particularly in forensic anthropology. Matt Cartmill took a sampling of articles published in the *American Journal of Physical Anthropology (AJPA)* between 1965 and 1996, which showed that 46% of the papers were on topics pertaining to human racial variation.[33] But despite anthropology's longtime attachment to race and racial classifications, using race designations is problematic when forced onto data. Indeed, this commitment to racial specificity of samples contributed to the obfuscation of Trotter's 1952 tibia error for decades. This is evidenced by responses to Mexican anthropologist Genovés's discrepancies in stature estimations based on the tibia, which were blamed on racial variation of the respective samples, instead of on the tibia measurement itself.

In 2016, John Albanese, et al. undertook a study to test if stature estimation equations based on grouped populations are useful.[34] In a group-specific estimation of stature, an analyst must select a reference group (such as "Black females") on which to base the stature calculation from measurements of bones. This is the process that Trotter and Gleser used. Albansese et al. found that these group-specific equations do not provide better results than entire sample-based equations which do not group by race and sex. Furthermore, these group-specific equations are more difficult to apply because, in forensic cases, at least one unknown, but anthropologically determined characteristic (race or sex), must be applied in order to estimate yet another unknown (height). A decade before Albanese et al.'s findings, anthropologist Marc Feldesman had reported similar conclusions for stature formulas, that there are only "slight" benefits to using categorized equations, and only when the "unknown" data (race and/or sex) is fairly certain.[35] Anthropologists have often, however, remained committed to using group-specific data for stature estimation, in spite of some evidence that this practice is not necessarily more reliable or more accurate, is dependent on assumptions of biological meaning in categorization, and introduces unnecessary variables.

Despite anthropologists recognizing that biological race is a fallacy, the concept of variation by geographical origins as it corresponds to social race is still actively used throughout the discipline, for practical purposes. Determining ancestry/race is important socially, as is made obvious by law enforcement and the public asking forensic anthropologists specifically for racial information. Physical features known to vary by ancestry can and do correlate to socially constructed race. Anthropologists can therefore, by assessing morphology, sometimes determine the likely race that a person would have been perceived as in life. Ousley, Jantz, and Freid (2009) further explain this arbitrariness of samples: that any groupings, such as those defined by social race and even by linguistics, can be differentiated in physical studies.[36] One only has to categorize reference samples that way, and then test individuals will be classified somewhere within that paradigm. In America, "Black" and "White" are two socially meaningful groups, and because of the discipline's practical applications, forensic anthropology often actively reinforces that this is biologically meaningful too.

Regardless of the intent or of the personal or professional beliefs of an author, when samples are divided by race, this opens up the research for interpretation as supporting the concept of discrete biological races. In 1960, Trotter and colleagues published "Densities of Bones of White and Negro Skeletons," in which the authors determined, among other results, that "the bones of the Negro skeleton are denser than bones of the White skeleton; and that bones of the male skeleton are denser than bones of the female skeleton."[37] Others used this work, fairly immediately and for decades following, as a reference to support that: 1) there are physiological differences between White and Black populations and 2) that osteoporosis is a disease *not* typically found in Black populations. In 1962, an anatomist described the article's results writing that "Trotter and her associates have found that … bones of the Negro skeleton are denser than bones of the White skeleton…. [I]t is significant in that it illustrates the pervasive nature of racial differences."[38] This anatomist was, not surprisingly, the UNC segregationist, Wesley Critz George, who had incited the AAPA debate to address "race propaganda" in 1956. But the fact that Trotter et al. had divided the samples by race, and characterized them in the manner they did, provided the possibility of differentiating between the two groups, which could therefore be used to support biological race concepts and validate beliefs of racial differences.

Trotter et al.'s data did not, despite their claims, actually support this division of groups. In 1974, Trotter and Hixon revisited the 1960 paper to increase the sample in size and age range.[39] As anthropologist Alan Goodman pointed out, the scatter plots used in this update further demonstrate the invalidity of dividing the samples by race for this data.[40] The plots show no real race and sex groupings, and indeed Trotter and Hixon themselves stated that "it is a challenge… to discern any difference between the densities of bone from blacks and those from whites. The six lowest densities, for example, were found in bones of blacks." This does not, however, stop the authors from imposing race- and sex-grouped variation onto the results and discussion, stating that "Negro skeletons exceed White skeletons and male skeletons exceed female skeletons in mean weight and density."[41] Even recognizing that the data did not justify subdivisions, the authors persisted in presenting the reference sample divided by race and sex and made unsupportable categorizations.

Trotter et al. (1960) has been widely cited as supporting versions of the argument that "it is a well-known fact that blacks do not suffer from osteoporosis."[42] Trotter et al. never stated this, their data did not support this, and they never discussed osteoporosis specifically but rather bone density across ages. By dividing the sample by race though, the data was left open to the inference. Indeed the authors, even in the 1974 re-examination, pointed readers to that conclusion by making the unsubstantiated claim that Black individuals as a group have greater bone density across ages than White individuals as a group. Of course, the continued uses of their data specifically as regards osteoporosis are cases of overinterpretation of the original source, but this overinterpretation has had real effects on medical care. As Goodman (1997) and Fausto-Sterling (2008) explain, the indirect results of this research have been insufficient medical care for Black individuals in regard to osteoporosis.[43] When medical professionals incorrectly identify a disease as being associated with specific populations, as opposed to associating it with underlying social, dietary, or other risk factors, they do not expect to find it in individuals from other populations. This leads to reduced screening for specific diseases, and in some cases, a requirement that an individual from one race be sicker than an individual from another race before they are considered for treatment, due to baseless traditions of considering different clinical measurement levels as normal in different races. This thereby reduces the care provided to individuals from the populations in which it is not expected to find a disease.

Furthermore, as Banks describes, individuals who do not fit into simplified racial schemes (like Black or White), must still be forcibly placed within one of the categories during medical testing in order to fulfill the dogma of separately analyzing bone density data based on race.[44] Though Trotter et al.'s 1960 data has been supplanted by Trotter's own (insufficient) re-clarifications, and by larger-scale studies and newer methods, this had not, by that point, resulted in a wide-scale shift away from using race as a factor in medical practice regarding osteoporosis. To confront issues such as this one, guidelines developed by a multidisciplinary group at Stanford University in 2008 recommend that when using ethnicity and race in medical studies one must ask: why it is relevant, how race will be determined, and whether this categorization is a relevant variable for the research.[45] While Trotter's work was produced decades before these guidelines existed, was not clinical, and was certainly not beholden to later standards, we can see that she and most other anthropologists at the time perhaps did not ask any of these questions.

In earlier papers, Trotter was sometimes more explicit in her descriptions of race and sex divisions as natural categories that are supported by anatomical evidence. In a 1934 publication on the septal aperture of the humerus, Trotter divided her samples by race and sex. Trotter confirmed an earlier statement from Hrdlička by commenting that the aperture is "hindered from manifesting itself in the stronger bone of the stronger limb or stronger individual, [which is] is in accord with the greater incidence of the aperture in the left side, the female sex and the negro race."[46] In this statement, she rank orders men as stronger than women, and White people as stronger than Black people. She also aligns herself with a recognized supporter of the race concept (Hrdlička) and makes the baseless and un-examined claim of the greater anatomical strength of White populations writ large. No consideration is given to the influence of occupational use, nutrition, and social disparities experienced by the populations she studied.

This is also a particularly telling example of the arbitrariness and social dependency of racial myths, which can fluctuate over time and circumstances, as suits any preferred argument. Trotter et al. would later, in 1960, claim that Black males had *denser* bones than White males from her sample. And the supposed physical superiority of Black bodies, which Cobb addressed in regard to Olympian Jesse Owens, as opposed to Trotter's comments in 1934, was another unfounded claim du jour.

This attachment to race categorizations also extended to Trotter's work with the military. In a 1949 military publication related to her US war dead identification work that demonstrates this conflict, Trotter wrote that "The bones are then appraised for *race*: Pure racial strains are relatively easy and the skull gives the best evidence. Where the race is not pure, the various characters must be weighed."[47] She then provides a list of traits for racial groups. Even though she was aware that individuals did not always fall into discrete racial types, she continued to use them and the AGRS required their use. While in Hawaii, Trotter also followed the collecting patterns common for her time of finding 'representative' samples of different races for skeletal collections. She wrote to Stewart that she would be able to obtain skeletons of native Hawaiians from a specific area.[48] Her only concern would be to check with the Bishop Museum before shipping them to St. Louis as museum specimens. Charles E. Snow, her predecessor at the AGRS in Hawaii, had assisted the Bishop Museum in collecting Hawaiian remains from a cemetery on Oahu.[49] Stewart's response was that the Smithsonian had skulls of Hawaiians, but not full skeletons, so "if you can salvage any specimens for science you have a right to do so. Be sure to keep a record of cultural associations."[50] I have found no record of whether she followed through. But apparently the careful concerns that Trotter and others had for the legal and rightful ownership of the Terry Collection of skeletons in the late 1960s did not apply to their potential plans for collecting the remains of native Hawaiians in the late 1940s.

Trotter was aware that races are not simple, discrete categories, but she also reinforced the use of race as a biological fact in scientific research. In this contradiction, Trotter was very much like her contemporaries, including individuals who were explicitly opposed to the race concept. Indeed, she was operating like many anthropologists do to this day, for a variety of practical reasons. Like others, Trotter also reinforced sex differences even when the data did not bear this out, in the very same papers. Certainly her academic and personal treatment of race and sex may have varied over time, just as her personal recognition of sexism had varied.

RACE, HAIR, AND APPLIED SCIENCE

Trotter's research and professional activities concerning hair were not only related to growth patterns, but also, unlike most of her skeletal research, usually directly involved race determination and variation. Trotter knew that hair was "considered by physical anthropologists to be one of the chief features for distinguishing between races."[51] For this reason, she had aimed to undertake such research since at least 1925 with her abandoned proposal for a National Research Council fellowship at Oxford correlating race with hair types and climate. But she and other anthropologists never did accomplish any large, comprehensive study correlating race and hair types. She had, however, published several articles describing the hair of populations (including White Americans, indigenous Australians, Iraqis, French Canadians, and even Peruvian mummies) and the hair of individuals (such as that of an Indian woman). To do this work, she also solicited and collected hair from global populations through her colleagues for decades. She looked at hair color, texture, and form. It seems she and others always believed the work would be valuable, but an actual project never took off. As she once commented to Charles Snow, while diplomatically declining to join him on a grant studying hair and race, "it's a terribly tedious job."[52] But in addition to the difficulty of such research, and despite her and other anthropologists' assumptions of the value of such work, there was just never enough evidence to merit it.

In the 1940s and 1950s, she and a former FBI agent who later completed a PhD in anatomy at Washington University, Oliver Duggins, attempted to study hair for the purposes of individual identification, as well as for age and race determination. Trotter even received a personal letter of thanks from the first FBI Director, J. Edgar Hoover, in 1945 for her contributions, though no specific research project was ever fully undertaken.[53] Despite the fact that her own research on this topic was lacking and existing research in anthropology was mostly anecdotal or based on small samples, Trotter directly applied her analyses of hair for race determination in a surprising undertaking. Various child welfare services from throughout Missouri and southern Illinois sought Trotter's expert advice in determining the races of infants and young children who were being placed for adoption. It is not clear how this consultation began, but she worked on at least 23 such cases between 1955 and 1969.

A child services worker would typically contact Trotter and then, partly at her request, provide detailed background on a child, the known mother, any 'alleged father', and other descriptions of family and circumstances. These details would focus on race and supposed racial physical features. The agencies sought to identify a child's race when they felt it was in question, for purposes of choosing their placement in an adoptive family. In uncertain cases, they wanted Trotter's outside, professional opinion. As one worker put it:

> Before placing any child with prospective adoptive parents, the agency informs the adopting couple of the baby's background so that they may determine if this is acceptable to them. Obviously, the desires of the adoptive parents must be considered, as adoption is a voluntary step on their part. We do not place children with applicants who tell us they cannot accept that child's heritage, be it a question of race, medical background, or whatever problem they feel doubt as to their acceptance. It is for this reason that we need to determine as far as possible a child's race and/or nationality before attempting to select a suitable home.[54]

The task was to make sure no child was placed with a family of a different race, and in the case of one child, a social worker claimed that "no negro couple would accept a child with her appearance; placement with a white family is equally impossible unless we know she is not of mixed blood."[55]

The process of adoption had undergone recent changes during this time period. By 1955, children who were adopted outnumbered, for the first time in the US, children who were institutionalized (at orphanages, for example). In 1957 in Missouri, laws began to pressure placement through adoption agencies instead of through independent means.[56] Social workers took on a higher authority, becoming selective in placing children by physical, racial, and other characteristics to "match" a child with an adoptive family that would resemble a biological family.[57] This endeavor was influenced by legal concerns. In one case from Boston, a Catholic woman was prevented from legally transferring her son to the Jewish family that had fostered him for 4 months, on the basis of their religion.[58] In New York, a family had to petition the courts for years after being refused permission to adopt a 4-year-old girl, whom they had fostered since she was 5 days old, because "she is blond and blue-eyed and they are swarthy Italian-Americans."[59] One adoptive family in Missouri returned a child after discovering that the baby's parents were both deaf, because they suspected she might also be deaf.[60] In Vermont, a judge denied the adoption of a 5-year-old girl who had one Black grandparent, citing his refusal to "make birth records show a Negro child with white parents."[61]

Anti-miscegenation laws of this time period, which prohibited interracial marriage and procreation, contributed to the social workers' avid interest in determining a child's race. Missouri had even enacted an additional provision that "an adoption may be set aside within five years when a person shall prove to be a member of a race, the members of which are prohibited by the laws of this state from marriage with members of the race to which the parents by adoption belong."[62] Missouri repealed its anti-miscegenation law in 1969, perhaps not coincidentally the same year as the last adoption case on which Trotter consulted. In 1968, the first few official "trans-racial" adoptions had already begun.[63] Apparently, international adoptions (or perhaps race combinations that were not considered Black and White) had not been subject to these laws, because there were at least a small number of children born in Japan and Korea who were adopted in Missouri following World War II and the Korean War, long before the repeal.[64]

This practice of anthropologists evaluating children for race in adoption cases was apparently also in place in another country which Trotter, perhaps hypocritically, had criticized. Under apartheid in South Africa in 1966, physical anthropologist Hertha de Villiers at the University of Witwatersrand examined, as was common practice, a baby for race. But, due to not receiving a definitive racial determination, the child had then spent months waiting for placement with a family.[65] De Villiers later adopted the baby and named her Phillippa, after colleague Phillip Tobias.

In the interest of finding long-term, legal homes for these children in Missouri, social workers were quite earnest in their endeavors to determine the race of a child prior to placement. The seriousness of these concerns was evident in at least one case Trotter consulted for, where a White foster mother became adamant that a baby be removed from her home as quickly as possible once she believed his skin was becoming darker.[66] The boy was moved to a Black foster family soon after. Adoption services wanted expert opinions in cases where they were uncertain of how the child would be culturally and legally perceived. Anthropology had identified itself as the authority on race, and Trotter had positioned herself as an expert on hair as a racial characteristic. From this position, she assisted social workers in their efforts to conform to both societal norms and the segregationist laws of the time.

The extremely detailed personal histories for the children which were provided to Trotter reflect the sincere worries of these social workers. In all of the cases with a known biological mother, she was described as 'Caucasian'. It seems that if a woman was considered Black, her child's race was not further questioned. Nationalities were specified for the woman's parents and often grandparents, her physical appearance, education, and marital status were described. Her medical, religious, and job histories were detailed. Furthermore, her alleged behavior and personality traits were given, particularly as related to the social workers' analysis of her sexual promiscuity and intelligence. The biological father was sometimes unknown, or for whatever reason was suspected to not be White.

To give an idea of the variety of backgrounds for these cases, the following are some examples. One set of adoptive parents was concerned that their child had a dark complexion, despite the known biological mother and father both being identified as Caucasian.[67] One baby was immediately placed for adoption by her White parents after the mother had been raped "by two Negro men" just under 9 months prior (and the social worker felt the need to note that this was "verified by police record").[68] Later, the White foster family received an unsolicited comment from a neighbor that "with that flat nose [the baby] might have come from Kinloch," which was the earliest African-American community incorporated in Missouri.[69] In one case the mother was a ninth grader who was "retarded and attended Special Education Classes," yet was somehow also described as "rather immature and it is possible that she is the type of person who is easily led and who could easily become involved with the less desirable types of people."[70] Another child was found abandoned in a parked car with no information known about his family history, for whom social workers sought an opinion on both his race and age.[71] One baby looked like "the child of two white parents" but his father was "known to be Negro;" in such a cultural dilemma, the service was worried to place him with either a Black or a White family.[72]

Along with this background information and hair samples, Trotter preferred to physically examine the child at Washington University, along with Oliver Duggins and a pediatrician when possible. They charged no fee for this service and were "anxious to help if we can" in order to expedite the placement of these children into successful, permanent homes.[73] They would inspect the body for skin coloration, presence or absence of a "Mongolian spot" (a slate gray birthmark), facial features, and would assess the hair macroscopically and microscopically for alleged racially identifying characteristics. Morphoscopic features included texture and color; microscopic features seem to have only consisted of assessment of "pigment clumping" and shape, as determined from a cross-sectional index. When the child could not be brought to St. Louis, Trotter would sometimes assess just a mailed hair clipping. Her response would include a summary of their findings.

In the final determination, Trotter regularly included a caveat such as, "I must emphasize that our help would constitute nothing more than an opinion. There is no scientific method for the determination of racial admixture" and that "both Dr. Duggins and I wish to emphasize, however, that determination of race, based on hair, is extremely difficult and always uncertain, particularly when the sample comes from a very young individual and the heritage is a mixed one. There is no characteristic, so far as is known, which is limited to one race. Rather, there is overlap of all characters between the races with certain ones occurring to a greater degree in one than in the others."[74] Trotter knew that races were not discrete categories and that no physical assessment could provide precisely the answers the social workers were seeking. She was very careful in expressing this to the adoption agencies. However, Trotter and her colleagues still provided determinations such as, "we are in complete agreement in the opinion that [the child] does not show evidence of Negroid ancestry."[75] For many responses, Trotter provided only an equivocal listing of all the characteristics that were observed.

Trotter almost invariably noted that determination of race in infants is particularly difficult. Some infants were so young that Trotter had to note that lanugo (the fine, soft hair present on many newborns) was "not as useful" as more mature, terminal hairs in determining race, though Trotter and Duggins still provided assessments in these cases anyway.[76] Trotter would often note that she would like to see children again when they were a few years older. Her interest in receiving updates on these children was worded less as a curiosity in their welfare or ultimate placement, and more so in assessing if and how her race determination may have changed with the child's increasing age. In a few cases, she was able to have this kind of follow-up, and she made notes to herself such as, "child has become more negroid" and that "characteristics which were barely suggestive of Negro admixture a year ago... are now quite definite."[77] She warned another social worker in regard to a baby with a White mother and Black father that "even though no Negro characteristics are apparent at this age, we could only say that they might appear as he grows older."[78] Indeed some of the social workers already expressed concerns about this possibility, one stating "I have heard somewhere that research has been done which proves that an infant can be no darker than his darkest grandparent. Is this really so and does it follow thru for the offsprings of the child?"[79] Trotter responded that "I can only say that this is generally believed but that I know of no specific long-term study bearing on this subject."[80]

The social workers' physical descriptions of the children were sometimes directly derived from racial stereotypes. One girl's hair was called "unmanageable" and "wiry."[81] Another infant arose apparent suspicion because he "responded to Negroes at the clinic."[82] For a hair sample from one baby, just one and a half months old, the child services worker asked Trotter to "notice the odor of this hair – [the baby] smells like this constantly, even when she is freshly bathed. The hair has a stronger odor than one notices on her, so perhaps the odor emanates from the hair."[83] The child's father was suspected to be "Negro and Indian." Trotter replied that she and others detected no odor (so, evidently they had actually justified this concern by smelling the hair), provided a summary of her findings, and indicated that "there is evidence to suggest an admixture of Caucasian and Negro characteristics."[84] Interestingly, the summary of findings Trotter presented relative to this infant's hair are very similar to those for another infant's hair who had a completely unknown father, and had come without such influencing language in the social worker's background information. But Trotter and Duggins's overall assessment for the other baby was a little bit more conservative, instead claiming that "a guarded conclusion would have to be that the hair is predominantly Caucasian but that it is impossible to rule out a trace of Negroid characteristics."[85] Trotter was certainly biased by the detailed background information provided to her, and in some cases her assessments reflect this bias.

Of course, Trotter and her colleagues were already working with a flawed and unproven hypothesis. Racial bias in these cases, and throughout much work in early physical anthropology, resulted in scientific error. Though anthropologists in the late 19th and early 20th centuries believed that hair held great promise for racial determination, it never fulfilled its perceived potential. Anthropologists had widely agreed that hair has, in Trotter's words, "long been considered to be one of the deciding criteria in the classification of races."[86] But they never found agreement on how to classify hair or exactly how it might correlate with race, the history of which Trotter herself described in 1939.[87] Trotter had rebuffed this as a problem even when in 1936 when one of her papers was rejected after receiving the critique that such studies should be deferred until better techniques for classifying hair were developed.[88]

Trotter remained, even later in life, reluctant to question the validity of the broad characterizations of hair texture, such as 'curly, kinky, straight, or wavy', particularly as were expected to correspond to particular populations. After listening to a description of a paper that criticized these ill-defined terms and that Trotter had recently peer-reviewed and recommended for rejection, Trotter's oral history interviewer in 1972 asked for a clarification. The interviewer wondered why indeed there were not better, more scientific terms for hair types. Trotter responded, "who's to say that hasn't been scientific?"[89] She went on to more clearly explain the specific shortcomings of the paper, and only conceded that the author perhaps had a point, but that he had not proven it. Instead of questioning the overall paradigm, Trotter pinpointed the (perhaps valid) shortcomings of the particular argument.

Anthropologist Emma Tarlo (2019) traced the history of studies on hair, particularly related to the collections of hair clippings of global populations now held in museums.[90] As Tarlo described it, "hair is a rebellious fibre."[91] She found that, paradoxically, anthropologists did not view hair's resistance to racialized categorization as evidence against the existence of race. So certain were they of the value of hair as a characteristic of race, and of the inherence of race, that they instead interpreted this as an incentive to develop more rigorous studies and methods to pinpoint hair as a racial determiner. That commitment, however, only led to a dead end. Koch, Jablonski, and Shriver (2018) studied Trotter's own collection of hair samples and found that hair shape and melanosome distribution did not distinguish hairs by geographic ancestry, and therefore recommended that such racial classifications as Trotter had used be excluded in forensic contexts.[92]

Publications in the *AJPA* on hair as a racial characteristic would decline in the 1960s and 1970s, with the last study of hair as specifically relates to race appearing in 1978.[93] Microscopic hair analysis to positively identify a single individual has been abandoned in legal cases. Starting in 2012, it prompted the FBI's largest post-conviction review of questioned forensic evidence, which found an extremely high number of wrongful convictions (approaching 100%) based on hair analyses for various purposes.[94] But broad claims that assessing characteristics of hair such as cross-sectional shape and pigmentation are useful as methods to not just to distinguish between racial groups, but also to identify individuals, have remained in the forensic literature until even recently.[95]

Trotter also received requests for racial determination from hair in other contexts. In 1959, Stewart wrote to Trotter after an FBI consultation that concerned the determination of race in a child with a known Korean mother and suspected "Negro GI father."[96] An assessment was made on a photo and hair sample only, and Stewart sought Trotter's thoughts on how reliable microscopic examination of hair might be in determining race, particularly in regard to "mixture." He hoped to use grant money to study this topic, though I do not see a record of that happening in any large-scale way. But clearly at this time, anthropologists working on forensic cases particularly still held out a great deal of untested and unproven faith in the usefulness of hair as a means of determining race.

Other requests were more specific, and one, in particular, is perplexing. In 1961, Wilton M. Krogman sent a letter to Trotter and Duggins detailing a recent story. A White man had come to Krogman asking to determine the race of his wife; after 11 years of marriage he had become suspicious that she was Black. The man's evidence included that she had recently admitted infidelity, took less care of her hygiene and the cleanliness of the apartment, and "smells like a Negro."[97] The man had covertly collected hair from his wife's hairbrush. Krogman seems to have found this story humorous and stated that he would owe Trotter and Duggins drinks the next time he saw them in return for the favor. Absurdly, Krogman did actually send along the hair sample. I found no record of if or how Trotter replied to Krogman's letter.

These consultations regarding hair for race determination fit within Trotter's other consulting and applied work within the community. She, like many other physical anthropologists, including Stewart, consulted on criminal investigations involving skeletal remains. In just one example from 1964, she provided a biological profile (age at death, sex, and race) for the remains of a woman unearthed during a construction project in St. Louis, which helped identify the victim.[98] In at least some cases, these anthropologists may have been quite zealous in this contribution, as evidenced by Stewart's self-congratulation in a handwritten update to Trotter that he "got the death sentence" after testifying in a recent murder trial.[99] In one more casual circumstance, Stewart advised a young Jewish man who was worried about marrying a woman he had met while stationed in Puerto Rico, because his friends believed she might have some Black ancestry. Stewart judged from photographs alone that she "'was a good Latin type'," and so the man should feel free to marry her.[100]

Trotter also received other types of requests for help or guidance in regard to racial determination and variability, for both social curiosity and academic purposes. In 1966, an instructor at Ohio University asked for Trotter's and several other anthropologists' assistance in determining for a graduate student's thesis "why Negroes in general have greater difficulty in learning to swim than Caucasians. We believe this to be due to anatomical differences and not to any lack of motor ability or learning capacity per se; nor to any lack of opportunity, since our basis for comparison is whites who have also lacked opportunity."[101] Trotter responded that she had no expertise in this, since she studied bones, but commented that "everybody in the department was especially interested in learning that Negroes in general have greater difficulty in learning to swim than Caucasians, but no one of us has any idea of the reason."[102] The comment is a bit baffling, because it is unclear whether Trotter and her colleagues had never heard this racial stereotype, if they actually believed that the graduate student had acquired reliable data confirming this myth, or both. Other language in these informal, though professional, interactions also confirm that she assumed a biological basis for race. To one physician who wondered if the alleged higher density of the bones of Black individuals in Trotter's 1960 paper could be caused by vocation or musculature, Trotter responded that "work habits may play a small part in increased density but the differences between Whites and Negros is a more deep seeded [sic] characteristic than can be attributed to activity during life."[103]

Perhaps Sherwood Washburn had already spelled it out clearly in a 1956 letter to Trotter in which he politely criticized part of her already published article, coauthored with Duggins and Frank M. Setzler, on the hair of indigenous Australians. He believed their argument tacitly relied on the "typological fallacy" of "three primary races, which is clearly nonsense."[104] He continued, stating that most contributions to the *AJPA* are "too specialized to consider the basic assumptions on which they are based. It is because the fundamentals do not get discussed that physical anthropology can keep doing the darndest things." It is interesting that Trotter allowed unproven assumptions about race to pass muster, when in other cases, like in her basic research on hair growth and bone mineral content, establishing the fundamentals was so important to her. Trotter, like many of her contemporaries, apparently held multiple, conflicting views on race, most of which at that time were accepted without scrutiny. Her views affected not just her personal and professional relationships, but also her research and its more widespread applications, such as stature estimations, criminal consult cases, osteoporosis screening, and adoption decisions. And despite Trotter's interests in the history of anthropology and of women in science, this curiosity did not extend into the history of social and scientific racism. But satisfactory coverage of her life necessarily includes the concepts that Trotter and the discipline of physical anthropology were deeply immersed in, even if they did not properly acknowledge them or recognize the value of their investigation at the time.

NOTES

1 Susan C. Antón, Ripan S. Malhi, and Agustín Fuentes, "Race and Diversity in US Biological Anthropology: A Decade of AAPA Initiatives," *American Journal of Physical Anthropology* 165 (2018): 158–180; Jennifer K. Wagner, Joon-Ho Yu, Jayne O. Ifekwunigwe, Tanya M. Harrell, Michael J. Bamshad, and

Charmaine D. Royal, "Anthropologists' Views on Race, Ancestry, and Genetics," *American Journal of Physical Anthropology* 162, no. 2 (2017): 318–327.

2 "Proceedings of the Twenty-fourth Annual Meeting of the American Association of Physical Anthropologists," *American Journal of Physical Anthropology* 13, no. 2 (1955): 377–378.

3 Letter, J. Lawrence Angel to William L. Strauss, June 6, 1955, series 3, box 4, folder 7, Mildred Trotter Papers, Becker Medical Library, Washington University School of Medicine.

4 Lesley M. Rankin-Hill and Michael L. Blakey, "W. Montague Cobb (1904–1990): Physical Anthropologist, Anatomist, and Activist," *American Anthropologist* 96 (1994): 74–96, p. 83.

5 Marta P. Alfonso and Michael A. Little (translation and editing), "Juan Comas's Summary History of the American Association of Physical Anthropologists (1928–1968)," *American Journal of Physical Anthropology* 128, no. S41 (2005): 163–195.

6 "Proceedings of the Twenty-Fifth Annual Meeting of the American Association of Physical Anthropologists," *American Journal of Physical Anthropology* 14, no. 2 (1956): 366.

7 "Proceedings of the Twenty-fifth Annual Meeting of the American Association of Physical Anthropologists," *American Journal of Physical Anthropology* 14, no. 2 (1956): 366–367.

8 Letter, John Gillin to Trotter, April 8, 1956, series 3, box 6, folder 3, Mildred Trotter Papers, Becker Medical Library, Washington University School of Medicine.

9 Letter, Trotter to T.D. Stewart, March 19, 1956, series 3, box 7, folder 19, Mildred Trotter Papers, Becker Medical Library, Washington University School of Medicine.

10 Sherwood L. Washburn, "Section of Anthropology: The New Physical Anthropology," *Transactions of the New York Academy of Sciences* 13, no. 7 Series II (1951): 298–304.

11 Leonard Lieberman, "Gender and the Deconstruction of the Race Concept," *American Anthropologist* 99, no. 3 (1997): 545–558.

12 Leonard Lieberman, "Gender and the Deconstruction of the Race Concept," *American Anthropologist* 99, no. 3 (1997): 545–558, pp. 549, 551.

13 Goldine C. Gleser, *Getting It All* (Seattle, WA: Keepsake Editions, 2000), p. 36.

14 Mary Lucas Powell, Della Collins Cook, Georgieann Bogdan, Jane E. Buikstra, Mario M. Castro, Patrick D. Horne, David R. Hunt, Richard T. Koritzer, Sheila Ferraz Mendonqa de Souza, Mary Kay Sandford, Laurie Saunders, Glaucia Aparecida Malerba Sene, Lynne Sullivan, and John J. Swetnam, "Invisible hands: Women

in Bioarchaeology," in *Bioarchaeology: The Contextual Analysis of Human Remains*, ed. Jane Buikstra and Lane Beck (Routledge, 2017).

15 Leonard Lieberman, "Gender and the Deconstruction of the Race Concept," *American Anthropologist* 99, no. 3 (1997): 550.

16 See, for example, Mildred Trotter, "The Vertebral Column in Whites and in American Negroes," *American Journal of Physical Anthropology* 13, no. 1 (1929): 95–107; and Mildred Trotter, "The Level of Termination of the Popliteal Artery in the White and the Negro," *American Journal of Physical Anthropology* 27, no. 1 (1940): 109–118.

17 Rachel J. Watkins, "Biohistorical Narratives of Racial Difference in the American Negro: Notes toward a Nuanced History of American Physical Anthropology," *Current Anthropology* 53, no. S5 (2012): S196–S209, S197.

18 Sung C. Choi and Mildred Trotter, "A Statistical Study of the Multivariate Structure and Race-sex Differences of American White and Negro Fetal Skeletons," *American Journal of Physical Anthropology* 33, no. 3 (1970): 307–312.

19 Letter, Trotter to Norman E. Waldron, March 4, 1949, series 3, box 4, folder 16, Mildred Trotter Papers, Becker Medical Library, Washington University School of Medicine.

20 Mildred Trotter and Goldine C. Gleser, "Estimation of Stature from Long Bones of American Whites and Negroes," *American Journal of Physical Anthropology* 10, no. 4 (1952): 463–514, p. 466.

21 Mildred Trotter and Goldine C. Gleser, "Estimation of Stature from Long Bones of American Whites and Negroes," *American Journal of Physical Anthropology* 10, no. 4 (1952): 463–514, p. 468.

22 Paul Huston Stevenson, "On Racial Differences in Stature Long Bone Regression Formulae, with Special Reference to Stature Reconstruction Formulae for the Chinese," *Biometrika* (1929): 303–321.

23 Aleš Hrdlička, *Practical Anthropometry*, T.D. Stewart, ed., (Philadelphia: *The Wistar Institute of Anatomy and Biology*, 1947); C. Wesley Dupertuis and John A. Hadden, "On the Reconstruction of Stature from Long Bones," *American Journal of Physical Anthropology* 9, no. 1 (1951): 15–54.

24 Mildred Trotter and Goldine C. Gleser, "Estimation of Stature from Long Bones of American Whites and Negroes," *American Journal of Physical Anthropology* 10, no. 4 (1952): 463–514, p. 510.

25 Letter, Trotter to Joseph Velo, October 16, 1968, series 13, box 8, folder 7, Mildred Trotter Papers, Becker Medical Library, Washington University School of Medicine.

26 Mildred Trotter and Goldine C. Gleser, "Estimation of Stature from Long Bones of American Whites and Negroes," *American Journal of Physical Anthropology* 10, no. 4 (1952): 463–514, p. 513.
27 David R. Hunt and John Albanese, "History and Demographic Composition of the Robert J. Terry Anatomical Collection," *American Journal of Physical Anthropology* 127 (2005): 406–417, p. 414.
28 Letter, Goldine Gleser to Trotter, July 19, 1973, series 3, box 6, folder 6; and letter, Trotter to T.D. Stewart, July 27, 1973, series 3, box 6, folder 6, Mildred Trotter Papers, Becker Medical Library, Washington University School of Medicine.
29 Letter, Trotter to T.D. Stewart, May 21, 1954, series 13, box 6, folder 11, Mildred Trotter Papers, Becker Medical Library, Washington University School of Medicine.
30 Stephen D. Ousley and Richard L. Jantz, "Fordisc 3 and Statistical Methods for Estimating Sex and Ancestry," in *Companion to Forensic Anthropology*, ed. Dennis Dirkmaat (West Sussex: Wiley, 2015).
31 Mildred Trotter, interview by Estelle Brodman, May 19, 1972 and May 23, 1972, transcript, Becker Medical Library, Washington University School of Medicine.
32 Aleš Hrdlička, "Physical Anthropology: Its Scope and Aims: Its History and Present Status in America," *American Journal of Physical Anthropology* 1 (1918): 3–23, pp. 18–19.
33 Matt Cartmill, "The Status of the Race Concept in Physical Anthropology," *American Anthropologist* 100, no. 3 (1998): 651–660, p. 554.
34 John Albanese, Stephanie E. Osley, and Andrew Tuck, "Do Group-Specific Equations Provide the Best Estimates of Stature?" *Forensic Science International* 261 (2016): 154–158.
35 Marc R. Feldesman and Robert L. Fountain, "'Race' specificity and the femur/stature ratio," *American Journal of Physical Anthropology* 100, no. 2 (1996): 207–224.
36 Stephen Ousley, Richard Jantz, and Donna Freid, "Understanding Race and Human Variation: Why Forensic Anthropologists are Good at Identifying Race," *American Journal of Physical Anthropology* 139, no. 1 (2009): 68–76.
37 Mildred Trotter, George E. Broman, and Roy R. Peterson, "Densities of Bones of White and Negro Skeletons." *Journal of Bone and Joint Surgery* 42-A (1960): 50–58, p. 50.
38 Wesley Critz George,."The Biology of the Race Problem," Report Prepared for the Governor of Alabama (1962), p. 14.
39 Mildred Trotter and Barbara B. Hixon, "Sequential Changes in Weight, Density, and Percentage Ash Weight of Human Skeletons from an Early Fetal Period through Old Age," *The Anatomical Record* 179, no. 1 (1974): 1–18.

40 Alan H. Goodman, "Bred in the Bone?," *The Sciences* 37, no. 2 (1997): 20–25.
41 Mildred Trotter and Barbara B. Hixon, "Sequential changes in Weight, Density, and Percentage Ash Weight of Human Skeletons from an Early Fetal Period through Old Age," *The Anatomical Record* 179, no. 1 (1974): 1.
42 Susan Helene Scherf Wasserman and Uriel S. Barzel, "Osteoporosis: The State of the Art in 1987: A Review," *Seminars in Nuclear Medicine* 17 (1987): 285.
43 Alan H. Goodman, "Bred in the Bone?," *The Sciences* 37, no. 2 (1997): 20–25; and Anne Fausto-Sterling, "The Bare Bones of Race," *Social Studies of Science* 38 (2008): 657–694.
44 Taunya L. Banks, "Funding Race as Biology: The Relevance of Race in Medical Research," *Minnesota Journal of Law, Science, and Technology* 12, no. 2 (2011): 571–618.
45 Sandra Soo-Jin Lee, Joanna Mountain, Barbara Koenig, Russ Altman, Melissa Brown, Albert Camarillo, Luca Cavalli-Sforza et al., "The Ethics of Characterizing Difference: Guiding Principles on Using Racial Categories in Human Genetics," *Genome Biology* 9, no. 7 (2008): 404, Statement 3.
46 Mildred Trotter, "Septal Apertures in the Humerus of American Whites and Negroes," *American Journal of Physical Anthropology* 19, no. 2 (1934): 213–227, p. 226.
47 Document, Mildred Trotter, "Operations at Central Identification Laboratory, A.G.R.S." series 5, box 15, folder 5, Mildred Trotter Papers, Becker Medical Library, Washington University School of Medicine.
48 Letter, Trotter to T.D. Stewart, August 6, 1948, series 3, box 7, folder 17, Mildred Trotter Papers, Becker Medical Library, Washington University School of Medicine.
49 Donald S. Marshall and Charles E. Snow, "An Evaluation of Polynesian Craniology," *American Journal of Physical Anthropology* 14, no. 3 (1956): 405–427.
50 Letter, Stewart to Trotter, August 10, 1948, series 3, box 7, folder 17, Mildred Trotter Papers, Becker Medical Library, Washington University School of Medicine.
51 Draft, Trotter, "The Department of Anatomy in My Time," p. 45, no date, series 1, box 1, Mildred Trotter Papers, Becker Medical Library, Washington University School of Medicine.
52 Letter, Trotter to Charles Snow, no date (1963), series 13, box 6, folder 9, Mildred Trotter Papers, Becker Medical Library, Washington University School of Medicine.
53 Letter, J. Edgar Hoover to Trotter, November 27, 1945, series 3, box 5, folder 41, Mildred Trotter Papers, Becker Medical Library, Washington University School of Medicine.

54 Letter, Terry Fillmore to Trotter, September 19, 1968, series 13, box 6, folder 4, Mildred Trotter Papers, Becker Medical Library, Washington University School of Medicine.
55 Letter, Hazel B. Hamilton to Trotter, December 9, 1955, series 13, box 6, folder 4, Mildred Trotter Papers, Becker Medical Library, Washington University School of Medicine.
56 Clarissa Start, "Trend to Adoptions through Agencies," *St. Louis Post-Dispatch*, January 22, 1957, 3D.
57 Michelle Kahan, "Put Up on Platforms: A History of Twentieth Century Adoption Policy on the United States," *Journal of Sociology and Social Welfare* 33 (2006): 51–57, p. 61.
58 "Law May Bar Return of Catholic Baby," *St. Louis Post-Dispatch*, August 26, 1951, 3D.
59 "New York Judge for Adoption of Child in Hair Color Case," *St. Louis Post-Dispatch*, January 7, 1967, 3A.
60 Clarissa Start, "Trend to Adoptions through Agencies," *St. Louis Post-Dispatch*, January 22, 1957, 3D.
61 "Judge Calls Girl Negro, Bans Adoption by Whites," *St. Louis Post-Dispatch*, October 19, 1961, 14D.
62 Pearl S. Buck, *Children for Adoption* (New York: Random House, 1964), 138–139. See also Randall Kennedy, *Interracial Intimacies: Sex, Marriage, Identity, and Adoption* (New York: Random House, 2003).
63 Sally Bixby Defty, "Trans-Racial Adoptions Rise Here," *St. Louis Post-Dispatch*, September 14, 1969, 3G.
64 "St. Louis Church Woman Served Orphans of Japan and Korea," *St. Louis Post-Dispatch*, December 13, 1958, 5A; "Woman Here Glows over Waif Airman Son Adopted in Korea," *St. Louis Post-Dispatch*, April 24, 1956, 3A.
65 Mike Alfred (interviewer and editor), *Twelve + One, Some Jo'burg Poets: Their Artistic Lives and Poetry* (Braamfontein: Botsotso, 2017), p. 35.
66 Letter, Larry A. Propst to Trotter, January 31, 1964, series 13, box 6, folder 4, Mildred Trotter Papers, Becker Medical Library, Washington University School of Medicine.
67 Letter, Shirley E. McArthur to Trotter, September 21, 1962, series 13, box 6, folder 4, Mildred Trotter Papers, Becker Medical Library, Washington University School of Medicine.
68 Letter, Louise Fairchild to Trotter, July 5, 1960, series 13, box 6, folder 4, Mildred Trotter Papers, Becker Medical Library, Washington University School of Medicine.
69 Letter, Louise Fairchild to Trotter, July 5, 1960, series 13, box 6, folder 4, Mildred Trotter Papers, Becker Medical Library, Washington University School of Medicine.

70 Letter, Cynthia Gieringer to Trotter, October 17, 1967, series 13, box 6, folder 4, Mildred Trotter Papers, Becker Medical Library, Washington University School of Medicine.
71 Letter, Larry A. Propst to Trotter, January 31, 1964, series 13, box 6, folder 4, Mildred Trotter Papers, Becker Medical Library, Washington University School of Medicine.
72 Letter, Betty Gilmore to Trotter, March 27, 1957, series 13, box 6, folder 4, Mildred Trotter Papers, Becker Medical Library, Washington University School of Medicine.
73 Letter, Trotter to Cynthia Gieringer, November 1, 1967, series 13, box 6, folder 4, Mildred Trotter Papers, Becker Medical Library, Washington University School of Medicine.
74 Letter, Trotter to Mona Platter, September 10, 1956; and Trotter to Jeanne Nahm, April 28, 1969, series 13, box 6, folder 4, Mildred Trotter Papers, Becker Medical Library, Washington University School of Medicine.
75 Letter, Trotter to Cynthia Gieringer, September 21 ,1967, series 13, box 6, folder 4, Mildred Trotter Papers, Becker Medical Library, Washington University School of Medicine.
76 Letter, Trotter to Grace B. Nelson, March 16, 1965, series 13, box 6, folder 4, Mildred Trotter Papers, Becker Medical Library, Washington University School of Medicine.
77 Letter, Trotter to Leon Foster October 15, 1959 [with handwritten notes by Trotter]; and Letter, Trotter to Evelyn Johnston, October 15, 1959, series 13, box 6, folder 4, Mildred Trotter Papers, Becker Medical Library, Washington University School of Medicine.
78 Letter, Trotter to Betty Gilmore, April 1, 1957, series 13, box 6, folder 4, Mildred Trotter Papers, Becker Medical Library, Washington University School of Medicine.
79 Letter, Kathleen Hassenplue to Trotter, April 17, 1964, series 13, box 6, folder 4, Mildred Trotter Papers, Becker Medical Library, Washington University School of Medicine.
80 Letter, Trotter to Kathleen Hassenplue, May 13, 1964, series 13, box 6, folder 4, Mildred Trotter Papers, Becker Medical Library, Washington University School of Medicine.
81 Letter, Ingrid Reuter to Trotter, February 2, 1965, series 13, box 6, folder 4, Mildred Trotter Papers, Becker Medical Library, Washington University School of Medicine.
82 Letter, Larry A Propst to Trotter, January 31, 1964, series 13, box 6, folder 4, Mildred Trotter Papers, Becker Medical Library, Washington University School of Medicine.
83 Letter, Barbara Clemons to Trotter, January 29, 1965, series 13, box 6, folder 4, Mildred Trotter Papers, Becker Medical Library, Washington University School of Medicine.

84 Letter, Trotter to Barbara Clemons. February 3, 1965, series 13, box 6, folder 4, Mildred Trotter Papers, Becker Medical Library, Washington University School of Medicine.
85 Letter, Trotter to Grace B. Nelson, March 16, 1965, series 13, box 6, folder 4, Mildred Trotter Papers, Becker Medical Library, Washington University School of Medicine.
86 Mildred Trotter, "A Review of the Classification of Hair," *American Journal of Physical Anthropology* 24, no. 1 (1938): 105–126, p. 105.
87 Mildred Trotter, "Classifications of Hair Color," *American Journal of Physical Anthropology* 25 no. 2 (1939): 237–260.
88 Letter, Henry Field to Trotter, May 13, 1936, series 2, box 2, folder 37; and Letter, Trotter to Henry Field, June 3, 1936, Mildred Trotter Papers, Becker Medical Library, Washington University School of Medicine.
89 Mildred Trotter, interview by Estelle Brodman, May 19, 1972 and May 23, 1972, audio, Becker Medical Library, Washington University School of Medicine.
90 Emma Tarlo, "Racial Hair: The Persistence and Resistance of a Category," *Journal of the Royal Anthropological Institute* 25, no. 2 (2019): 324–348.
91 Emma Tarlo, "Racial Hair: The Persistence and Resistance of a Category," *Journal of the Royal Anthropological Institute* 25, no. 2 (2019): 324–348, p. 346.
92 Koch, Sandra, Nina Jablonski, and Mark D. Shriver, "Reanalysis of the Trotter Collection for a Study on Variation in Human Hair," abstract, *American Journal of Physical Anthropology* 165, no. S65 (2018): 143.
93 The article is Daniel B. Hrdy, "Analysis of Hair Samples of Mummies from Semna South (Sudanese Nubia)," *American Journal of Physical Anthropology* 49, no. 2 (1978): 277–282.
94 FBI Testimony on Microscopic Hair Analysis Contained Errors in at Least 90 Percent of Cases in Ongoing Review, FBI (April 20, 2015), https://www.fbi.gov/news/pressrel/press-releases/fbi-testimony-on-microscopic-hair-analysis-contained-errors-in-at-least-90-percent-of-cases-in-ongoing-review.
95 For example, Robert R. Ogle Jr and Michelle J. Fox, *Atlas of Human Hair: Microscopic Characteristics* (Boca Raton, FL: CRC Press, 2017); and Cary T. Oien, "Forensic Hair Comparison: Background Information for Interpretation," *FBI Forensic Science Communications* 11, no. 2 (April 2009).
96 Letter, T.D. Stewart to Trotter, November 24, 1959, series 13, box 6, folder 12, Mildred Trotter Papers, Becker Medical Library, Washington University School of Medicine.

97 Letter, W.M. Krogman to Trotter, July 13, 1960, series 13, box 46, folder 8, Mildred Trotter Papers, Becker Medical Library, Washington University School of Medicine.
98 Letter, Curtis Brostron to Trotter, September 30, 1964, series 3, box 7, folder 5, Mildred Trotter Papers, Becker Medical Library, Washington University School of Medicine.
99 Letter, T. Dale Stewart to Trotter, December 20, 1948, series 3, box 7, folder 17, Mildred Trotter Papers, Becker Medical Library, Washington University School of Medicine.
100 Virginia Irwin, "Smithsonian: More than Super Museum," *St. Louis Post-Dispatch*, January 22, 1948, 3D.
101 Letter, B.L. Allen to Chairman of the Department of Anatomy, July 5 ,1966, series 13, box 1, folder 1, Mildred Trotter Papers, Becker Medical Library, Washington University School of Medicine.
102 Letter, Trotter to B.L. Allen, July 7, 1966, series 13, box 1, folder 1, Mildred Trotter Papers, Becker Medical Library, Washington University School of Medicine.
103 Letter, Trotter to William C. Thomas, November 23, 1964, series 13, box 7, folder 1, Mildred Trotter Papers, Becker Medical Library, Washington University School of Medicine.
104 Letter, Sherwood Washburn to Trotter, September 15, 1956, series 13, box 1, folder 8, Mildred Trotter Papers, Becker Medical Library, Washington University School of Medicine.

CHAPTER 9

Later Years

Even if Trotter did not recognize every topic that would become of interest to others, she did leave a trail so that all these subjects could later be discovered. Charles Danforth had encouraged her to save work for decades after she thought she needed it, though she stated that "I'm afraid I haven't always followed his advice."[1] One step that Trotter did take was to document her experiences in an oral history, from her perspective, late in her career. In 1972, Trotter was interviewed over 2 days by Washington University's Bernard Becker Medical Library historian, Estelle Brodman, for an oral history project designed to preserve personal accounts of faculty experiences.[2] The contents of her oral history have been woven throughout this entire book. The recording is approximately 1.5 hours long, with variable, but overall extremely poor, audio quality. This oral history gives an otherwise inaccessible window into Trotter's mannerisms and brings her words to life.

Trotter speaks briskly, but mindfully, with a neutral American accent that is easily intelligible. Her style is very matter-of-fact and unpretentious. Though she was not soft-spoken, she has a somewhat wavery voice and frequently clears her throat, being at that point 73 years old. She and Brodman enjoyed coffee and cake as they talked. Trotter's frequent laughter tends to be quick and choppy and is immediately blended into continued speech. Sometimes a breathy voice or short pauses indicate just a smile. The transcript of the conversations is not a perfect documentation of the audio. Sometimes it paraphrases, clarifies, omits, and appears out of chronological order, but it is an overall representative record of the conversations. It appears as though she, Brodman, and an archivist in 1985 contributed to the many edits and clarifications made to the written version of the conversation. Among more significant differences, there were some small, but amusing, omissions to the transcript. Trotter is occasionally dubious as to whether certain topics they discuss would actually be of any interest to listeners ("you know you don't want this stuff"), but she notes that they were having fun talking either way. She also made an aside, after criticizing the condition of

DOI: 10.4324/9781003252818-9

the skeletal collection at Case Western Reserve University, that "I hope the Cleveland people don't ever hear this." And when Brodman asked what Trotter's plans were for the future, she joked that "I'm still working on the Nobel Prize," before launching into a detailed description of her macaque bone weight project.[3]

This sense of humor, ability to give and take jabs, and enjoyment of phrasing is also evident throughout all of Trotter's correspondence. During World War II, and presumably due to rationing of materials, Trotter discovered one day that her tires were stolen and her car was propped up on cinder blocks outside the medical school. At least 37 such tire thefts had taken place within a few days.[4] She quipped that the ride home she received was her "only experience in a police car."[5] In 1949, Trotter replied to a former colleague in Hawaii that "knowledge of the existence of San Veno has not reached this part of the country and I am endeavoring not to mention it. Please don't put it in a letter again because it just might leak out in some way and get on my new car. That would remind me of too many painful experiences" [referring to San Veino, a disinfectant fluid used during embalming].[6] She and Stewart regularly joked back and forth about their extensive and rapid correspondence. Once he questioned her, "do you really worry about people's reactions to your ideas or do you just like to get letters so that the mailman will think you are important?"[7] She retorted that she didn't care what the mailman thought, but just to make sure he did not get the wrong idea, Stewart should address all future mail to a man in the department or to her secretary.[8] When using Stewart's recommendations for a letter to an Army General, she flattered him by writing that "everything you do is good and if I have made sassy remarks to you I here-by take them all back."[9] And while waiting for a response to her offer of her macaque skeletal collection to the Smithsonian in 1978, Trotter prodded Stewart to intervene: "tell him the life expectancy of my age category is almost nil and these skeletons won't get sent if I die tomorrow."[10]

When writing to Wu Rukang, who had changed the English spelling of his name since she had last written to him, she wrote "isn't it good of me to reform my spelling of your name? Even at my age I can make a change!"[11] And to Frank Spencer, in reference to his dissertation on Hrdlička, she questioned the tentative subtitle: "What do you mean by 'The Anatomy of the Man'? Wasn't his body cremated? I suspect my question will demonstrate to you my literal mindedness."[12] While discussing her bone weight and density studies, Trotter noted "I would like to have denser bones myself."[13]

Trotter enjoyed cooking, mainly for the fun of experimentation, and saved a recipe for barium molasses cookies, complete with a warning to not add baking soda.[14] She even tried her hand at Chinese cuisine after her 1979 trip to China.[15] She also seems to be a fan of some now-uncommon idioms, writing that something "warms the cockles of my heart," and that a colleague is "going great guns."[16] During times of relative hardship too, she maintained a clear perspective and sense of humor. In 1978, a jewelry case filled with items of high sentimental, if not also monetary, value (including a watch given to her by her parents for her high school graduation) was stolen from her suitcase during a train ride. In response, Trotter wrote that she was "trying to be philosophical about losing only material things."[17]

Her words to close colleagues also occasionally reveal anxiety and sometimes perfectionism or cautiousness, which is perhaps expectable for someone with such a high-achieving career. One news article called her a "quiet-spoken perfectionist."[18] She often expressed it with that same humor. To Stewart regarding some mysterious topic, she wrote, "My next subject is the worry which is now making me bald headed. I can't get any grayer."[19] She also asked Stewart, while in the throes of her American Association of Physical Anthropology (AAPA) Presidency, for "any other advice that will help me keep my shirt on."[20] Writing to Larry Angel after she accidentally sent a speech draft directly to the *American Journal of Physical Anthropology (AJPA)* publisher she signed off, "Yours in distress."[21] During their meticulous draft revisions ahead of the difficult 1958 stature article, Trotter brooded to Gleser, "Will this ever end?/Yours in a feeble state."[22] Gleser then encouraged Trotter, insisting that she should "stop getting yourself into a stew over minor questions of wording. I think maybe you are procrastinating because you are afraid to send it to Russell [Newman]. Our reputations are not at stake because of the choice of a word. Let us get on with it! (All said with a smile though I can't draw cute little pictures like you do.)"[23] Sometimes Trotter simply expressed exasperation: "How do I get myself into these situations!"[24] She was also a lifelong blusher, which may have made it difficult to conceal some of these responses.

But Trotter was also firm, and she did not hesitate to assert herself in personal and professional matters. As she wrote once, "I hate to be a nuisance, but here I am again."[25] In 1936, Henry Field had asked her to contribute a chapter about the hair of Arabs for a Field Museum publication. When he sent her the final monograph which excluded Trotter's chapter, he apologized that the editor had found it to be of insufficient quality for this purpose, and Field sent along some hair samples as consolation.[26] Trotter responded that, since her paper was questioned, she had sent it to Charles Danforth to review, who instead felt it should be published in full. In light of this, she asked that the Field Museum pay for the expensive tables Field had originally requested for inclusion in its *AJPA* publication.[27] Field paid for it out of his own pocket. In 1956, she corrected Stewart on his terminology of broadly the "pubic symphysis" when he was referring specifically to the "symphyseal surface of the pubis" in a publication. She wondered if he agreed, or if he thought she was just being a "fussy old maid."[28]

To some, Trotter may have even come across as intimidating. One former student recalled that

> both Mildred Trotter and [associate professor of biochemistry] Ethel Ronzoni were considered formidable. It took me a little time to realize that this was kind of an exterior...but they both had this brusque, slightly aggressive, challenging way of talking so that you felt always that they weren't sure you really measured up... I got along fine with both of them, though it took a little time for me to have enough confidence to talk to them.[29]

When, in 1977, she noticed that her name and that of another colleague had been removed from the 12th edition of American Men and Women of Science (which had only changed its title to include women in 1971), Trotter wrote to the editor asking, "what is considered to be 'no apparent activity'?" and went on to detail her extensive continuing service and publications, ending with "how can this mistake be set right?"[30] And in 1975, Trotter noticed that a new car title had never arrived. It had been mistakenly put in the name of her nephew, Robert J. Trotter, whom she had requested to be listed as the secondary co-owner. Because of this expectation to place a man's name ahead of a woman's regardless of the circumstances, the title had been returned to sender in the mail. When she discovered the cause, she wrote to the state title administrator, wondering "why in the world" they would put the car in his name and clarified that "the purpose of this letter is to ask you to correct your mistake and to return my dollar."[31]

With retirement, Trotter wrote to Gleser that "I'm not finding the days longer, but I am finding the years shorter."[32] She claimed in her oral history to have no real hobbies of note, but she was indeed a devoted symphony patron, active birdwatcher and member of the Audubon Society (and for 5 years a board member), swimmer, and she enjoyed privately singing. She felt that her interest in birds was stimulated by Ann Haven Morgan, and fortified by Robert J. Terry.[33] She enjoyed keeping plants because, as she stated "that's the farmer in me."[34]

She also seems to have had a rich social life and kept in close contact with her family in Pennsylvania. During visits to her brother's farm, she enjoyed paring apples and taking long walks. Her nephew, James, remembers eagerly hoping for toys at Christmas, but always receiving a

Trotter birdwatching with binoculars, October 1958. VC170-i170033, Becker Medical Library, Washington University School of Medicine.

book from his Aunt Mamie instead.[35] Her great-nephew David remembers her as being "so, so full of energy" and infatuated with nature.[36] She also continued to invite family members out to tour St. Louis when they turned 16.[37] David remembers his trip from 1980, when his Aunt Mamie wanted to expose him to something other than farm life. They attended the symphony (for which she had small opera glasses), botanical gardens, and an art museum where he saw a Monet painting and bought prints, which he framed and has given to his daughters. David noted her emphasis on starting the day with a nutritious meal, and that she had two very hard twin beds in her room, which she believed were better for one's back. On a tour of the anatomy department, Aunt Mamie explained her previous work with the Army identifying the remains of war dead.

Despite her protestations that she was unexceptional, she also knew that for her, "life hasn't been so dull. I haven't been lazy."[38] Throughout her later years, Trotter found more opportunities to combine her work with travel. In 1963, Trotter spent those 3 months in a visiting professorship at Makerere University in Uganda, training young surgeons for their specialty boards as part of the Rockefeller Foundation's Medical

Samuel L. Clark, Louis Leakey, and Mildred Trotter, January 18, 1968. VC170-i170181, Becker Medical Library, Washington University School of Medicine.

and Natural Sciences program. Though this was only a short time, she followed the young men's careers for years, noting that "I'm interested in the welfare of every single one of those men."[39] During this appointment in Uganda she visited Raymond Dart at the University of Witwatersrand in South Africa. She officially retired in 1967, but remained professionally active, keeping her office at Washington University.[40] She also served as Associate Editor for the *AJPA* in 1944, 1956–1960, and 1968–1972, and maintained a grant from the US Public Health Service until 1976. In the early 1980s she served on Washington University's Human Studies Committee, which oversaw the approvals of research involving human subjects.[41] She also took undergraduate courses in sociocultural anthropology, archaeology, art, and music. And she continued to guest lecture in the anatomy department.

Trotter received honorary degrees from the Western College for Women (1956), Mount Holyoke (1960), and Washington University (1980). As she stated to Stewart, "I was terribly excited about it [the Mount Holyoke honorary degree] but I am realizing more and more how little they mean. Nevertheless, it was fun."[42] And yet, Virginia Apgar (of the Apgar Score for newborns) congratulated Trotter on her honorary degree from Mount Holyoke, noting that when she first heard the news from a friend, she was so positively stunned that she almost crashed her car.[43] In 1975, Washington University endowed a lectureship in her name to bring a scientist who is a woman to the University each year. In 1979, the medical school started a scholarship in her name for students in financial need, funded by her former students.[44] Since 1977 the

American Association of Physical Anthropologists has dedicated one of its four student awards in her honor, the Mildred Trotter Prize.

In 1977, she traveled to South America and, though she was in her late 70s, a former student who accompanied her on the trip felt he could not keep up with her. She knew many colleagues along the way and had looked up historical background information in advance on every place they visited.[45] She was able to visit the Galapagos Islands, and even (very briefly) Antarctica. On the Argentina leg of this trip Trotter, with her interest in birds, was particularly captivated by the penguins.[46] She jumped at all professional excuses to travel during these years, visiting many countries, including China, Taiwan, Egypt, Mexico, Greece, and Israel. With her lifetime of travel, it is interesting to note that she experienced intense motion sickness, and would later take along a non-drowsy antiemetic because, as she stated, "my security goes up 150% with this in my purse."[47] And as she aged, the travel could physically wear on her: "at the moment [my physical difficulty] is accumulation of fluid in the subcutaneous tissues. My vanity makes me dislike it especially around the eyes and ankles."[48] It was Trotter's opinion that "it's better to travel when you're young."[49] She had never attempted to learn another language. By the 1960s she felt that, "I have been lazy about learning foreign languages, and now I think I am too old to begin."[50] From all this travel and correspondence, Trotter created a stamp collection, which she later sent to her great-nephew David, as well as a coin collection.[51]

Trotter made a second trip to South Africa in 1984, joined by Stewart and Cobb. In a memorable moment for her, she held the Taung skull, an *Australopithecus africanus* fossil specimen, at the 60th anniversary

Trotter in Luxor, Egypt, September 24, 1963. VC170-i170438, Becker Medical Library, Washington University School of Medicine.

Group portrait of Frances Wheelhouse, Raymond Dart, Mildred Trotter, and Phillip Tobias at the Taung Jubilee, Johannesburg, South Africa, 1984. VC170-i170615, Becker Medical Library, Washington University School of Medicine.

celebration of its discovery.[52] During this trip, Trotter suffered a stroke while in the company of Phillip Tobias. She spent the next 6 weeks at the Johannesburg Hospital before being able to fly home.[53] The stroke impaired her ability to speak and understand language, though she could still sing. After another stroke in early 1985, one day before her 86th birthday, Trotter completely lost her capacity for speech and never recovered it. She spent the next 6.5 years at the Bethesda-Dilworth nursing home in St. Louis, and also served as a clinical research patient, until her death on August 23, 1991.[54] As a friend and former student described at her Washington University memorial service, "words [were] very important" to Trotter, "especially during the 6½ years she lived without them."[55] In her 1972 oral history Trotter had expressed her expectation to stay in St. Louis for the rest of her life, and so she did. She also donated her body to the Washington University School of Medicine, true to her long-term efforts toward the 1956 Missouri Uniform Anatomical Gift Act. Trotter is memorialized with a headstone at Beaver Cemetery and Mausoleum, near her hometown in Pennsylvania, where her family interred a portion of her hair.[56] She was able to will a substantial amount of money to her family, which, in light of her decades of a relatively smaller salary and pension, is a further testament to her lifetime of frugality.[57]

Over her 92 years Trotter had indeed, as she put it, "establish[ed] an endurance record."[58] As one might expect over time, much of her and her contemporaries' research has been superseded or relatively abandoned. This is not surprising for work that is decades old, in an academic field that has made previously unimaginable changes with the advent of genomic and virtual studies (so much so that the name for the field has become 'biological anthropology'). But what is somewhat incredible is that some of Trotter's work does remain relevant and is in continued, active use, such as her stature estimation project and her foundational work in hair growth that underlies all subsequent medical and scientific advancements. Mildred Trotter's enduring legacy further resonates through her profound influence on her thousands of students and their subsequent medical practices, her contributions to the Terry Anatomical Collection and its preservation, the impact of the original Missouri Uniform Anatomical Gift Act, her pioneering roles as a woman on staff at the medical school and as the first woman to be President of the American Association of Physical Anthropologists, and in her reshaping of the military's ongoing process of human identification. Her portrait continues to serenely look out over the forensic anthropologists, now more women than men, who are still, more than 7 decades later, undertaking the formidable task of identifying the remains of fallen US service members.

NOTES

1 Letter, Trotter to T.D. Stewart, January 20, 1970, series 13, box 6, folder 12, Mildred Trotter Papers, Becker Medical Library, Washington University School of Medicine.

2 The oral history transcript is available on the University's website, here: http://beckerexhibits.wustl.edu/oral/interviews/trotter.html. The audio file was made available on my request.

3 Mildred Trotter, interview by Estelle Brodman, May 19, 1972 and May 23, 1972, audio, Becker Medical Library, Washington University School of Medicine.

4 "9 More Auto Tires Taken by Thieves," *St. Louis Post-Dispatch*, January 7, 1942, 3.

5 Draft, Trotter, "The Department of Anatomy in My Time," p. 73, no date, series 1, box 1, Mildred Trotter Papers, Becker Medical Library, Washington University School of Medicine.

6 Letter, Trotter to Don C. Herr, September 20,1949, series 3, box 4, folder 16, Mildred Trotter Papers, Becker Medical Library, Washington University School of Medicine.

7 Letter, T.D. Stewart to Trotter, May 16, 1958, series 13, box 6, folder 11, Mildred Trotter Papers, Becker Medical Library, Washington University School of Medicine.

8 Letter, Trotter to T.D. Stewart, May 19, 1958, series 13, box 6, folder 11, Mildred Trotter Papers, Becker Medical Library, Washington University School of Medicine.
9 Letter, Trotter to T.D. Stewart, May 3, 1955, series 13, box 6, folder 11, Mildred Trotter Papers, Becker Medical Library, Washington University School of Medicine.
10 Letter, Trotter to T.D. Stewart May 19, 1978, series 13, box 1, folder 5, Mildred Trotter Papers, Becker Medical Library, Washington University School of Medicine.
11 Letter, Trotter to Wu Rukang, April 13, 1982, series 13, box 7, folder 11, Mildred Trotter Papers, Becker Medical Library, Washington University School of Medicine.
12 Letter, Trotter to Frank Spencer, October 13, 1975, series 13, box 6, folder 10, Mildred Trotter Papers, Becker Medical Library, Washington University School of Medicine.
13 Letter, Trotter to William C. Thomas Nov 23 1964, series 13, box 7, folder 1, Mildred Trotter Papers, Becker Medical Library, Washington University School of Medicine.
14 Letter, Trotter to Janet Bryan, November 22, 1978, series 3, box 6, folder 45; and Letter, Sylvia Hensley to Trotter, January 25, 1955, series 13, box 2, folder 3, Mildred Trotter Papers, Becker Medical Library, Washington University School of Medicine.
15 Letter, Cynthia Ling to Trotter, October 22, 1979, series 3, box 6, folder 33, Mildred Trotter Papers, Becker Medical Library, Washington University School of Medicine.
16 Letter, Trotter to Peggy C. Caldwell, October 17, 1980, series 13, box 7, folder 9; Trotter to Eleanor, April 16, 1954, series 13, box 4, folder 2; and Trotter to Jane, November 9, 1961, series 13, box 6, folder 6, Mildred Trotter Papers, Becker Medical Library, Washington University School of Medicine.
17 Letter, Trotter to Sarah E. Finnegan, April 24, 1978, series 3, box 8, folder 5, Mildred Trotter Papers, Becker Medical Library, Washington University School of Medicine.
18 Mary Kimbrough, "Bone Detective," *The Everyday Magazine in the St. Louis Post-Dispatch*, May 8 1955, 1G.
19 Letter, Trotter to T.D. Stewart, February 1, 1956, series 3, box 10, folder 7, Mildred Trotter Papers, Becker Medical Library, Washington University School of Medicine.
20 Letter, Trotter to T.D. Stewart, March 26, 1956, series 3, box 17, folder 9, Mildred Trotter Papers, Becker Medical Library, Washington University School of Medicine.
21 Letter, Trotter to J. Lawerence Angel, June 8, 1956, series 3, box 4, folder 7, Mildred Trotter Papers, Becker Medical Library, Washington University School of Medicine.

22 Letter, Trotter to Goldine Gleser, November 14, 1957, series 5, box 12, folder 7, Mildred Trotter Papers, Becker Medical Library, Washington University School of Medicine.
23 Letter, Goldine Gleser to Trotter, November 27, 1957, series 5, box 13, folder 16, Mildred Trotter Papers, Becker Medical Library, Washington University School of Medicine.
24 Letter, Trotter to T.D. Stewart, April 2, 1957, series 13, box 8, folder 11, Mildred Trotter Papers, Becker Medical Library, Washington University School of Medicine.
25 Letter, Trotter to Frank E. Poirier, April 2, 1957, series 3, box 6, folder 52, Mildred Trotter Papers, Becker Medical Library, Washington University School of Medicine.
26 Letter, Henry Field to Trotter, May 13, 1936, series 2, box 2, folder 37, Mildred Trotter Papers, Becker Medical Library, Washington University School of Medicine.
27 Letter, Trotter to Henry Field, June 3, 1936, series 2, box 2, folder 37, Mildred Trotter Papers, Becker Medical Library, Washington University School of Medicine; Mildred Trotter, "The hair of the Arabs of central Iraq," *American Journal of Physical Anthropology* 21, no. 3 (1936): 423–428.
28 Letter, Trotter to T. Dale Stewart, November 6, 1956, series 13, box 1, folder 8, Mildred Trotter Papers, Becker Medical Library, Washington University School of Medicine.
29 Samuel B. Guze, interviewed by Marion Hunt, 1994, transcript, Becker Medical Library, Washington University School of Medicine.
30 Letter, Trotter to Renee Lautenback, April 25, 1977, series 3, box 4, folder 12, Mildred Trotter Papers, Becker Medical Library, Washington University School of Medicine.
31 Letter, Trotter to Certificate of Title Administrator (Jefferson City, MO), December 16, 1975, series 13, box 7, folder 5, Mildred Trotter Papers, Becker Medical Library, Washington University School of Medicine.
32 Letter, Trotter to Goldine C. Gleser, August 20, 1973, series 3, box 6, folder 6, Mildred Trotter Papers, Becker Medical Library, Washington University School of Medicine.
33 Letter, Trotter to Janet Bryan, November 22, 1978, series 3, box 6, folder 45, Mildred Trotter Papers, Becker Medical Library, Washington University School of Medicine.
34 Letter, Trotter to Janet Bryan, November 22, 1978, series 3, box 6, folder 45, Mildred Trotter Papers, Becker Medical Library, Washington University School of Medicine.
35 Trotter, James. Interview by author. Phone conversation. December 18, 2020.

36 Trotter, David. Interview by author. Phone conversation. October 21, 2020.
37 Barbara Vancheri, "At 81, a County Native Goes Strong in the Lab," *Beaver County Times*, Wednesday, August 20, 1980, B-1.
38 Barbara Vancheri, "At 81, a County Native Goes Strong in the Lab," *Beaver County Times*, Wednesday, August 20, 1980, B-1.
39 Letter, Trotter to David Allbrook, February 12, 1964, series 13, box 1, folder 14, Mildred Trotter Papers, Becker Medical Library, Washington University School of Medicine.
40 Glenn Conroy, Jane Phillips-Conroy, Roy Peterson, Robert Sussman, and Steven Molnar, "Obituary. Mildred Trotter, Ph.D. (Feb. 2, 1899–Aug. 23, 1991)," *American Journal of Physical Anthropology* 87, no. 3 (1992): 373–374.
41 Letter, Helen Stoskopf to Trotter, November 10, 1980, series 5, box 12, folder 2, Mildred Trotter Papers, Becker Medical Library, Washington University School of Medicine.
42 Letter, Trotter to T.D. Stewart, September 9, 1960, series 13, box 6, folder 12, Mildred Trotter Papers, Becker Medical Library, Washington University School of Medicine.
43 Letter, Virginia Apgar to Trotter, June 5, 1960, series 13, box 1, folder 1, Mildred Trotter Papers, Becker Medical Library, Washington University School of Medicine.
44 "Bulletin of the Washington University School of Medicine," *Publications of Washington University* 78, no. 5 (June 30, 1980), p. 22.
45 No author, "A tribute to Mildred Trotter, Ph.D.," *Outlook Magazine, Washington University School of Medicine* 12, no. 3 (Summer 1975), p. 154.
46 Letter, Trotter to David B. Allbrook, February 28, 1977, series 13, box 1, folder 1, Mildred Trotter Papers, Becker Medical Library, Washington University School of Medicine.
47 Letter, Trotter to Tess Bresnehan, March 16, 1965, series 13, box 2, folder 1, Mildred Trotter Papers, Becker Medical Library, Washington University School of Medicine.
48 Letter, Trotter to Robert J. Terry, December 6, 1963, series 13, box 7, folder 6, Mildred Trotter Papers, Becker Medical Library, Washington University School of Medicine.
49 Letter, Trotter to Loy E. Cramer, July 8, 1964, series 13, box 2, folder 9, Mildred Trotter Papers, Becker Medical Library, Washington University School of Medicine.
50 Letter, Trotter to Nina Dzhavakhishvili, May 6, 1960, series 13, box 3, folder 1, Mildred Trotter Papers, Becker Medical Library, Washington University School of Medicine.

51 Trotter, David. Interview by author. Phone conversation. October 21, 2020; and Trotter, James. Interview by author. Phone conversation. December 18, 2020.
52 Marion Hunt, "Mildred Trotter: 'With Honor in Her Own Country'," *Outlook Magazine, Washington University School of Medicine* 17, no. 1 (Spring 1980): 8–13, p. 11.
53 Phillip Tobias, *Into the Past: A Memoir* (Johannesburg: Picador Africa and Wits University Press, 2005), p. 117.
54 Ann Randolph Flipse Gerber, "Remarks Prepared for the Memorial Service for Mildred Trotter, Ph.D. 1899–1991," October 9, 1991, http://beckerexhibits.wustl.edu/mowihsp/bios/FlipseMemTrotter.htm.
55 Ann Randolph Flipse Gerber, "Remarks Prepared for the Memorial Service for Mildred Trotter, Ph.D. 1899–1991," October 9, 1991, http://beckerexhibits.wustl.edu/mowihsp/bios/FlipseMemTrotter.htm.
56 Trotter, David. Interview by author. Phone conversation. October 21, 2020.
57 Trotter, James. Interview by author. Phone conversation. December 18, 2020.
58 Quoted in Twink Cherrick, "Named Lectureship, Portrait to Honor Anatomy Professor Mildred Trotter," *Washington University Record* (May 22, 1975), p. 4.

Index

Note: *Italic* page numbers refer to figures.